PRENTICE-HALL FOUNDATIONS OF FINANCE SERIES

John C. Burton

The Management of Working Capital

Alan Coleman

The Financial Management of Financial Institutions

Herbert E. Dougall

Capital Markets and Institutions

Jack Clark Francis and Stephen H. Archer

Portfolio Analysis

Robert K. Jaedicke and Robert T. Sprouse

Accounting Flows: Income, Funds, and Cash

James T. S. Porterfield

Investment Decisions and Capital Costs

Alexander A. Robichek and Stewart C. Myers

Optimal Financing Decisions

Ezra Solomon and Jaime C. Laya

Measuring Profitability

J. Fred Weston

The Scope and Methodology of Finance

PRENTICE-HALL FOUNDATIONS OF FINANCE SERIES

Ezra Solomon, *Editor*

Portfolio Analysis

Jack Clark Francis

Finance Department
Wharton School of Finance and Commerce
University of Pennsylvania

Stephen H. Archer

Finance Department
Graduate School of Business
University of Washington

Prentice-Hall, Inc., Englewood Cliffs, New Jersey

P 13—686287—X

C 13—686295—0

Library of Congress Catalog Card No. 79-130977

Printed in the United States of America

Current Printing (last digit):

10 9 8

PRENTICE-HALL INTERNATIONAL, INC., *London*

PRENTICE-HALL OF AUSTRALIA, PTY. LTD., *Sydney*

PRENTICE-HALL OF CANADA, LTD., *Toronto*

PRENTICE-HALL OF INDIA PRIVATE LIMITED, *New Delhi*

PRENTICE-HALL OF JAPAN, INC., *Tokyo*

To our parents

Editor's Note

The subject matter of financial management is in the process of rapid change. A growing analytical content, virtually nonexistent ten years ago, has displaced the earlier descriptive treatment as the center of emphasis in the field.

These developments have created problems for both teachers and students. On the one hand, recent and current thinking, which is addressed to basic questions that cut across traditional divisions of the subject matter, do not fit neatly into the older structure of academic courses and texts in corporate finance. On the other hand, the new developments have not yet stabilized and as a result have not yet reached the degree of certainty, lucidity, and freedom from controversy that would permit all of them to be captured within a single, straightforward treatment at the textbook level. Indeed, given the present rate of change, it will be years before such a development can be expected.

One solution to the problem, which the present Foundations of Finance Series tries to provide, is to cover the major components of the subject through short independent studies. These individual essays provide a vehicle through which the writer can concentrate on a single sequence of ideas and thus communicate some of the excitement of current thinking and controversy. For the teacher and student, the separate self-contained books provide a flexible up-to-date survey of current thinking on each subarea covered and at the same time permit maximum flexibility in course and curriculum design.

EZRA SOLOMON

Preface

This book has two primary objectives. The first and most obvious objective is to teach portfolio analysis. Chapters 1, 2, and 3 seek to lay the foundation for portfolio analysis. Chapter 4 presents portfolio-analysis techniques. Chapters 5 through 10 explore various implications of portfolio analysis. The last chapter takes up some unanswered questions and ventures a few subjective conclusions. Several mathematical appendices (A through F) at the end of the book are included as a helpful refresher of relevant topics from freshman college algebra and elementary statistics.

The second objective of this book is to "sell" a pedagogical point of view. We believe the most important things a business student can learn are mathematics, economics, and computer programming—the tools of business analysis. Having mastered these, the student may learn the functional areas of business (such as finance) more easily. Tools, models, and concepts can be carried through life, whereas all but the most important institutional and descriptive facts are often forgotten unless they are used regularly.

This book stresses economic rationale, mathematical definitions, numerical examples, and "how to do it yourself" math pointers to the exclusion of institutional and descriptive material. The book reflects our approach to teaching investments. Every undergraduate and graduate student who took our investments course at the University of Washington in 1968 and 1969 did a portfolio analysis term project. It will be clear at several points in the text that we believe it is more important to stress the tools with which the answers may be found than to "give the answers." We believe this is true for both research oriented students and students who are training to be line managers. The analytical tools are as useful in solving cases as they are in research.

The amount of math and econometrics used in this book exceeds that which is found in most finance books. This represents a compromise. We tended toward less discussion and more analysis. Our students and reviewers, however, persuaded us to decrease the level of mathematics. Thus, Hessian matrices, which appeared earlier, are absent here; what mathematics remains has been largely segregated into appendices; and the chapters have been expanded with subjective discussion and numerical examples. This was done in hopes that the book may be read on several levels. Undergraduates may read the chapters and omit the appendices. More advanced readers may skim the chapters and confine their attention to the appendices and references.

We are indebted to many people for assistance in preparing this manuscript. Secretaries, undergraduate students, graduate students, reviewers, and faculty members—in Philadelphia, Seattle, and elsewhere—have provided beneficial help at numerous points. Marshall Blume, Nancy Jacob, and Jim Walter were particularly helpful reviewers. Don Hoflin, Bob Floch, and Earl Keller made helpful contributions. Dr. Harry Markowitz provided the seminal work upon which this effort is based; the profession is in debt to him for that. Of course, any errors are the sole property of the authors.

J. C. F.
S. H. A.

Table of Contents

Portfolio Analysis

SECTION ONE

DEFINITIONS AND MEASUREMENTS

Introduction

THE stock market has long captured most people's curiosity and imagination. Its mysteries and its stories of sudden wealth are tantalizing—so much so that many are moved to "play" the market.[1] Although the stock market is a complex subject, the potential rewards are great and an investor's interest usually grows. Recently academicians, whose credentials suggest they seek to satisfy their intellectual curiosity as well as supplement their modest means, have become interested in the stock markets. Some of the relationships and facts that these men have uncovered are reported in this book.

Investments as a Subject of Study Is Changing

Changes are occurring rapidly in the teaching of investments.[2] Investigation of the legal intricacies of the various securities, the tax status of different sources of income, how a stock exchange operates, the needs of

---

[1] For a discussion of "playing" the stock market read *The Money Game* by "Adam Smith" (New York: Random House, 1967). The book puts rigorous analysis into an entertaining perspective.

[2] Sauvain says: "A book that almost literally ushered in a new era in the theory of diversification and portfolio structure is the study by Harry Markowitz . . .", H. Sauvain, *Investment Management*, 3rd ed. (Englewood Cliffs, N.J.: Prentice-Hall, Inc., 1967), p. 407.

3

the various investing institutions, and other descriptive and institutional matters are giving way to deeper analysis. The newer courses treat problems on a more abstract and general level. They seek more efficient methods of achieving investment objectives. They are more concerned with the "why" and less with the "who" and "where."

Some instructors and researchers are attempting to reduce the portion of the study of investments that previously had been left to judgment. Models of investor and market behavior have been constructed for manipulation and study. Consequently, a new body of conceptual relationships and principles has evolved. It is felt that this approach has more applications in more different areas and can be retained by students better than the so-called descriptive and institutional material. A course comprised entirely of descriptive and institutional material is likely to be too vocationally oriented. Since students pursuing careers in investments can quickly pick up the folklore of the vocation, and they forget such material equally as fast if it isn't used, it might as well be minimized in college-level instruction. These are the conclusions of the Ford Foundation and the Carnegie Corporation studies of the efficacy of business school curricula in general.[3] In particular, these are the personal views of many of the instructors of the new investments courses.

Of course, some of the traditional material must remain. As potential operating executives, business students need to be able to relate the concepts and analysis learned directly to the problems they will face after graduation. To effectively apply his knowledge the student should be somewhat familiar with the vocabulary and institutions with which he must deal. And, the student should be shown how to use the tools he has learned to make managerial decisions.

Characteristics of New Developments in Investments

The new developments that are reshaping investments courses have common elements. First, the important new developments are all mathematical to some extent.[4] To those uninitiated in mathematics this must be a source of frustration. Those who are able to use mathematics recognize the following advantages of such theorizing:

1. All hypothesized relationships are explicit.
2. Definitions are clearer and in measurable terms.
3. The model readily yields to numerous forms of analysis which may result in subtle and revealing discoveries.
4. The model may be well suited for prediction.
5. Mathematics permits more succinct, and at the same time, more complete statements than verbal language.

---

[3] "New Report on the Business Schools," *Fortune*, December 1964. This is a readable discussion of the Ford and Carnegie studies and the shortcomings of the typical business school curriculum.

[4] The first Nobel Prize ever awarded to economics or business scholars was awarded for econometric model-building in November 1969. The second, given a year later, was also for mathematical economics.

A second element common to the newly developing models is their simplicity. They all abstract from reality. Rather than become bogged down in numerous real and imagined eventualities, these theorists do not hesitate to assume ambiguities away. Then on the basis of their assumptions they deduce conclusions. There is nothing wrong with such model-building. After all, if a theory indulged every eventuality, it wouldn't be a theory—it would be description. Rigorous analysis requires models. Models are by definition abstractions of reality. They must be simplified versions of reality that focus on only the important and fundamental relationships. If an analyst steps outside his model, he usually finds himself standing on the street arguing with laymen who are prone to ignore their implicit assumptions and make untestable assertions. After a model has been worked rigorously through to its logical conclusions, then unrealistic assumptions can be relaxed to allow insights into more realistic situations.

A third common element is the background of the theorists. In addition to being mathematically proficient, these men are either economists or have strong backgrounds in the discipline. Economics has a tractable model which often can be useful in financial analysis. The large amount of new financial literature being written by economists attests to the usefulness of such training.

Finally, the theories are often very general. The perceptive student of these theories can readily adapt them to purposes unrelated to finance. Unfortunately, space does not permit a pursuit of the wide application of the theories discussed. Even the Markowitz model of portfolio analysis, to which this book is primarily directed, will not be extended into other fields. But a little imagination will allow the reader to see that Markowitz' analysis is adaptable for any decision involving risk, such as selecting an auto, a home, a career, or even a spouse!

Direction of this Book

The primary topic of this book is a segment of the field of investments known as portfolio management. Portfolio management includes the following three activities:

1. Security analysis (predicting the rates of return of individual securities).
2. Portfolio analysis (determining a portfolio's future return and risk possibilities).
3. Portfolio selection (selecting from among those portfolios deemed worthy of further consideration in stage two that single portfolio most suitable for the owner's particular purposes).

The analysis in this book will primarily embrace stage two of portfolio management and its implications. Stages one and three will also be discussed briefly.

The Security Analyst's Job

The demands on the security analyst are not as stringent as they may sound. For example, the forecaster need not forecast a security's returns for many periods into the future. In fact, he need only forecast "one period" into the future, since portfolio analysis deals with only one time period. The length of that time period can vary within wide limits. It definitely may not be a short-run period (portfolio analysis is not designed for speculative trading) or a very long-run period. But between, say, three months and ten years, the portfolio managers can select any planning horizons that fit the owner's needs.[5]

The security analyst's forecast should be in terms of rates of return:

$$\text{rate of return} = \frac{(\text{ending price} - \text{beginning price}) + \text{dividends}}{\text{beginning price}}. \quad (1.1)$$

Equation (1.1) defines the rate of return on a common-stock investment for "one period." Other definitions for the rate of return are given in the appendix to this chapter.

The security analyst needn't make point estimates. Rather, it is necessary that he furnish the portfolio analyst with an estimated probability distribution of returns for each security. These may be estimated using historical data. The distribution may then need to be adjusted to reflect anticipated factors that were not present historically. Consider Fig. 1.1—an example of a probability distribution of rates of return for some security.[6]

The security analyst must also estimate correlation coefficients or covariances between all securities under consideration. His task will be discussed more extensively in Chapter 3. Given these pieces of information (input data), portfolio analysis can determine the optimal portfolio for any investor who is adequately described by the assumptions listed next.

Possible return	Estimated probability
−10%	0.1
−5%	0.1
0	0.1
+5%	0.2
+10%	0.4
+15%	0.1
	1.0

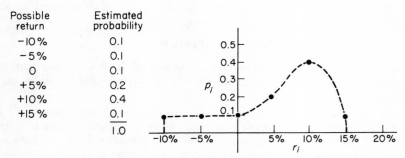

Fig. 1.1   Finite Probability Distribution of Rates of Return

---

[5] K. V. Smith, "Alternative Procedures for Revising Investment Portfolios," *Journal of Financial and Quantitative Analysis*, December 1968, pp. 371–405. Smith makes some suggestions about the length of time that seems appropriate.

[6] This probability distribution is a finite distribution, since the outcomes (rates of return) do not assume all possible values in the relevant range. The distribution is skewed left.

Assumptions Underlying Portfolio Analysis

The assumptions below are the basis for the entire analysis that follows:

1. All investors maximize one-period expected utility and exhibit diminishing marginal utility of wealth. This implies that they visualize each investment opportunity as being represented by a probability distribution of additions to their terminal wealth. Or, equivalently, all investors visualize assets as probability distributions of expected returns over some holding period.
2. Investors' risk estimates are proportional to the variability of the expected returns.
3. Investors are willing to base their decisions solely in terms of expected return and risk. That is, utility (U) is a function of variability of return (σ) and expected return $(E(r))$. Symbolically, $U = f(\sigma, E(r))$.
4. For any given level of risk, investors prefer higher returns to lower returns. Symbolically, $\delta U/\delta E(r) > 0$. Or, conversely, for any given level of rate of return, investors prefer less risk over more risk. Symbolically, $\delta U/\delta\sigma < 0$.

These assumptions will be maintained throughout the discussion of portfolio analysis and capital market theory. Investors described by these assumptions will prefer "Markowitz efficient assets."

In essence, portfolio analysis is based on the premise that the most desirable assets are those which have:

1. the minimum expected risk at any given expected rate of return, or, conversely,
2. the maximum expected rate of return at any given level of expected risk.

Such assets are usually portfolios rather than individual assets. These assets are called "efficient portfolios" whether they contain one or many assets. Investors described by the assumptions above will prefer efficient portfolios to nonefficient portfolios.

In the "real world" many investors are observed holding nonefficient portfolios. Furthermore, portfolio analysis is based on some simplified assumptions about reality. This raises questions as to the efficacy of the analysis. Before proceeding further, it might be wise to examine the validity of these assumptions underlying portfolio analysis.

The first assumption about probability distributions of terminal wealth or rates of return may be violated in several respects. First, many investors simply do not forecast assets prices or know how to define the rate of return from an investment. Second, investors are frequently heard discussing the "growth potential," the "glamour" of a stock, the "ability of management," and numerous other considerations other than terminal wealth or rates of return. Third, investors often base their decisions on estimates of the "most likely" outcome rather than considering a probability distribution.

These seeming disparities with assumption one are not serious. If investors are interested in a security's "glamour" or "growth," it is probably because they (consciously or subconsciously) believe these factors affect the asset's rate of return or terminal wealth. And, even if investors cannot define rate of return, they may still try to maximize it merely by trying to maximize additions to their terminal wealth: the two objectives are equivalent. Furthermore, visualizing probability distributions need not be explicit. "Most likely" estimates are undoubtedly prepared either explicitly or implicitly from a subjective probability distribution.

The risk definition given in assumption two does not conform to the risk measures compiled by some popular financial services. The published quality ratings seem implicitly to define risk to be the probability of default. However, if firms' probability of default is highly correlated with their variability of return, assumption three is not invalid.

As pointed out above, investors sometimes discuss concepts such as the "glamour" or "image" of a security. This may seem to indicate that the third assumption is an oversimplification. However, if these factors affect the expected value and variability of a security's rate of return, this assumption is not violated either.

The fourth assumption may also seem inadequate. Behavioralists have pointed out to economists that businessmen infrequently, if ever, maximize or minimize. The behavioralists explain that businessmen usually strive only to do a satisfactory or sufficient job. Rarely, if ever, do businessmen work to attain the optimum of complete maximization or minimization, whichever may be the appropriate objective. However, if some highly competitive businessmen attain near-optimization of their objective and other businessmen follow these leaders, then this assumption also turns out to be not unrealistic.

In any event, all the assumptions underlying portfolio analysis have been shown to be inadequate to at least some extent. This raises questions as to the validity of portfolio analysis.

Although it would clearly be better if none of the assumptions underlying the analysis were ever violated, this condition is not necessary to establish the value of the analysis. If the analysis rationalizes complex behavior that is observed (such as diversification), if the analysis yields worthwhile predictions, then it can be valuable in spite of fallacious assumptions. Furthermore, if the assumptions are only slight oversimplifications, as are the four above, they are no cause for alarm. People need only behave *as if* they were described by the assumptions for a theory to be valid.

Taxes

The analysis presented here can be conducted to fit the needs of an investor in a given tax situation. That is, equation (1.1) may be adapted to treat any tax differential between dividends and capital gains that the analyst considers appropriate. This would require restating equation (1.1) in the form of (1.1′):

rate of return =

$$\frac{(\text{ending price} - \text{beginning price})(1 - T_G) + \text{dividends}(1 - T_O)}{\text{beginning price}},$$

$$(1.1′)$$

where T_G is the relevant capital gains tax rate and T_O is the relevant ordinary income tax rate to the particular investor. To conduct the analysis in this manner will obviously require additional calculation. To avoid this calculation, tax considerations will not be incorporated explicitly throughout the analysis. However, the effects of taxes will be discussed later.

Mathematics Segregated into Appendices

What follows will be partially mathematical. However, the reader who is uninitiated in mathematics can master the basic material. All that is needed is a remembrance of freshman college algebra, one course in classical statistics, and patience—mostly patience. The material is presented at the simplest possible level which a fair coverage of the model will allow. The basic material is presented completely in terms of elementary finite probability theory and algebra supplemented with graphs, explanation, and references where more complete explanations may be found.

Differential calculus and matrix algebra are used in some of the appendices. The reader is hereby forewarned and may avoid this material if he wishes. The book is written so its continuity will not be disturbed by skipping these appendices. Little, if any, of the vocabulary or basic concepts necessary for an acquaintance with the subject is found in these parts of the book. Most of the appendices contain practical solution techniques for large problems, proofs, derivations, and other material of interest only to the devout.

The appendices at the end of the chapters contain material tangential to the topic of the chapter. The material in Appendix 2A is essential for comprehension of the rest of the book. This material on finite probability is relegated to an appendix only because so many readers have already had courses in this area.[7] In contrast, Appendices 1A, 2B, 4A, 4B, 4C, 4D, 4E, 5A, 5B, and 7A may be omitted with no loss of continuity.

The appendices at the rear of the book are of a more general nature. They are furnished to provide assistance with the mathematics found in the chapters and in other appendices. Regardless of the level of the student, the authors believe this book can provide a report on important developments within the area of portfolio analysis.

---

[7] Throughout the rest of this book the equations derived in Appendix 2A will recur and be referred to by the equation numbers from that appendix.

Appendix IA
Various Rates of Return

Definitions

Rate of return may be defined several ways. Consider the following three possible definitions of rates of return:

$$\text{market return} = \frac{\text{capital gains or loss plus dividend income}}{\text{purchase price}}.$$

$$\text{earnings return} = \frac{\text{earnings per share}}{\text{market value per share}}.$$

$$\text{accounting return} = \frac{\text{earnings per share}}{\text{book value per share}}.$$

The three different rates of return above are typically not even highly correlated with each other for the same firm and over the same periods. Thus, it makes a big difference how rate of return is defined. The vagaries of the accounting procedure and an investigation of how income should be defined will not be undertaken here.[1] Suffice it to say, for investment decisions the investor is primarily concerned with the rate at which wealth or value increases. Since the market rate of return measures the rate at which the investor's wealth or the investment's value grows (or shrinks), this is the definition used throughout this book.

Calculating the Market Rate of Return Per Period

If an investor pays the price P_0 at the beginning of some period (say a year) and gets back dividends (D) or interest plus the price P_1 at the end of the period, the rate of return (r) for that period is the discount rate which equates the present value of all cashflows to the cost of the investment. Symbolically,

$$P_0 = \frac{P_1 + D}{1 + r},$$

$$P_0(1 + r) = P_1 + D,$$

$$P_0 r = (P_1 - P_0) + D,$$

$$r = \frac{(P_1 - P_0) + D}{P_0}$$

$$= \frac{\text{capital gains plus dividends for the period}}{\text{beginning price}}. \tag{1.1}$$

---

[1] R. K. Jaekicke and R. T. Sprouse, *Accounting Flows: Income Funds and Cash* (Englewood Cliffs, N.J.: Prentice-Hall, Inc., 1965); A. A. Robichek and S. C. Myers, *Optimal Financing Decisions* (Englewood Cliffs, N. J.: Prentice-Hall, Inc., 1965), chaps. 1 and 2. These sources deal with the problem of how income should be defined.

Thus, if \$100 is invested for one year and returns the principle plus \$7 capital gains, plus \$8 dividends, the return $r_1 = 15$ percent is found as follows:

$$P_0 = \$100 = \frac{107 + 8}{1 + r} = \frac{115}{1 + r},$$

$$r_1 = \frac{7 + 8}{\$100} = \frac{\$15}{\$100} = 15 \text{ percent} = \text{annual rate of return}$$

by equation (1.1).

And, if the \$115 is invested and returns the \$115 principle plus $-\$13.75$ capital loss plus \$8 dividend, the annual return is $r_2 = -5$ percent.

$$\$115 = P_0 = \frac{115 - 13.75 + 8.00}{1 + r} = \frac{109.25}{1 + r},$$

$$r_2 = \frac{-13.75 + 8}{115} = \frac{-5.75}{115} = -5 \text{ percent annual rate of return.}$$

The rate of return defined by equation (1.1) is thus seen to be identical to the internal rate of return, the holding-period yield, or the marginal efficiency of capital for investments of "one period" duration.

Equation (1.1) is defined in terms of the income sources from common-stock investment since this analysis is primarily concerned with portfolios of common stocks. However, the rate of return on other forms of investment is easily defined, and this analysis is general enough so that assets other than merely common stocks may be considered. For example, the rate of return on a real estate investment could be defined as

$$r = \frac{V_1 - V_0}{V_0} \tag{1A.1}$$

where V_1 is the investor's end-of-period value for a real estate holding and V_0 is the beginning-of-period value or cost.

Continuous Compounding

Equations (1.1) and (1A.1) define a holding-period yield which is compounded once per period. These equations must be restated if continuous compounding is assumed. The continuous analogue to equation (1.1) is

$$r_t = \ln\left(\frac{P_{t+1} + D_t}{P_t}\right) = \ln(P_{t+1} + D_t) - \ln P_t \tag{1A.2}$$

where ln denotes the natural or naperian logarithm.[2] The continuous

---

[2] Natural logarithms are used because they offer advantages over common logarithms. First, the natural logarithm of the value relatives is a good estimate of the rate of return for returns below 15 percent—for example, ln (\$110/\$100) = .095. Second, the differentiation rule for natural logarithms is simple. However, common base-10 logs may be used to calculate the geometric mean.

analogue to (1A.1) is

$$r = \ln \left(\frac{V_1}{V_0}\right) = \ln V_1 - \ln V_0. \tag{1A.3}$$

The rate of return computed with continuous compounding is smaller than the return calculated with less frequent compounding. For example, one dollar invested at the beginning of some period that returns \$1.10 at the end of the period would have a rate of return of 10 percent by equation (1A.1)—namely:

$$\frac{V_1 - V_0}{V_0} = \frac{1.10 - 1.00}{1.00} = \frac{.10}{1.00} = 10 \text{ percent.}$$

But, by equation (1A.3), the return on this same investment is 9.5 percent, calculated as follows:

$$\ln \left(\frac{V_1}{V_0}\right) = \ln \left(\frac{1.10}{1.00}\right)$$

$$= \ln (1.1) - \ln (1.00) = .095 - 0 = .095 = 9.5 \text{ percent.}$$

The advantage of using equations (1A.2) and (1A.3) is that they are adapted to calculation of the geometric mean return.

Geometric Mean Rate of Return

The geometric mean return (gr) over n period is defined as follows:

$$\text{gr} = \left[\prod_{t=1}^{n} (\text{VR}_t)\right]^{1/n} - 1$$

where

$$\text{VR}_t = \left(\frac{P_{t+1} + D_t}{P_t}\right) = \left(\frac{V_{t+1}}{V_t}\right) = (1 + r_t)$$

and is called the "value relative" at time t. Equivalently,

$$\text{gr} = (\sqrt[n]{(1 + r_1)(1 + r_2) \cdots (1 + r_n)}) - 1.$$

Since it is cumbersome to evaluate the nth root, the following definitions of the geometric mean return (are entirely equivalent and) are suggested for use in actual computations.[3]

$$\text{gr} = \left\{\exp\left[\frac{1}{n} \sum_{t=1}^{n} \ln (\text{VR}_t)\right]\right\} - 1$$

$$= \left\{\exp\left[\frac{1}{n} \sum_{t=1}^{n} \ln (1 + r_t)\right]\right\} - 1. \tag{1A.4}$$

---

[3] Using natural logarithms, the antilogarithm of x equals e^x. This operation is frequently indicated by writing exp (x), where exp (is a Fortran library function which) means evaluate e with an exponent of x.

The geometric mean return over n periods has the virtue that when compounded, it equals the ratio V_n/V_0 at the nth period. More specifically, if V_0 dollars are left invested for n periods and grow to an ending value of V_n, the geometric mean return (gr) is that number which causes the following equation to hold: $V_0(1 + \text{gr})^n = V_n$. The arithmetic average of the n rates of return calculated for the same investment over the same n periods would be larger than or equal to the geometric mean. Denoting the average of the n rates of return calculated by equations (1.1) and (1A.1) by ar for arithmetic average return, the following inequality holds: $\text{ar} \geq \text{gr}$.

For example, consider the inadequacy of the arithmetic average return when the price of a stock doubles in one period and then depreciates 50 percent in the next period. For simplicity, assume dividends are zero.

	Time periods		
	$t = 0$	$t = 1$	$t = 2$
Price at end of period	$40	$80	$40
The ar per period by eq. (1.1)	—	$\text{ar}_1 = 100\%$	$\text{ar}_2 = -50\%$
The natural logarithm[4] of the value relatives, ln (VR)	—	$\ln(\text{VR}_1) = .693$	$\ln(\text{VR}_2) = -.693$

The average return for periods 1 and 2 using equation (1.1) is (the average of 100 percent and -50 percent, that is: (100 percent $-$ 50 percent)/2 = 25 percent. But, using equation (1A.4), the geometric mean is zero

$$\left(\exp\left[\frac{(.693) + (-.693)}{2}\right]\right) - 1 = 0.$$

Certainly an investment purchased for $40 and sold for $40 two periods later did not have an average return of 25 percent. Rather, the geometric mean return of zero is the correct return.[5] The geometric mean of several periods r_t's is the true mean rate of return over the entire time span.

---

[4] Using natural logarithms, $\ln(80/40) = \ln 2 = .693$ and $\ln(40/80) = \ln(.5) = -.693$.

[5] For more information on these returns as they relate to portfolio analysis see: H. M. Markowitz, *Portfolio Selection* (New York: John Wiley & Sons, Inc., 1959), chap. 6; "Criteria for Choice Among Risky Ventures," by H. A. Latane, *Journal of Political Economy*, April 1959, pp. 144–155; L. Fisher's, "An Algorithm for Finding Exact Rates of Return," *Journal of Business*, Supplement, January 1966, pp. 111–119; also, M. C. Jensen discusses some relevant points in his dissertation, "Risk, the Pricing of Capital Assets, and the Evaluation of Investment Portfolios," unpublished Ph.D dissertation, 1968, University of Chicago; E. Fama, "The Behavior of Stock Market Prices," *Journal of Business*, January 1965, see pp. 45–46.

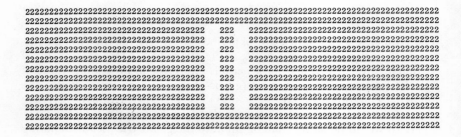

Risk, Efficiency, and Diversification

THE purpose of this chapter is to define a few words and concepts needed later. Terms such as risk, dominant, efficient, opportunity set, capital market line (CML), naive diversification, efficient Markowitz diversification, and others will be discussed in an intuitive fashion. Later, they will be examined in more depth.

What Is Risk

Webster's New World Dictionary defines risk as the chance of injury, damage, or loss. Although this definition is certainly good and correct, it is unsuitable for this study.

The topic of this study is portfolio *analysis*. Analysis cannot proceed very far using verbal definitions, for several reasons. (1) Verbal definitions are not exact; different people interpret them in different ways. (2) Verbal definitions do not yield to analysis; they can only be broken down into more verbose verbal definitions and examples. (3) Verbal definitions do not facilitate cardinal (or sometimes even ordinal) comparisons because they aren't usually explicit enough to allow measurement of the item defined.[1] Suffice it to say that a quantitative risk surrogate is needed

---

[1] Most physical and social sciences are moving to refine and quantify their studies. For example, biometrics, econometrics, and psychometrics are focusing on quantification of the studies of biology, economics, and psychology.

to replace the verbal definition of risk if portfolio analysis is to proceed very far.

The model used here for analyzing risk focuses on more or less subjective probability distributions of some quantifiable outcome. Since the rate of return on an investment is the most important outcome of an investment, financial risk analysis will focus on probability distributions on rates of return like the one shown in Fig. 2.1.

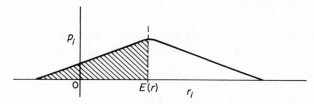

Fig. 2.1   Probability Distribution of Rates of Return

The mean or expected value of the probability distribution of returns, $E(r)$, represents the mathematical expectation of the various possible rates of return. The expected return is defined in equation (2.1):

$$E(r) = \sum_i p_i r_i, \qquad (2.1)$$

where p_i is the probability of the ith rate of return.[2]

Rates of return below $E(r)$ represent disappointing outcomes to the investor studying the asset's probability distribution of returns. The area within the probability distribution that lies to the left of $E(r)$ graphically represents the investor's chance of injury, loss, or damage—that is, risk. The semivariance of returns (svr) defined in equation (2.2) is a quantitative risk surrogate which measures the area below $E(r)$ in the probability distribution of returns.

$$svr = \sum_i p_i [bar_i - E(r)]^2, \qquad (2.2)$$

where bar_i's are rates of return that are less than $E(r)$. The bar_i's are below average rates of return. The square root of (2.2) is called the semideviation of returns and is an equivalent financial risk surrogate which may be more intuitively pleasing.[3]

The semivariance and semideviation of returns are special cases of the variance and standard deviation of returns. The variance of returns,

---

[2] Continuous probability distributions will be ignored here. The estimated returns will assume only finite values.

[3] H. Markowitz, *Portfolio Selection* (New York: John Wiley & Sons, Inc., 1959), chap. 9.

defined in equation (2.3), measures the dispersion or width of the entire

$$\sigma^2 = \sum_i p_i [r_i - E(r)]^2 \qquad (2.3)$$

probability distribution, rather than merely the portion of it lying below $E(r)$. The standard deviation of returns is the square root of (2.3).

Symmetric Probability Distributions of Returns

Consider Figs. 2.2, 2.3, and 2.4, which show three different types of skewness in probability distributions of returns. If assets' probability

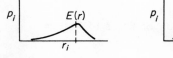
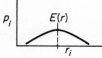
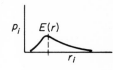

Fig. 2.2	Fig. 2.3	Fig. 2.4
Probability Distribution Skewed Left	Symmetric Probability Distribution	Probability Distribution Skewed Right

distributions of rates of return are symmetric, as shown in Fig. 2.3, rather than skewed to the left or right, "an analysis based on (expected return) and (standard deviation) would consider these . . . (assets) as equally desirable" relative to an analysis based on expected return and semi-deviation.[4] Since most studies published thus far indicate the distributions of returns are symmetric,[5] the semideviation will be abandoned here in favor of the standard deviation of returns. As Markowitz points out, the standard deviation (or variance) "is superior with respect to cost, convenience, and familiarity" . . . and "will produce the same set of efficient portfolios" . . . as the semideviation (or semivariance) if the probability distributions are symmetric.[6]

[4] *Ibid.*, p. 190.

[5] M. G. Kendall, "The Analysis of Economic Time Series, I: Prices," *Journal of the Royal Statistical Society*, ser. A., 1953, pp. 11-25; M. F. M. Osborne, "Brownian Motion in the Stock Market," *Operations Research*, vol. VII, 1959, pp. 173–195; H. V. Roberts, "Stock Market 'Patterns' and Financial Analysis: Methodological Suggestions," *Journal of Finance*, Vol. 14, 1951, pp. 1–10. Arditti seems to have found some skewness, however. F. D. Arditti, "Risk and the Required Rate of Return on Equity," *Journal of Finance*, March, 1967, p. 25; M. E. Blume, "Portfolio Theory: A Step Toward Its Practical Application," *Journal of Business*, April 1970, p. 163.

[6] Markowitz, *Portfolio Selection*, pp. 193–194.

Thus, the variance or standard deviation of returns is the risk surrogate that will be employed throughout the remainder of this book. This is equivalent to defining financial risk as variability of return.

Fundamental Security Analysis

The logic of analyzing only a firm's rate of return may seem oversimplified compared with more fundamental security analysis techniques that stress ratio analysis of financial statements, management interviews, industry forecasts, the economic outlook, and so on. However, there is no contradiction in these two approaches. After the fundamental security analyst completes his task, he need only convert his estimates into several possible rates of return and attach probability estimates to each. The security analyst's consideration of such matters as how highly the firm is levered (that is, how much debt is used relative to the equity), its ability to meet fixed obligations, instability within the industry, the possibility of product obsolescence, the aggressiveness of competitors, the productivity of research and development, management depth and ability, and macroeconomic conditions are all duly reflected in the forecasted rates of return and their probabilities. Thus, the variability of the expected returns is a measure of risk grounded in fundamental analysis of the firm, its industry, and the economic outlook.

Utility Foundations of Portfolio Analysis

In economic analysis the ultimate objective of human behavior is assumed to be utility maximization. Of course, utility is considered to be a function of many things. But, since consumption embraces those variables determining utility over which man has some control, utility is typically assumed to be a function of consumption goods (such as food, leisure, health care, and education). Because the consumption goods that man can control to some extent have a cost, consumption is assumed to be a function (namely, a linear transformation) of wealth. Thus, utility can be restated as a function of wealth.

Investment activity affects utility through its effects on wealth. Since the rate of return is a measure of the rate at which wealth is accumulated, the utility from investment activity can be restated as a function of the rate of return on invested wealth. This can all be summarized symbolically as follows, where U denotes utility and g, h, and j are some positive functions.

$$\begin{aligned} U &= g(\text{consumption}) \\ &= g[h(\text{wealth})] \quad \text{since consumption} = h(\text{wealth}) \\ &= g\{h[j(\text{rate of return})]\} \quad \text{since wealth} = j(\text{rate of return}). \end{aligned}$$

In a world of certainty where all outcomes were known in advance, a utility maximizer would simply invest his wealth in the one asset with the highest expected rate of return. However, in an uncertain world, men can only maximize what they expect utility to be—not what it will actually turn out to be, since this is an unknown. Thus, with the advent of uncertainty, risk considerations enter the picture. Symbolically, equation (2.4), representing portfolio analysis assumption three, summarizes the relation between an investor's utility and his investments in a world of uncertainty.

$$E(u) = f(E(r), \text{risk}) \qquad (2.4)$$

$$= f(E(r), \sigma).$$

Consider the following example of how rational investment decisions can be made within the context of the two-parameter model (that is, considering only risk and return of the securities).

Numerical Example

Assume an investor is trying to select one security from among five securities. The securities and their estimated return and risk are:

Name of Security	Expected Return, $E(r)$	Risk (σ)
American Telephone Works (ATW)	7.0%	3.7%
General Auto Corp. (GAC)	7.7%	4.9%
Fuzzyworm Tractor Co. (FTC)	15.0%	15.0%
Fairyear Tire & Rubber (FTR)	3.0%	3.7%
Hotstone Tire Corp. (HTC)	7.7%	12.0%

The five securities are compared in the two-dimensional Fig. 2.5 with expected return on the vertical axis and risk on the horizontal axis.[7] Clearly, GAC *dominates* HTC, since they both offer the same expected return but GAC is less risky.[8] And FTR is dominated by ATW, since they are both in the same risk class (that is, $\sigma = 3.7$ percent) but ATW offers a higher expected return. Thus, FTR and HTC can be eliminated from consideration: they would not make good purchases individually.

It appears that the number of choices has been narrowed from five to three. This is not true. Portfolios of the three dominant securities create an infinite number of choices which lie *approximately* along the line RZ,

---

[7] The authors decided to put the dependent variable $E(r)$ on the vertical axis rather than the horizontal axis as many other authors have done. This decision was based on a desire to provide the reader graphs consistent with those shown in mathematical statistics texts, where the dependent variable is customarily placed on the vertical axis.

[8] A dominant security has one of the following: (i) the lowest risk (σ) in its $E(r)$ class, or, (ii) the highest $E(r)$ in its risk class, or (iii) both an $E(r)$ that is above another security's $E(r)$ and a σ that is below the other security's risk.

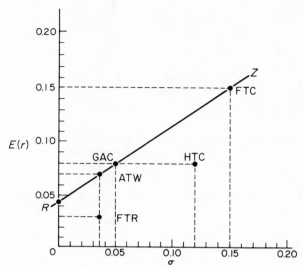

Fig. 2.5   Opportunities in Risk-Return Space

or left of it—depending on the correlation coefficients between the securities.[9]

For example, a portfolio composed 50–50 of ATW and GAC has an expected return of 7.35 percent [by equation (2A.8)] and a standard deviation of 4.3 percent [by equation (2A.9) and assuming perfect positive correlation]. The expected return on this portfolio is calculated as follows:

$$E(r_p) = w_{\text{ATW}}E(r_{\text{ATW}}) + w_{\text{GAC}}E(r_{\text{GAC}})$$

$$= \tfrac{1}{2}(7\%) + \tfrac{1}{2}(7.7\%) = 7.35 \text{ percent.}$$

The standard deviation of returns is calculated as follows:

$$\sigma_p = \sqrt{\begin{aligned}&w_{\text{ATW}}^2\sigma_{\text{ATW}}^2 + w_{\text{GAC}}^2\sigma_{\text{GAC}}^2\\ &+ 2w_{\text{ATW}}w_{\text{GAC}}r_{\text{ATW,GAC}}\sigma_{\text{ATW}}\sigma_{\text{GAC}}\end{aligned}}$$

$$= \sqrt{(\tfrac{1}{2})^2(3.7\%)^2 + (\tfrac{1}{2})^2(4.9\%)^2 + 2(\tfrac{1}{2})(\tfrac{1}{2})(1)(3.7\%)(4.9\%)}$$

$$= \sqrt{.00184} \simeq 4.3 \text{ percent.}$$

If the reader is not already familiar with these formulas for the return

---

[9] Actually, correlation coefficients between securities in a given portfolio that are below $+1$ will produce points that dominate the line RZ and may even represent portfolios containing the two dominated securities HTC and FTR. These and other possibilities will be discussed later in this chapter.

and risk of a portfolio, he should study Appendix 2A before reading Chapter 2. Plotting this portfolio on Fig. 2.5 would produce a point about halfway between ATW and GAC. Likewise, letting the point R denote investing in risk-free assets at 4 percent return (for example, short-term government bonds), the points between points R and ATW represent portfolios of varying proportions of government bonds and ATW shares. By borrowing at rate R and investing in ATW, GAC, or FTC, the investor creates points on RZ that lie out past FTC (that is, by using leverage).

By elimination of dominated securities the choice has been limited to points ATW, GAC, FTC, and the *infinite* number of portfolios containing some combination of securities, which is assumed, to keep things simple, to lie along the line RZ in Fig. 2.5. Exactly which point along RZ an investor selects depends on the personal preferences in the trade-off between risk and return.

Investor Preferences and Indifference Curves

Indifference curves can be used to represent investors' preferences. Indifference curves are drawn such that investors' satisfaction is equal all along their length; they are sometimes called utility isoquants. Assuming investors dislike risk and like larger expected returns, the indifference curves are positively sloped. The exact amount of slope depends on the investors' particular preferences for a safe return versus a larger risky return. The indifference map of a timid, risk-fearing investor is shown in Fig. 2.6. Figure 2.7 depicts an aggressive, risk-averting investor who will accept large risks for a small increase in return. Both the timid and aggressive investors dislike risk. However, the timid investor in Fig. 2.6 dislikes risk more than the aggressive investor in Fig. 2.7. A risk lover (such as an inveterate gambler) would have indifference curves convex to the expected-return axis.

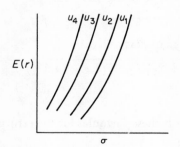

Fig. 2.6
Timid Risk-Averter's Indifference
Map

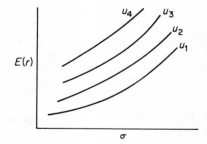

Fig. 2.7
Aggressive Risk-Averter's Indifference
Map

The higher-numbered utility isoquants represent higher levels of satisfaction. These curves grow more vertical as they rise, reflecting a diminishing willingness to assume risk.

Reproducing line RZ from Fig. 2.5, the analysis can be made determinate with the addition of an indifference map as in Fig. 2.8. The investor will seek the highest indifference curve tangent to the dominant opportunity locus, RZ, and thus reach a point like O where his satisfaction is maximum.

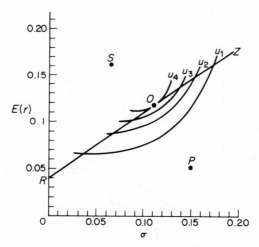

Fig. 2.8   A Risk-Return Preference Ordering

Assets like P in Fig. 2.8, which are dominated, will suffer from lack of demand, and their price will fall.[10] The rate of return is the ratio of dividends plus capital gains or losses, all over the purchase price. After a price fall the denominator of the ratio will be reduced enough to increase the value of the rate of return. This means the equilibrium return on P will move toward RZ after the temporary capital losses cease. Points above the line RZ (like S) represent undervalued assets whose prices will be bid up. The resulting higher equilibrium price (that is, higher denominator in rate-of-return ratio) will lower the expected rate of return on the previously undervalued asset, and it will tend to be relocated on RZ.[11]

---

[10] Technically, P could represent an individual security in equilibrium if that security were held in an efficient portfolio.

[11] An equilibrium rate of return is a rate of return on the ray RZ. Equilibrium returns have no tendency to change. Note, however, that price changes may be necessary to maintain equilibrium rates of return.

The Opportunity Set

Plotting all investments $E(r)$ and σ in Fig. 2.9 and connecting these possible investments with lines representing possible combinations (portfolios) of the individual assets generates an *opportunity set* which might take on the escalloped quarter-moon shape shown. Within the opportunity set are all individual securities, as well as all portfolios not containing R. Thus, all points within this space are feasible investments. The

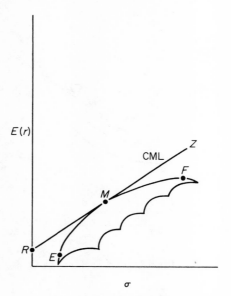

Fig. 2.9   The Opportunity Set

left side of the opportunity set between points E and F is the *efficient frontier* of the opportunity set. It is comprised of all "efficient investments."

An *efficient investment* has either (1) more return than any other investment in its risk class (that is, any other security with the same variability of returns), or (2) less risk than any other security with the same return. The efficient frontier of the opportunity set *dominates* all other investments in the opportunity set. These investments are sometimes said to be *Markowitz efficient*, referring to Harry Markowitz, the originator of two-parameter portfolio analysis.

Hirshleifer expressed the reason for the particular shape of the efficient frontier of the opportunity set as follows:

> The curvature shown for the efficient frontier—opposite to that of the $(E(r), \sigma)$ indifference curves—follows also from the covariance effect, since

moving to higher values of portfolio $E(r)$ progressively reduces the number of securities that can be held in combination so as to lower σ.[12]

Adding the possibility of borrowing or lending at rate R a new opportunity set, the line RMZ, is created. The line RMZ represents the continuum of possible portfolios an investor could construct from R and M by borrowing and lending at rate R. RMZ is called the *capital market line* (CML). As graphed in Fig. 2.9 the CML is the true efficient frontier—it dominates the efficient frontier of the opportunity set. The CML can be viewed as the locus of the maximum rates of returns for each risk class. The CML represents the opportunity foregone by investing in less efficient investments.

Each point on the CML is determined by values for $E(r)$ and σ. The σ determines the *risk class* of the investment. The $E(r)$ is the cost of capital, or capitalization rate, appropriate for that particular risk class.

Diversification

Markowitz diversification is the particular form of diversification activity implied by portfolio analysis. This type of diversification differs from the *naive definition of diversification* used widely by security salesmen and traditional investments texts. These sources define diversification as "not putting all your eggs in one basket" or "spreading your risks." The possible benefits of naive diversification will be discussed later. Naive diversification ignores the covariance between securities and results in superfluous diversification.

Markowitz efficient diversification involves combining investments with less than perfect positive correlation in order to reduce risk in the portfolio without sacrificing any of the portfolio's return. In general, the lower the correlation of the assets in a portfolio the less risky the portfolio will be. This is true regardless how risky the assets of the portfolio are when analyzed in isolation.

Markowitz puts it this way:[13]

> Not only does [portfolio analysis] imply diversification, it implies the "right kind" of diversification for the "right reason." The adequacy of diversification is not thought by investors to depend on the number of different securities held. A portfolio with sixty different railway securities, for example, would not be as well diversified as the same size portfolio with

---

[12] Jack Hirschleifer, "Efficient Allocation of Capital in an Uncertain World," *American Economic Review*, May 1964, p. 79.

[13] H. Markowitz, "Portfolio Selection," *Journal of Finance*, vol. VII, no. 1 (March 1952), p. 89. Reprinted in Archer and D'Ambrosio, *The Theory of Business Finance: A Book of Readings* (New York: The Macmillan Company, 1967), p. 599; E. B. Frederickson, *Frontiers of Investment Analysis* (Scranton, Pa.: International Textbook Co., 1966), p. 364; Wu and Zakon, *Elements of Investments* (New York: Holt, Rinehart and Winston, Inc., 1965), p. 310. Parenthetical phrase added.

some railroad, some public utility, mining, various sorts of manufacturing, etc. The reason is that it is generally more likely for firms within the same industry to do poorly at the same time than for firms in dissimilar industries.

Similarly, in trying to make variance [of returns] small it is not enough to invest in many securities. It is necessary to avoid investing in securities with high covariances among themselves.

Diversification Demonstration

Consider the following two securities:

Investments	$E(r)$	σ
A	5%	20%
B	15%	40%

Combining securities A and B, the expected return of the resulting portfolio is given below:

$$E(r_p) = \sum_{i=1}^{2} w_i E(r_i) = w_A E(r_A) + w_B E(r_B)$$

$$= (w_A)\ .05 + (w_B)\ .15$$

$$= (\tfrac{2}{3})\ .05 + (\tfrac{1}{3})\ .15 = .083 = 8.3 \text{ percent,} \qquad (2.5)$$

if $w_A = \tfrac{2}{3}$ and $w_B = \tfrac{1}{3}$.[14] The risk of the portfolio is given by the following function:

$$SD(r_p) = \sqrt{w_A{}^2 \sigma_{AA} + w_B{}^2 \sigma_{BB} + 2 w_A w_B \sigma_{AB}}$$

$$= \sqrt{w_A{}^2 \sigma_{AA} + w_B{}^2 \sigma_{BB} + 2 w_A w_B r_{AB} \sigma_A \sigma_B}$$

$$\text{since } \sigma_{AB} = r_{AB} \sigma_A \sigma_B. \qquad (2.6)$$

---

[14] The minimum variance weights may be found by trial and error. However, the standard calculus optimization techniques are much more efficient. The variance of the portfolio of A and B is given by the following equation:

$V = \text{Var}\ (r_{A+B}) = w_A{}^2 \sigma_{AA} + w_B{}^2 \sigma_{BB} + 2 w_A w_B \sigma_{AB}$

$= .04 w_A{}^2 + .16 w_B{}^2 + 2(-1)(.2)(.4) w_A w_B, \qquad$ when $r_{AB} = -1$

$= .04 w_A{}^2 + .16(1 - w_A)^2 - .16 w_A (1 - w_A), \qquad$ since $w_B = (1 - w_A)$ in this two-asset portfolio

$= .04 w_A{}^2 + .16 - .32 w_A + .16 w_A{}^2 - .16 w_A + .16 w_A.$

To minimize this variance set $dV/dw_A = 0$ and solve for w_A.

$$dV/dw_A = 2(.04) w_A - .32 + (2)(.16) w_A - .16 + (.16) 2 w_A{}^2 = 0$$

$$= .08 w_A - .48 + .64 w_A = 0$$

$$= .72 w_A - .48 = 0$$

$$w_A = .48/.72 = 2/3.$$

Thus, w_B must equal $1/3$ to minimize this portfolio's variance (that is, risk).

The reader who is not familiar with equations (2.5) and (2.6) should read all of Appendix 2A before proceeding. Using the values for assets A and B:

$$\sigma_p = \sqrt{(\tfrac{2}{3})^2(20\%)^2 + (\tfrac{1}{3})^2(40\%)^2 + 2(r_{AB})(\tfrac{2}{3})(\tfrac{1}{3})(20\%)(40\%)}$$
$$= \sqrt{.0175 + .0175 + .035(r_{AB})} = \sqrt{.035 + .035(r_{AB})}.$$

Although the expected return of this portfolio is fixed at 8.3 percent for these proportions of A and B, the risk of the portfolio varies with r_{AB}, the correlation coefficient. Thus, if $r_{AB} = +1$, then $\sigma_p = \sqrt{.07} = 25.4$ percent. If $r_{AB} = 0$, then $\sigma_p = \sqrt{.035} = 18.7$ percent. And, if $r_{AB} = -1$, then $\sigma_p = \sqrt{0} = 0$. The locus of all possible proportions (w_A and w_B) for investments A and B are plotted in Fig. 2.10 for $r_{AB} = 1$, 0, and -1.

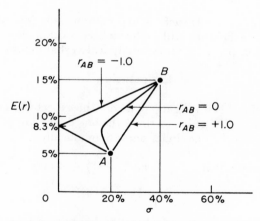

Fig. 2.10   The Effects of Markowitz Diversification

Figure 2.10 graphically depicts how Markowitz diversification affects risk in the portfolio.[15] Figure 2.10 shows that the lower the r_{AB} the more risk is reduced by combining A and B into a portfolio. The straight line between A and B defines the locus of $E(r)$ and σ combinations for all possible portfolios of A and B when $r_{AB} = +1$. Considering the effects of diversification as depicted in Fig. 2.10, the reader is invited to reexamine Fig. 2.9. The particular shape [that is, curves convex to the $E(r)$ axis] given the opportunity set in Fig. 2.9 is the result of diversification.

---

[15] Figure 2.10 was published in Professor W. Sharpe's article, "Capital Asset Prices: A Theory of Market Equilibrium Under Conditions of Risk," *The Journal of Finance*, September 1964.

Risk can be reduced via Markowitz diversification without decreasing return at all.[16] Such diversification is surely a good thing! It is possible that naive diversification would reduce risk. However, naive diversification cannot be expected to *minimize* risk, since it ignores the most important variable, the correlation (or covariance) between assets. Naive diversification only concentrates on owning many assets—that is, "not putting all your eggs in one basket."

Appendix 2B discusses how diversification can affect the value of a portfolio. Chapter 7 discusses the extent to which diversification is useful.

Appendix 2A

Defining Risk Via Finite Probability

In this appendix words such as expectation and risk will be defined formally. These definitions will be formalized so that they may be used instead of the less precise and less analytical verbal definitions.

Expectation

For a one-dollar bet on the flip of a coin the expected value of the outcome is the probability of heads times the one dollar loss plus the probability of tails times the one-dollar gain. Symbolically,

$$\text{expected value} = p(\text{heads})(-\$1) + p(\text{tails})(+\$1)$$

$$= .5(-1) + .5(+1) = 0,$$

where $p(\text{heads})$ represents the probability that heads occurs. The symbols above are a very definitive statement of what is meant by the phrase, "we expect the gamblers will break even." Writing this expression for expected value in even more general and compact form yields equation (2A.1).

$$E(X) \equiv \sum_{i=1}^{N} p_i x_i$$

$$\equiv (p_1)(x_1) + (p_2)(x_2) + \cdots + (p_n)(x_n). \tag{2A.1}$$

---

[16] The authors have found that their students sometimes misinterpret Fig. 2.10 and think that the correlation between securities also affects the portfolio's return. The error of this conclusion is easily seen by noting that the correlation coefficient is not to be found in the formula for the portfolio's return, equation (2.5). Thus, $E(r_p)$ is independent of the benefits of Markowitz diversification.

It is assumed that the probabilities sum to one, $\sum_{i}^{n} p = 1.0$. In words, equation (2A.1) says expected value of the random variable x (for example, x might be the dollar outcome of the gamble or any other number resulting from an experiment involving chance) equals the sum of all n products of (p_i) and (x_i), where p_i is the probability of the ith outcome [for example, p (heads) $= p_i = \frac{1}{2}$ when flipping coins] and x_i is the ith outcome (for example, $x_i = -\$1$ or $+\$1$ might represent heads or tails).[1]

Mathematicians say that the letter "E" as used in equation (2A.1) is an *operator*. They mean the letter E specifies the operation of multiplying all outcomes times their probabilities and summing those products to get the expected value.

Finding the expected values of a set of numbers is roughly analogous to finding the weighted average of the numbers—using probabilities for weights. Do not be confused, however; although the arithmetic is the same, an average is conceptually different from an expectation. An expectation is determined by its probabilities and it represents a hypothesis about an unknown outcome. An average, however, is a summarizing measure. There is no conceptual connection between the average and the expectation—only the mechanical similarity of the calculations.

The operator E will be used to derive several important formulas. Therefore, consider several elementary properties of expected values, which will be used later:

(i) The expected value of a constant number is that constant. Symbolically, if c is any constant number (for example, $c = 2$ or 99 or 1064),

$$E(c) = pc + pc + \cdots + pc = c.$$

This simple statement is almost a tautology.

(ii) The expected value of a constant times a random variable[2] equals the constant times the expected value of the random variable. Thus, if x is a random variable where $x = -1$ represents a loss and $x = +1$ represents a win in a coin flip and c is the constant number of dollars bet on each toss, this situation may be restated as follows:

$$E(cx) = cE(x).$$

The proof follows:

$$E(cx) = \sum_{i=1}^{n} p_i(cx_i) = p_1(cx_1) + \cdots + p_n(cx_n)$$

$$= p_1 cx_1 + \cdots + p_n cx_n$$

$$= c(p_1 x_1 + \cdots + p_n x_n) = c\sum_{i=1}^{n} p_i x_i = cE(x)$$

---

[1] Appendix A is provided at the end of this book for readers who would like to review the mathematical operator sigma (Σ)—the summation sign. Appendix B briefly examines the different types of probabilities. Appendix C shows some important proofs that can be accomplished with the expectation operator.

[2] A random variable is a rule or function that assigns a value to each outcome of an experiment.

(iii) The expected value of the sum of n independent random variables is simply the sum of their expected values. For example, if $n = 2$ for random variables called x and y,

$$E(x + y) = E(x) + E(y).$$

The proof follows:

$$
\begin{aligned}
E(x + y) &= \sum_{i=1}^{n} p_i \cdot (x_i + y_i) \\
&= p_i \cdot (x_1 + y_1) + p_2 \cdot (x_2 + y_2) + \cdots + p_n(x_n + y_n) \\
&= p_1 x_1 + p_1 y_1 + p_2 x_2 + p_2 y_2 + \cdots + p_n x_n + p_n y_n \\
&= [p_1 x_1 + p_2 x_2 + \cdots + p_n x_n] + [p_1 y_1 + p_2 y_2 + \cdots + p_n y_n] \\
&= \sum_{i=1}^{n} p_i x_i + \sum_{i=1}^{n} p_i y_i = E(x) + E(y),
\end{aligned}
$$

where p_i is the joint probability of x_i and y_i occurring jointly.

(iv) The expected value of a constant times a random variable plus a constant equals the constant times the expected value of the random variable plus the constant. Symbolically, if b and c are constants and x is a random variable,

$$E(bx + c) = bE(x) + c.$$

The proof is a combination of the proofs for i, ii, and iii.

The reader who has trouble with this brief development of expected-value operators is encouraged to consult an elementary text on finite probability theory[3] or the appendix on expected-value proofs at the back of the book.

Risk

The phrase "dispersion of outcomes around the expected value" could be substituted for the word "risk" as used here. The word "riskier" simply means "*more* dispersion of expected outcomes around the expected value." The "dispersion of outcomes" definition of risk squares with the common but less precise use of the word in everyday conversation. Consider a more formal version of the same definition, which lends itself well for analysis.

The mathematics terms variance and standard deviation measure dispersion of outcome about the expected value. Symbolically, the variance of the random variable x is

$$
\begin{aligned}
\sigma_i^2 = \sigma_{ii} &= \sum_{i=1}^{n} p_i (x_i - E(x))^2 = E(x_i - E(x))^2 \\
&= p_1 (x_1 - E(x))^2 + p_2 (x_2 - E(x))^2 + \cdots + p_n (x_n - E(x))^2.
\end{aligned}
\qquad (2A.2)
$$

---

[3] A book such as Mosteller, Rourke, and Thomas, *Probability with Statistical Applications* (Reading, Mass.: Addison-Wesley Publishing Co., Inc., 1961), would be an excellent source for self-taught finite probability theory and a handy reference for readable definitions. Appendix C shows how to prove some important relations using the expected-value operator.

In words, the variance (σ_{ii}) is the sum of the products of the squared deviations times their probabilities. If all n outcomes are equally likely, $p_i = 1/n$. If a coin-flipping gamble is fair [that is, $E(x) = 0$] and the stakes are five dollars, the variance is computed as follows.

$$\text{Var (\$5 gamble)} = p_i(x_1 - E(x))^2 + p_2(x_2 - E(x))^2,$$
$$\text{Var (\$5 gamble)} = (\tfrac{1}{2})(-5 - 0)^2 + (\tfrac{1}{2})(+5 + 0)^2$$
$$= 12.50 + 12.50 = 25.$$

The variance of the $5 gamble is 25 "dollars squared." To convert this measure of risk into more intuitively appealing terms the standard deviation (σ), which is simply the square root of the variance, will be used.

$$\sigma = \sqrt{\sum_{i=1}^{n} p_i(x_i - E(x))^2} = \sqrt{\sigma_{ii}} = \sqrt{E(x - E(x))^2} = \sqrt{\sigma^2}. \quad (2A.3)$$

Thus, $\sqrt{25}$ "dollars squared" $= \$5 =$ standard deviation of the $5 gamble.

Notice that in equations (2A.2) and (2A.3) the variance and standard deviations are both defined two ways. First, they are defined using the summation sign $(\sum)$ and probabilities. Second, they are defined using the expected-value operator (E), which equation (2A.1) showed means the same thing as the summation sign and probabilities. The definitions will be used interchangeably. Consider another example—one more appropriate for portfolio analysis.

Example 2A.1 Two securities' annual rates of return for a ten-year period are shown below. Assume this is historical data.

Year (t)	American Telephone Works (ATW)	General Auto Corp. (GAC)	Joint Probability*
1	7%	5%	.1
2	4	0	.1
3	0	−5	.1
4	7	5	.1
5	10	10	.1
6	14	16	.1
7	7	16	.1
8	4	10	.1
9	10	10	.1
10	7	10	.1
			1.0

* See Appendix B at the rear of the book for definition of joint probability.

From the data a security analyst computes the following relative frequencies—or, in our usage, probability distributions.

American Telephone Works (ATW)		General Auto Corp. (GAC)	
Forecasted return	Marginal probability*	Forecasted return	Marginal probability
0	.1	−5%	.1
4%	.2	0	.1
7	.4	5	.2
10	.2	10	.4
14	.1	16	.2
	1.0		1.0

* See Appendix B at rear of book for definition of marginal probability.

To derive the probability distributions above, the security analyst could have ignored the historical data or paid little attention to it. He could have made a subjective probability distribution based on his experience and intuition. The security analyst's tools are examined in Chapter 3. However, assuming the processes determining the historical returns will not change in the future, the expected probability distribution is derived directly from the historical data.

Expected Return

The expected return of ATW is calculated using equation (2A.1) and substituting the random variable r for the random variable x in the equation as follows:

$$E(x) = \sum_{i=1}^{n} p_i x_i, \tag{2A.1}$$

$$E(r_{\text{ATW}}) = \sum_{t=1}^{10} p_i r_t. \tag{2A.1'}$$

Or, using the marginal probabilities instead of the joint probabilities, equation (2A.1') may be written as

$$E(r_{\text{ATW}}) = \sum_{1}^{5} pr$$

$$= (.1)(0) + (.2)(.04) + (.4)(.07) + (.2)(.1) + (.1)(.14)$$

$$= 0 + .008 + .028 + .02 + .014 = .07 = 7 \text{ percent.}$$

The reader may check his understanding of formula (2A.1') by verifying $E(r_{\text{GAC}}) = .077 = 7.7$ percent = the expected return for GAC.

Risk in a Security

Risk was generally defined as the expected dispersion of the outcomes. In discussing securities it will be assumed that the rate of return is the single most meaningful outcome associated with the securities' performance.

Thus, discussion of the risk of a security will focus on dispersion of the security's rate of return around its expected return. That is, one might equate a security's risk with its "variability of return."[4] The standard deviation of rates of return (or variance of rates of return) is a possible measure of the phenomenon defined above as the risk of a security. Symbolically, this can be written by substituting r_i's in the place of x_i's in equation (2A.2).

$$\sigma_i{}^2 = \sigma_{ii} = \sum_{t=1}^{n} p_{it}(r_{it} - E(r_i))^2 = E(r_i - E(r))^2. \qquad (2A.2')$$

Equation (2A.2') defines the variance of returns for security i. The value of σ_{ii} is in terms of a "rate of return squared." The standard deviation of returns is the square root of the variance.

$$\sigma \text{ or } \sigma_i = \sqrt{\sum_{t=1}^{n} p_{it}(r_{it} - E(r_i))^2} = \sqrt{E(r - E(r))^2} = \sqrt{\sigma_{ii}}. \qquad (2A.3')$$

Thus, for the returns on ATW in Example 2A.1, using the marginal probabilities, the variance and standard deviation of returns are found as follows:

$$\sigma_{\text{ATW}}^2 = (.1)(0 - .07)^2 + (.2)(.04 - .07)^2 + (.4)(.07 - .07)^2$$

$$+ (.2)(.1 - .07)^2 + (.1)(.14 - .07)^2$$

$$= (.1)(.0049) + (.2)(.0009) + (.4)(0) + (.2)(.0009) + (.1)(.0049)$$

$$= .00049 + .00018 + 0 + .00018 + .00049 = .00134$$

$$\sigma_{\text{ATW}} = \sqrt{.00134} = .0368 = 3.68 \text{ percent.}$$

It is left as an exercise for the reader to verify that the standard deviation of returns from GAC is 6.28 percent.

Covariance of Returns

The covariance of returns on securities i and j will be denoted by σ_{ij} or Cov (r_i, r_j).

$$\sigma_{ij} = E\{[r_i - E(r_i)][r_j - E(r_j)]\}$$

$$= \sum_{t=1}^{n} p_t\{[r_{it} - E(r_i)][r_{jt} - E(r_j)]\}, \qquad (2A.4)$$

---

[4] Harry Markowitz, *Portfolio Selection: Cowles Foundation Monograph 16* (New York: John Wiley & Sons, Inc., 1959), p. 14.

where r_{it} is the tth rate of return for the ith firm. The ten ordered pairs of rates of return (r_{ATW}, r_{GAC}) from Example 2A.1 have been graphed in Fig. 2A.1, and a numerical example follows.

By making the assumption that all ten returns are equally likely to occur, $p_i = 1/n = \frac{1}{10}$ can be substituted for the probabilities in the formula for covariance. Thus, the formula can be rewritten

$$\sigma_{ij} = \sum_{t=1}^{10} (\tfrac{1}{10})[r_{ATC} - E(r_{ATC})][r_{GAC} - E(r_{GAC})].$$

The calculations are shown below. Notice that in Fig. 2A.1 all but one of the ordered pairs (r_{ATW}, r_{GAC}) are plotted in the first quadrant—the northeast quadrant.

ATW		GAC		Probabilities	Products Column
r_{it}	$[r_{it} - E(r)]$	r_{jt}	$[r_{jt} - E(r)]$	$p_t = 1/n$	$(p_t)[r - E(r_i)][r - E(r_j)]$
.07	0	.05	−.027	.1	0
.04	−.03	0	−.077	.1	+.000231
0	−.07	−.05	−.127	.1	+.000889
.07	0	.05	−.027	.1	0
.1	.03	.1	.023	.1	+.000069
.14	.07	.16	.083	.1	+.000581
.07	0	.16	.083	.1	0
.04	−.03	.1	.023	.1	−.000069
.1	.03	.1	.023	.1	+.000069
.07	0	.1	.023	.1	0
				1.0	.00177
$E(r_{ATW}) = .07$		$E(r_{GAC}) = .077$			$\sum_{t-1}^{n=10} p_t[r_{it} - E(r_i)][r_{jt} - E(r_j)]$

The first and third quadrants of Fig. 2A.1 contain the ordered pairs whose products (that is, r_{ATW} times r_{GAC}) are positive. The second and fourth quadrants contain the ordered pairs whose products are negative. However, in calculating the covariance the origin (the point where $r_{ATW} = 0$ and $r_{GAC} = 0$) is not used to determine whether the ten observed values of r_{ATW} and r_{GAC} are high (positive) or low (negative) deviations. The covariance uses deviations of the random variable from its expected value [that is, the ith deviation is $(r_i - E(r))$], which, in effect, shifts the point of reference from the origin to the *centroid*—the "center of gravity" for the ten points.[5]

Thus, points northeast and southwest of the centroid will have positive products [that is, $(p_t) \cdot (r_i - E(r_i)) \cdot (r_j - E(r_j))$] in the products column of the computations shown. Since only the eighth ordered pair

---

[5] The centroid is the point where the expected values of all variables occur. In (r_{ATW}, r_{GAC}) space $[E(r_{ATW}), E(r_{GAC})]$ is the centroid.

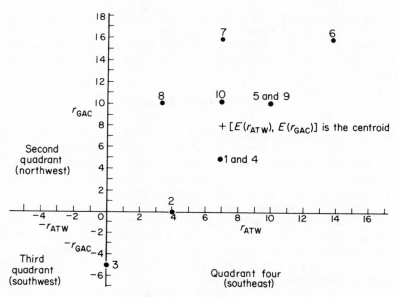

Fig. 2A.1   Ten Ordered Pairs (r_{ATW}, r_{GAC}) of Rates
of Return from ATW and GAC Data in
Example 2A.1

lies either northwest or southeast, it is the only negative product in the products column of the computation. Obviously, the positive products exceed the negative products; that is, there are more points southwest and northeast of the centroid. Thus, the sum of these products, which is the covariance of returns, is positive. The sign of the net total of these products determines the sign of the covariance.

If the ten ordered pairs had been further northeast and southwest of the centroid, the covariance would have been a larger positive number. If the majority of the plotted points were southeast and northwest of their centroid, their covariance would be negative because the two variables moved inversely (were negatively correlated).

The covariance of some variable with itself equals the variance of that variable: compare formulas (2A.2) and (2A.4). The covariance of returns on securities i and j is

$$\sigma_{ij} = E[(r_i - E(r_i)) \cdot (r_j - E(r_j))]. \qquad (2A.4)$$

Note that when $i = j$, equation (2A.4) becomes equation (2A.2').

when $i = j$, then $\sigma_{ij} = \sigma_{ii} = \sigma_{jj} = E(r_i - E(r_i))^2 = E(r_j - E(r_j))^2,$
$$\qquad (2A.2')$$

which shows that the covariance of i or j with themselves or with identical securities (that is, when $i = j$) equals the variance.

In calculating covariances it makes no difference which variable comes first. Thus, $\sigma_{ij} = \sigma_{ji}$ for any variables i and j.

If the reader is unsure of these assertions, he should take real numbers such as given in the numerical examples and calculate the values by hand.

Correlation of Returns

Within the context of portfolio analysis *diversification* can be defined as *combining securities with less than perfectly positively correlated* returns. In order for the portfolio analyst to construct a diversified portfolio, he must know correlation coefficients between all securities under consideration. Denote the correlation coefficient between securities i and j as r_{ij}.

A correlation coefficient can vary as follows: $-1 \leq r \leq +1$. If $r_{ij} = +1$, the returns on securities i and j are perfectly positively correlated; they move in the same direction at the same time. If $r_{ij} = 0$, the returns of i and j are uncorrelated; they show no tendency to follow each other. If $r_{ij} = -1$, securities i and j vary inversely; they are perfectly negatively correlated. The definition of r_{ij} is

$$r_{ij} = \frac{\text{cov}\,(r_i, r_j)}{\sigma_i \sigma_j} = \frac{E[(r_i - E(r_i))(r_j - E(r_j))]}{\sigma_i \sigma_j}$$

$$= \frac{\sum p_t[(r_{it} - E(r_i))(r_{jt} - E(r_j))]}{\sigma_i \sigma_j}, \tag{2A.5}$$

where σ_i is defined by equation (2A.3′) and cov (r_i, r_j) is the covariance of returns of the two securities i and j defined in equation (2A.4).

The covariance measures how the random variables vary together—how they covary. Thus, the covariance always has the same sign as the correlation coefficient. Using equation (2A.5), the correlation of returns for $i = \text{ATW}$ and $j = \text{GAC}$ can be computed as follows:

$$r_{ij} = \frac{\sigma_{ij}}{\sigma_i \sigma_j} = \frac{.00177}{(.0368)(.0628)} = \frac{.00177}{.00231} = +.77 = r_{\text{ATW,GAC}}.$$

Using circular definitions, the covariance can be defined in terms of the correlation coefficient and the standard deviations.

$$\sigma_{ij} = (r_{ij})(\sigma_i)(\sigma_j) \tag{2A.6}$$

Equation (2A.6) is derived by simple algebraic manipulation of equation (2A.5).

The Data Required for Portfolio Analysis

Portfolio analysis requires that the security analyst furnish the following estimates for every security to be considered:

1. the expected return,
2. the variance of returns, and
3. the covariances between all securities.[6]

The security analyst could obtain these inputs from historical data. Or, he can subjectively estimate these inputs. If the historical data are accurate and conditions in the future are expected to resemble those from the period in which the data were derived, the historical data may be the best estimate of the future. But if the security analyst is "expert" or the market is changing, subjective estimates may be preferable to historical data.

Since the security analyst can consider each security separately, he deals primarily with single random variables. The tools and concepts developed so far in this chapter are appropriate for such work.

The portfolio analyst must consider many securities at once when constructing the optimum portfolio. That is, he must be concerned with the expected return and risk of the weighted *sum* of many random variables. In the next few pages the statistical tools the portfolio analyst uses will be developed.

Weights Within the Portfolio

The portfolio-analysis technique that follows does not directly indicate the dollar amount that should be invested in each security. Rather, it yields the optimum *proportions* each security in the optimum portfolio should assume. These proportions, weights, or participation levels, as they are variously called, will be denoted by w_i's. Thus, w_i is the fraction of the total value of the portfolio that should be placed in security i. Assuming that all funds allocated for portfolio use are to be accounted for, the following constraint is placed on all portfolios:

$$\sum_{i=1}^{n} w_i = 1. \tag{2A.7}$$

In words, the n fractions of the total portfolio invested in n different assets sum up to one. This constraint cannot be violated in portfolio analysis, or the analysis has no rational economic interpretation.

---

[6] Using Sharpe's simplified model, covariances based on some market index may be used instead of covariances between all possible combinations of securities.

Expected Return from a Portfolio

Letting r_p denote some actual return from a portfolio and $E(r_p)$ its expected return, $E(r_p)$ may be defined as in equation (2A.8):

$$E(r_p) = \sum_{i=1}^{n} w_i E(r_i) = \sum_{i=1}^{n} w_i \left(\sum_{t=1}^{T} p_{it} r_{it} \right)$$

$$= w_1 E(r_1) + w_2 E(r_2) + \cdots + w_n E(r_n). \tag{2A.8}$$

In words, the expected return on a portfolio is the weighted average of the expected returns from the n assets in the portfolio.

Thus, the expected return of the portfolio with $w_{\text{ATW}} = .4$ and $w_{\text{GAC}} = .6$ is

$$E(r_p) = (.4)E(r_{\text{ATW}}) + (.6)E(r_{\text{GAC}}) = (.4)(.07) + (.6)(.077)$$

$$= .028 + .0462 = .0742 = 7.42 \text{ percent.}$$

Note that $\sum_{i=1}^{2} w_i = 1$.

Portfolio Risk

It is necessary to expand the mathematical definition of risk used for single securities into a form describing the returns of all securities in the portfolio. Following the "dispersion of outcome" or "variability of return" definitions of risk, the risk of a portfolio is defined as the variability of its return—that is, the variability of r_p. Denoting the variance of r_p by Var (r_p), it is possible to derive an analytical expression for Var (r_p) in terms of the r_i's of all securities in the portfolio. This is the form of the expression suitable for portfolio analysis.

Substituting r_p for r_i in equation (2A.2') yields equation (2A.2''), which will be denoted by Var (r_p).

$$\sigma_{ii} = E(r_i - E(r))^2 = \sigma_i^2, \tag{2A.2'}$$

$$\sigma_{r_p}^2 = \text{Var } (r_p) = E(r_p - E(r_p))^2. \tag{2A.2''}$$

A simple two-security portfolio will be used to analyze equation (2A.2''). However, the results are perfectly general and follow for an n-security portfolio where n is any positive integer. Substituting the quantity $(w_1 r_1 + w_2 r_2)$ for the equivalent r_p into equation (2A.2'') yields

$$\text{Var } (r_p) = E([w_1 r_1 + w_2 r_2] - E[w_1 r_1 + w_2 r_2])^2.$$

Removing the parentheses and using property (i) of the expectation (since the w_i's can be treated as constants) results in an equivalent form:

$$= E(w_1 r_1 + w_2 r_2 - w_1 E(r_1) - w_2 E(r_2))^2.$$

Collecting terms with like subscripts and factoring out the w_i's gives

$$= E(w_1[r_1 - E(r_1)] + w_2[r_2 - E(r_2)])^2.$$

Since $(ab + cd)^2 = (a^2b^2 + c^2d^2 + 2abcd)$, the above squared quantity can likewise be expanded by letting $ab = w_1[r_1 - E(r_1)]$ and $cd = w_2[r_2 - E(r_2)]$, which gives

$$= E(w_1^2[r_1 - E(r_1)]^2 + w_2^2[r_2 - E(r_2)]^2$$
$$+ 2w_1w_2[r_1 - E(r_1)] \cdot [(r_2 - E(r_2)]).$$

Using property (ii) of the E operator yields

$$= w_1^2 E[r_1 - E(r_1)]^2 + w_2^2 E[r_2 - E(r_2)]^2$$
$$+ 2w_1w_2 E([r_1 - E(r_1)] \cdot [r_2 - E(r_2)]),$$

and, recalling equations (2A.3') and (2A.4) which define σ_{ii} and σ_{ij}, we recognize the above expression as

$$= w_1^2\sigma_{11} + w_2^2\sigma_{22} + 2w_1w_2\sigma_{12}$$
$$= w_1^2 \operatorname{Var}(r_1) + w_2^2 \operatorname{Var}(r_2) + 2w_1w_2 \operatorname{cov}(r_1r_2). \qquad (2A.9)$$

In words, equation (2A.9) shows that the variance of a weighted sum is not always simply the sum of the weighted variances. The covariance term may increase or decrease the variance of the sum, depending on its sign.

The derivation of equation (2A.9) is repeated in a more coherent manner below.

$$\sigma_{r_p}^2 = \operatorname{Var}(r_p) = E(r_p - E(r_p))^2$$
$$= E(w_1r_1 + w_2r_2 - E(w_1r_1 + w_2r_2))^2$$
$$= E[w_1r_1 + w_2r_2 - w_1E(r_1) - w_2E(r_2)]^2$$
$$= E[w_1(r_1 - E(r_1)) + w_2(r_2 - E(r_2))]^2$$
$$= E[w_1^2(r_1 - E(r_1))^2 + w_2^2(r_2 - E(r_2))^2$$
$$+ 2w_1w_2(r_1 - E(r_1))(r_2 - E(r_2))]$$
$$= w_1^2 E(r_1 - E(r_1))^2 + w_2^2 E(r_2 - E(r_2))^2$$
$$+ 2w_1w_2 E[(r_1 - E(r_1))(r_2 - E(r_2))]$$
$$= w_1^2 \operatorname{Var}(r_1) + w_2^2 \operatorname{Var}(r_2) + 2w_1w_2 \operatorname{cov}(r_1r_2). \qquad (2A.9)$$

The derivation of equation (2A.9) is one of the main teaching points of this appendix. An understanding of equation (2A.9) is essential to a true understanding of diversification and portfolio analysis. Next, equation (2A.9) will be expanded (without proof) to measure the risk of more realistic portfolios (portfolios with more than two securities). However, even in its more elaborate versions equation (2A.9) is still simply the sum of the weighted variances and covariances.

Equation (2A.9) is sometimes written more compactly as

$$\text{Var}\ (r_p) = \sum_{i}^{n} w_i{}^2 \sigma_{ii} + \sum_{j}^{n} \sum_{i}^{n} w_i w_j \sigma_{ij},$$
$$\text{for } i \neq j$$

where $n = 2$ or any other positive integer. To clarify this notation consider the following table of terms. The subscript i is the row number and j is the column number.

	Column 1	Column 2	
$\text{Var}\ (r_p) =$	$+\ w_1 w_1 \sigma_{11}$	$+\ w_1 w_2 \sigma_{12}$	Row 1
	$+\ w_2 w_1 \sigma_{21}$	$+\ w_2 w_2 \sigma_{22} =$	Row 2

$$= w_1 w_1 \sigma_{11} + w_1 w_2 \sigma_{12} + w_2 w_1 \sigma_{21} + w_2 w_2 \sigma_{22}$$

$$= w_1{}^2 \sigma_{11} + 2 w_1 w_2 \sigma_{12} + w_2{}^2 \sigma_{22} \qquad (\text{since } w_1 w_2 \sigma_{12} = w_2 w_1 \sigma_{21})$$

$$= \sum_{i=1}^{2} w_i{}^2 \sigma_{ii} + \sum_{j=1}^{2} \sum_{i=1}^{2} w_i w_j \sigma_{ij} \qquad\qquad (2A.9')$$
$$\text{for } i \neq j$$

$$= \sum_{j}^{2} \sum_{i}^{2} w_i w_j \sigma_{ij} \qquad \text{since cov } (r_i, r_i) = \text{var } (r_i) \text{ for } i = j \qquad (2A.9'')$$

$$= \sum_{i=1}^{2} w_i{}^2 \sigma_{ii} + \sum_{i=1}^{2} \sum_{j=1}^{2} w_i w_j r_{ij} \sigma_i \sigma_j \qquad \text{since } \sigma_{ij} = r_{ij} \sigma_i \sigma_j. \qquad (2A.9''')$$
$$\text{for } i \neq j$$

The three factors that determine the risk of a portfolio are the weights of the securities, the standard deviation (or variance) of each security, and the correlation coefficient (or covariance) between the securities.

Expressions of Var (r_p) for a large number of securities take the following form.

	Col. 1	Col. 2	Col. 3		Col. $n-1$	Col. n	
$\text{Var}\ (r_p) =$	$w_1 w_1 \sigma_{11} +$	$w_1 w_2 \sigma_{12} +$	$w_1 w_3 \sigma_{13} +$	$\cdots +$	$w_1 w_{n-1} \sigma_{1,n-1} +$	$w_1 w_n \sigma_{1n} +$	Row 1
	$w_2 w_1 \sigma_{21} +$	$w_2 w_2 \sigma_{22} +$	$w_2 w_3 \sigma_{23} +$	$\cdots +$	$w_2 w_{n-1} \sigma_{2,n-1} +$	$w_2 w_n \sigma_{2n} +$	Row 2
	$w_3 w_1 \sigma_{31} +$	$w_3 w_2 \sigma_{32} +$	$w_3 w_3 \sigma_{33} +$	$\cdots +$	$w_3 w_{n-1} \sigma_{3,n-1} +$	$w_3 w_n \sigma_{3n} +$	Row 3
	$\cdot$	$\cdot$	$\cdot$		$\cdot$	$\cdot$	
	$\cdot$	$\cdot$	$\cdot$		$\cdot$	$\cdot$	
	$w_n w_1 \sigma_{n1} +$	$w_n w_2 \sigma_{n2} +$	$w_n w_3 \sigma_{n3} +$	$\cdots +$	$w_n w_{n-1} \sigma_{n,n-1} +$	$w_n w_n \sigma_{nn}$	Row n

The data above comprise a matrix. The matrix can be represented more compactly using the succinct summation symbols shown below.

$$\text{Var } (r_p) = \sum_{i}^{n} w_i^2 \sigma_{ii} + \sum_{\substack{i=1 \\ \text{for } i \neq j}}^{n} \sum_{j=1}^{n} w_i w_j \sigma_{ij} = \sum_{i=1}^{n} \sum_{j=1}^{n} w_i w_j \sigma_{ij}.$$

A matrix can be thought of as an array of numbers or a table of numbers.[7] The matrix above represents the weighted sum of all n variances plus all $n^2 - n$ covariances. Thus, in a portfolio of 100 securities ($n = 100$) there will be 100 variances and $100^2 - 100 = 9,900$ covariances. The security analyst must supply all of these plus 100 expected returns for the 100 assets being considered. Later, a simplified method will be shown to ease the securities analyst's work.[8]

Notice that the spaces in the matrix containing terms with identical subscripts form a diagonal pattern from the upper left-hand corner of the matrix to the lower right-hand corner. These are the n weighted variance terms (for example, $w_i w_i \sigma_{ii}$). All the other boxes contain the $n^2 - n$ weighted covariance terms (for example, $w_i w_j \sigma_{ij}$). Since $w_i w_j \sigma_{ij} = w_j w_i \sigma_{ji}$, the variance-covariance matrix is *symmetric*. Each covariance is repeated twice in the matrix. The covariances above the diagonal are the mirror-image of the covariances below the diagonal. Thus, the security analyst must actually estimate only $(\frac{1}{2})(n^2 - n)$ unique covariances.

If the two securities from Example 2A.1 are combined into a portfolio, the expected return $E(r_p)$ is found with equation (2A.8). To calculate the variance of such a portfolio recall that $\sigma_{12} = \sigma_{21} = .00177$, $\sigma_{11} = (\sigma_{\text{ATW}})^2 = (.368)^2 = .00134$, $\sigma_{22} = (\sigma_{\text{GAC}})^2 = (.0628)^2 = .00393$. Assuming that half the portfolio's funds were invested in ATW and half in GAC, then $w_1 = w_2 = \frac{1}{2}$. By equation (2A.9)

$$\text{Var } (r_p) = w_1^2 \sigma_{11} + w_2^2 \sigma_{22} + 2w_1 w_2 \sigma_{12}$$

$$= (.5)^2(.00134) + (.5)^2(.00393) + 2(.5)(.5)(.00177)$$

$$= (.25)(.00134) + (.25)(.00393) + 2(.25)(.00177)$$

$$= (.25)(.00134) + (.25)(.00393) + (.5)(.00177)$$

$$= .000335 + .000982 + .000885 = .002202.$$

The standard deviation of this security portfolio is

$$\sigma_{r_p} = \sqrt{\text{Var } (r_p)} = \sqrt{.0022} = .047 = 4.7 \text{ percent.} \qquad (2A.10)$$

---

[7] The matrix above is a special type of matrix based on the *variance-covariance matrix*.

[8] See Appendix 4E about a simplified method.

Summary of Notation and Formulas

A summary of notation and important equations concludes this appendix. A rate of return (r) is

$$r = \frac{\text{(ending price} - \text{beginning price)} + \text{dividends}}{\text{beginning price}} . \quad (1A.1)$$

The following notation will be used throughout the analysis:

p_i = probability of the ith outcome, $0 \leq p_i \leq 1$,

w_i = weight of ith security in portfolio, or the participation level of the ith security,

σ_{ii} = variance of ith random variable—for example, the variance of the ith security or the covariance of the ith random variable with itself,

σ_i = standard deviation of ith random variable,

σ_{ij} = cov (i, j) = covariance of ith and jth random variables,

r_i = rate of return on ith security,

r_{ij} = correlation coefficient between ith and jth random variables,

R = pure or riskless rate of interest,

σ_{r_p} = $SD(r_p)$ = standard deviation of portfolio = $\sqrt{\text{Var }(r_p)}$.

The expected rate of return is

$$E(r) = \sum_{t=1}^{n} p_t r_t = p_1 r_1 + p_2 r_2 + \cdots + p_n r_n = \sum_{i=1}^{n} p_i r_i. \quad (2A.1')$$

The variance of returns for a single random variable is:

$$\sigma_{ii} = \sum_{t=1}^{n} p_{it}(r_{it} - E(r_i))^2 = E(r - E(r))^2 \quad (2A.2')$$

$$= p_1(r_1 - E(r))^2 + p_2(r_2 - E(r))^2 + \cdots + p_n(r_n - E(r))^2.$$

The standard deviation of returns is

$$\sigma = \sqrt{\sum_{t=1}^{n} p_{it}(r_{it} - E(r))^2} = \sqrt{E(r - E(r))^2}. \quad (2A.3')$$

The covariance of returns of the ith and jth securities is denoted cov (r_i, r_j) and also as

$$\sigma_{ij} = E[(r_i - E(r_i)) \cdot (r_j - E(r_j))] = \sum_{t=1}^{n} (p_t)(r_{it} - E(r_i))(r_{jt} - E(r_j))$$

$$\quad (2A.4)$$

$$= (r_{ij})(\sigma_i)(\sigma_j). \quad (2A.6)$$

The correlation coefficient between the ith and jth securities rates of return is

$$r_{ij} = \frac{\text{cov } (i,j)}{\sigma_i \sigma_j} = \frac{E[(r_i - E(r_i)) \cdot (r_j - E(r_j))]}{\sigma_i \sigma_j}.$$ (2A.5)

The sum of all n weights in the portfolio must be one:

$$\sum_{i=1}^{n} w_i = 1.$$ (2A.7)

The expected return of the portfolio is the weighted average of the expected returns of the assets comprising the portfolio:

$$E(r_p) = \sum_{i=1}^{n} w_i E(r_i) = \sum_{i=1}^{n} w_i \left(\sum_{t=1}^{T} p_{it} r_{it} \right)$$ (2A.8)

$$= w_1 E(r_1) + w_2 E(r_2) + \cdots + w_n E(r_n).$$ (2A.8')

The variance of the portfolio can be defined simply for the two-security portfolio:

$$\text{Var } (r_p) = w_1{}^2 \sigma_{11} + w_2{}^2 \sigma_{22} + 2w_1 w_2 \sigma_{12}.$$ (2A.9)

For the n security portfolio the variance of the portfolio's returns can be denoted several ways, all of which are equivalent.

$$\text{Var } (r_p) = \sum_{i=1}^{n} w_i{}^2 \sigma_{ii} + \sum_{j=1}^{n} \sum_{i=1}^{n} w_i w_j \sigma_{ij} \qquad \text{for } i \neq j$$ (2A.9')

$$= \sum_{j=1}^{n} \sum_{i=1}^{n} w_i w_j \sigma_{ij}$$ (2A.9'')

$$= \sum_{i=1}^{n} w_i{}^2 \sigma_{ii} + \sum_{j=1}^{n} \sum_{i=1}^{n} w_i w_j r_{ij} \sigma_i \sigma_j \qquad \text{for } i \neq j.$$ (2A.9''')

The standard deviation of the n-security portfolio is

$$\sigma_{r_p} = SD(r_p) = \sqrt{\text{Var } (r_p)}.$$ (2A.10)

Different derivations of these same essential formulas may be found elsewhere.[9]

---

[9] Markowitz, *Portfolio Selection*, chaps. 3 and 4.

Appendix 2B

How Risk Affects Value

Consider information about investments A and B.

Investment	Cost[1]	Annual NCF[2]	$E(R)$[3]	σ	Life
A	\$2,000	\$100/yr	5%	20%	∞
B	\$666.66	\$100/yr	15%	40%	∞

According to the capital market line hypothesized in Fig. 2B.1, investment A, which is in risk class $\sigma_A = 20$ percent, should be discounted at 10 percent to determine its present value (PV).[4] And, investment B should be capitalized at 20 percent to find its present value. Assume the investments both have expected net cash flows, $(E(\text{NCF}))$, of \$100 per

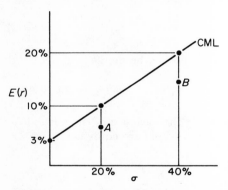

Fig. 2B.1   Hypothetical Values for CML

year for perpetuity. Their PV's are:

$$\text{PV}_A = \frac{\$100}{.1} = \$1,000, \qquad \text{PV}_B = \frac{\$100}{.2} = \$500.$$

---

[1] Costs equal present value of a perpetual \$100 annuity capitalized at the expected return for the investment. For example, for investment A, the cost is

$$\frac{\$100}{.05} = \$2,000 = \frac{\text{perpetual NCF}}{\text{capitalization rate}}.$$

[2] NCF stands for net cash flow.

[3] In this example the expected return is the interest rate that equates the cost of the investment to the present value of its NCF's. For example, for B the $E(r)$ is k in the formula

$$\sum_{t=1}^{\infty} \$100/(1 + k)^t = \$666.66.$$

[4] See any introductory finance textbook for an explanation of the present-value formulas.

The above calculations show the present values of A and B are less than their costs. They are both overpriced. The purchaser could expect returns of only 5 percent on A and 15 percent on B—based on their costs— rather than 10 percent on A and 20 percent on B, which is what the CML shows as appropriate returns for their risk classes.

To obtain an idea of how diversification affects present value, consider the value of a portfolio made of A and B. Assume $r_{AB} = -1$. The portfolio's risk is reduced to zero when $r_{AB} = -1$, $w_A = \frac{2}{3}$, and $w_B = \frac{1}{3}$— see Fig. 2.10. According to the CML in Fig. 2B.1, 3 percent is the discount rate appropriate for zero-risk investments. The net cashflows from a portfolio of $\frac{2}{3}$ of A and $\frac{1}{3}$ of B are $(\frac{2}{3})E(\text{NCF}_A) + (\frac{1}{3})E(\text{NCF}_B) = \$66.66 + \$33.33$ per year. The present value of the portfolio is calculated below:

$$\text{PV}_{(2/3)A+(1/3)B} = \frac{66.66 + 33.33}{.03} = \frac{100}{.03} = \$3,333.33.$$

It may seem as if putting some money in the less valuable investment B would decrease the value of the diversified portfolio below the value of an all-A portfolio. However, owing to the benefits of diversification, which reduces the portfolio's risk, the portfolio is discounted at a lower rate.[5]

---

[5] The desirability of an asset is proportional to θ, where $\theta = (r - R)/\sigma$. Consider θ' which is defined below.

$$\theta' = \frac{r - R}{k} = \frac{\text{risk premium}}{\text{cost of capital}},$$

where k is the cost of capital or capitalization rate for an asset. Here too, θ' is an index of desirability. In the numerical example above, k is a linear function (f) of σ as represented by the CML. Symbolically, $k = f(\sigma)$, where f is linear. Thus, θ' is some linear transformation of θ. Specifically,

$$\theta' = \frac{r - R}{k} = \frac{r - R}{f(\sigma)} = g\left(\frac{r - R}{\sigma}\right) = g(\theta).$$

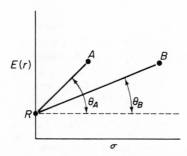

Fig. 2B.2   Assets in Risk-Return Space

Students of present-value theory should recognize that an asset's present value will vary directly with θ'. This formulation shows clearly that the benefits from diversification (namely, higher present values) depend on the *relation* of return and risk—not merely on risk alone. That is, diversification that reduces risk and also reduces θ or θ' is not necessarily beneficial—it may reduce the portfolio's value.

The increase in the value of the portfolio (to \$3,333.33) over the costs or values of its individual components (that is, \$2,000 and \$666.66) results from diversification.[6] Of course, these values are merely estimates. The actual value of investments A, B, and the portfolio would probably differ from these values owing to inefficiencies in the capital market. For example, investors' inability to measure risk, the existence of brokerage fees and taxes, and investor ignorance of the CML all tend to reduce the clarity of the above conclusions. The process through which Markowitz diversification increases value is summarized in Fig. 2B.3.

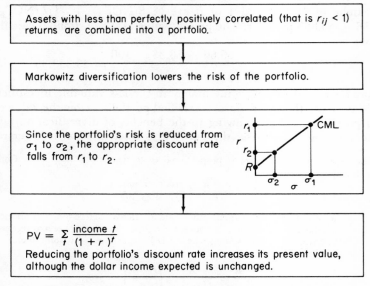

Fig. 2B.3   Flow Chart of how Diversification Increases
             Value

In any event, an important point about diversification is that the variability of the portfolio may be less than the variability of the least variable security in the portfolio. This surprising conclusion would be the result of a negative covariance term in equations (2A.9) or (2A.10).

Unfortunately, very few securities have returns that are negatively correlated with other securities.[7] Most securities' returns are positively

---

[6] W. W. Alberts and J. Segall, *The Corporate Merger* (Chicago: University of Chicago Press, 1966), pp. 262–272. Professor Alberts presents a similar type of numerical example of how diversification affects value. However, Professor Alberts uses a different risk surrogate. An interesting conclusion about mergers' diversification effects is reached in this book.

[7] Homestake Mining, Pan-Am World Airlines, General Portland Cement, and Pepsi Cola all had negative correlation with the market over a recent ten-year period. However, some of these firms may not be expected to be negatively correlated with the market indices in the future, owing to various changes within the firms.

correlated with each other and with the market indices. The rare security that has low or negative correlation will enjoy strong demand as wise investors seek to diversify. The price of such a security will be sustained at high levels relative to the other securities. Thus, the rate of return on negatively correlated securities can be expected to remain lower than the CML would indicate for the appropriate risk classes of the securities. That is, these points may be off of the CML in equilibrium.[8] Securities that are highly positively correlated with the market indices will not be in high demand.

---

[8] The perceptive reader may wonder if σ may not be an inappropriate measure of risk. If so, he is correctly anticipating the capital market theory. The covariance of returns between each security and the market is suggested as a measure of risk for individual securities.

Generating the Statistical Inputs for Portfolio Analysis

CHAPTER 4 and its appendices will explain various methods of performing portfolio analysis. In each case it will be assumed that a security analyst has furnished the portfolio analyst with the statistical inputs required for portfolio analysis. The purpose of this chapter is to show new approaches to security analysis that will yield the statistics needed for portfolio analysis.

The Required Statistical Inputs

If a portfolio analyst is going to derive the efficient frontier from a group of n assets, where n is any positive integer, the following statistics are required:

1. expected return estimates for all n assets under consideration;
2. expected standard deviation (or variance) of the rate of return for all n assets; and,
3. all the expected covariances between these various n assets rates of return. It can be shown that $[(\frac{1}{2})(n^2 - n)]$ different covariances are required for an n asset analysis.

The formulas for the expected rate of return, $E(r_i)$; standard deviation of returns, σ_i; and covariance of returns, $\sigma_{ij} = \text{cov}(r_i, r_j)$, were discussed in Appendix 2A.

The efficient portfolios generated by portfolio analysis are no better than the statistical inputs on which they are based. Thus, it is imperative that attention be devoted to this phase of portfolio management. In this chapter three different approaches will be suggested for generating the statistical inputs: (a) ex post data may be tabulated and projected into the future with or without being adjusted; (b) ex ante probability distributions can be compiled; or, (c) a simple econometric relationship may be used to forecast returns. Ideally, all three approaches should be pursued independently for each of the n assets. These independent forecasts could then be compared and contrasted by a committee of security analysts and a consensus of opinion reached as a final step in security analysis. This final consensus of opinion would represent the best attainable statistics and could be given to the portfolio analyst.

Ex Post Data

Gathering historical data on a firm's expected return, standard deviation and covariance is a good place to begin security analysis. Although these statistics may change with the passage of time, they can give the security analyst an objective point of reference from which he may proceed. The historical data needed are the market prices and dividends for each firm being considered.

Sources for Historical Data

Data on a security's market prices and dividends may be found in several different places:[1]

1. *Moody's Handbook of Widely Held Common Stocks* is a quarterly publication covering about 1,000 companies.
2. The Standard & Poor's *Stock Market Encyclopedia* and *Stock Guide* are handy compendiums published several times each year.
3. *ISL Daily Stock Price* is published quarterly and lists over 2,000 securities from the NYSE and AMEX.

There are many satisfactory sources for historical data on market prices and dividends.[2] The three sources above are suggested only because they

---

[1] Jerome B. Cohen and E. D. Zinbarg, *Investment Analysis and Portfolio Selection* (Homewood, Ill.: Richard D. Irwin, Inc., 1967). See Chapter 3 for a discussion of various "Sources of Investment Information."

[2] Electronic computers may be advantageously employed in tabulating historical statistics. The necessary data are available on magnetic tapes designed to use with computers. The University of Chicago has prepared such tapes. The Standard and Poor's Compustat tapes and the ISL tapes are also satisfactory. These tapes and others are used at the Wharton School: the University of Chicago tapes seem to be most suitable for this particular work. Any of these tapes may be purchased by individuals, schools, or corporations.

Name of firm researched—————————————— Researcher —————————————————

Type security —————————————————— Source of data ————————————————

Industry ————————————————————————

Quarter years	Reported Data			Changes in unit of account	Adjusted Data			Rate of return [1]	Growth in E.P.S. [2]
	Begin. mkt. price	Qtrly. div.	Qtrly. E.P.S.		Begin. mkt. price	Qtrly. div.	Qtrly. E.P.S.		
1970–IV	——	——	——	——	——	——	——	——	——
1970–III	——	——	——	——	——	——	——	——	——
1970–II	——	——	——	——	——	——	——	——	——
1970–I	——	——	——	——	——	——	——	——	——
1969–IV	——	——	——	——	——	——	——	——	——
1969–III	——	——	——	——	——	——	——	——	——
1969–II	——	——	——	——	——	——	——	——	——
1969–I	——	——	——	——	——	——	——	——	——
1968–IV	——	——	——	——	——	——	——	——	——
1968–III	——	——	——	——	——	——	——	——	——
1968–II	——	——	——	——	——	——	——	——	——
1968–I	——	——	——	——	——	——	——	——	——
1967–IV	——	——	——	——	——	——	——	——	——
1967–III	——	——	——	——	——	——	——	——	——
1967–II	——	——	——	——	——	——	——	——	——
1967–I	——	——	——	——	——	——	——	——	——
1966–IV	——	——	——	——	——	——	——	——	——
1966–III	——	——	——	——	——	——	——	——	——
1966–II	——	——	——	——	——	——	——	——	——
1966–I	——	——	——	——	——	——	——	——	——
1965–IV	——	——	——	——	——	——	——	——	——
1965–III	——	——	——	——	——	——	——	——	——
1965–II	——	——	——	——	——	——	——	——	——
1965–I	——	——	——	——	——	——	——	——	——
1964–IV	——	——	——	——	——	——	——	——	——
1964–III	——	——	——	——	——	——	——	——	——
1964–II	——	——	——	——	——	——	——	——	——
1964–I	——	——	——	——	——	——	——	——	——
1963–IV	——	——	——	——	——	——	——	——	——
1963–III	——	——	——	——	——	——	——	——	——
1963–II	——	——	——	——	——	——	——	——	——
1963–I	——	——	——	——	——	——	——	——	——
1962–IV	——	——	——	——	——	——	——	——	——
1962–III	——	——	——	——	——	——	——	——	——
1962–II	——	——	——	——	——	——	——	——	——
1962–I	——	——	——	——	——	——	——	——	——
1961–IV	——	——	——	——	——	——	——	——	——
1961–III	——	——	——	——	——	——	——	——	——
1961–II	——	——	——	——	——	——	——	——	——
1961–I	——	——	——	——	——	——	——	——	——

Variance in rates of return ———————————————— standard deviation————————

Average rate of return————————————————————————————————————

Regression coefficients for characteristic line A————————B————————Q ————

[1] $r_t = (P_{t+1} - P_t + D_t)/P_t$ = rate of return in period t.

[2] $g_t = (EPS_t - EPS_{t-1})/EPS_{t-1}$ = earnings growth in period t.

Average growth in EPS————————————————————————————————

Fig. 3.1   Form for Gathering Common-Stock Data

contain both price and dividend data and they are easy to read.[3] Forms like the one in Fig. 3.1 may expedite the data gathering.

Changes in the Unit of Account

For reasons that are dubious in many cases, corporations frequently declare stock dividends and/or stock splits. Although such paper shuffling does not change the market value of the firm,[4] it does require the security analyst to make adjustments for these changes in the unit of account. Consider the hypothetical data in Fig. 3.2.

Time Period	1	2	3	4	5
Beginning market price	$100	$100	50	25	25
Earnings per share	10	10	5	2.50	2.50
Dividends per share	5	5	2.50	1.25	1.25
Par value per share	1	1	.50	.25	.25
Book value per share	20	20	10	5	5
Multiplication adjustment	× 1	× 1	× 2	× 4	× 4
Division adjustment	× (1/4)	× (1/4)	× (1/2)	× 1	× 1
True rate of return	5%	5%	5%	5%	5%

Fig. 3.2   Hypothetical Market Data on a Per Share Basis

Assume the firm represented in Fig. 3.2 had no fluctuations in the market price of its stock. Also assume it had a 2-for-1 stock split, or equivalently, a 100 percent stock dividend between periods 2 and 3 and again between periods 3 and 4.[5] Realistically, this hypothetical firm had no capital gains or losses; the 5 percent dividend yield each period thus equals the true rate of return calculated by equation (1.1). The decrease in the market price per share between periods 2 and 3 and again between periods 3 and 4 reflects changes in the unit of account, not capital losses. To adjust for changes in the unit of account either the multiplication or the division adjustment factors (but not both) shown in Fig. 3.2 may be used. This converts the market data to comparable levels. The rate of return for each period may then be calculated with equation (1.1).

---

[3] The authors have had their investments students, undergraduate and graduate, gather data and perform portfolio analysis for over six quarters. The students seem to prefer *Moody's Handbook of Widely Held Common Stocks*.

[4] E. Fama, L. Fisher, M. Jensen, and R. Roll, "The Adjustment of Stock Prices to New Information," *International Economic Review*, February 1969, pages 1–21.

[5] Accountants and attorneys adhere to the fiction that a 2-for-1 stock split is not equivalent to a 100 percent stock dividend. However, these bookkeeping and legal technicalities may be ignored here.

Formulas for Ex Post Data

When estimating the ex ante input statistics for an asset from ex post data each historical observation is treated as being equally likely. Assume historical data are gathered for T periods. The probability of each observation is: $p = (1/T)$. Substituting this probability into equations (2A.1), (2A.3), and (2A.4) yields the formulas below.

The historical average return ($\bar{r}$) calculated as shown in equation (3.1) may be used as an estimate of the expected return, $E(r)$.

$$\bar{r}_i = \left(\frac{1}{T}\right) \sum_{t=1}^{T} r_t. \tag{3.1}$$

The historical standard deviation, $\hat{\sigma}$, may be used as an estimate of expected risk,

$$\hat{\sigma}_i = \left[\left(\frac{1}{T}\right) \sum_{t=1}^{T} (r_t - \bar{r})^2 \right]^{1/2}. \tag{3.2}$$

The historical covariance, $\hat{\sigma}_{ij}$, may be used as an estimate of the expected covariance, σ_{ij}.

$$\hat{\sigma}_{ij} = \left[\left(\frac{1}{T}\right) \sum_{t=1}^{T} (r_{ti} - \bar{r}_i)(r_{tj} - \bar{r}_j) \right]. \tag{3.3}$$

Subjective Adjustments for Historical Statistics

After historical data are tabulated and $\bar{r}_i$, $\hat{\sigma}_i$, and $\hat{\sigma}_{ij}$ are calculated, it may be desirable to adjust these statistics for some companies. If the firm under consideration has added or dropped product lines; entered large new sales territories or left old ones; had a complete management shake-up; experienced a significant technological breakthrough; been faced with tough, new competitors; obtained important new government permits, sanctions, or subsidies; won or lost important legal battles that set new precedents for the future; or experienced other changes that are expected to alter the firm's future average return, risk, and/or covariance, then the security analyst should make subjective adjustments in $\bar{r}_i$, $\hat{\sigma}_i$, and/or $\hat{\sigma}_{ij}$ for the firm. Consider a numerical example.

Imagine a (hypothetical) airline named West Coast Lines (WCL) which has been in operation for years. Assume WCL has been flying between Seattle, Los Angeles, and San Francisco and its operating statistics over the past decade have been tabulated. Further imagine another airline, say, Trans Continental Airlines (TCA), about the same size, which flies everyplace WCL flies. But, TCA also flies to Las Vegas and Hawaii. Figure 3.3 shows historical statistics gathered for the two hypothetical airlines over the past decade.

Ex Post Statistic	WCL	TCA
$\bar{r}_i$	$.15 = 15.0\%$	$.2 = 20.0\%$
$\hat{\sigma}_i$	$.4 \ = 40.0\%$	$.5 = 50.0\%$
$\hat{\sigma}_{ij}$	.25	.4

Fig. 3.3 Operating Statistics for Past Decade

Now, assume WCL obtains permission from the Civil Aeronautics Board to make passenger flights to Las Vegas and Hawaii like TCA. How will this change in WCL's product line and sales territory be expected to affect its average return, risk, and covariance in the next five years?

Flying affluent passengers on champagne flights and vacations to Hawaii and Las Vegas will likely increase WCL's sales, profits, and average return in the future. However, since champagne flights and vacations are luxury items that many people cancel during recession periods, it seems probable that WCL will experience more variability of return (that is, risk) in future years than it has in the past.

Nearly all stock prices are highly positively correlated with the national economy.[6] Since WCL's new flights will increase the correlation of its sales, profits, and returns with the national economy, it is likely that WCL's covariance of returns with most other stocks will also rise. Thus, WCL's average return, risk, and covariance can all be expected to rise as a result of the Civil Aeronautics Board's ruling.

The exact values forecasted for WCL's average return, risk, and covariance may be estimated subjectively by the security analyst. WCL's historical figures shown in Fig. 3.3 furnish the minimum estimates. And, the figures for TCA furnish good guidelines to follow when reevaluating WCL's return, risk, and covariance statistics. The forecasted statistics may not prove to be perfect. However, a qualified security analyst should be able to generate acceptable estimates to use as inputs for portfolio analysis.

Establishing Ex Ante Probability Distributions

A second approach to forecasting return, risk, and covariance statistics is to develop subjective probability distributions of returns for each firm over all the states of nature (economic conditions) that may pertain. This second approach is similar to the first, since historical experience and subjective hunches may be used. However, the second approach is different in that it focuses on developing a probability distribution from which the needed statistics are tabulated. The first approach concentrated directly on the needed statistics and tended to ignore the underlying probability distribution.

---

[6] B. J. King, "Market and Industry Factors in Stock Price Behavior," *Journal of Business*, vol. XXXIX, no. 1, II (January 1966), pp. 139–190.

The States of Nature and Their Probabilities

The states of nature that have the largest effect on securities rates of return are the economic conditions such as boom and recession. These states of nature may be meaningfully separated into, say, four categories as shown in Fig. 3.4.

The security analyst should fill in the estimated rate of return which will occur for——— company during the future period from———————to—————————for each of the four possible economic conditions. The economist should fill in the probabilities associated with each economic condition.

Economic Condition	Probability	Forecasted Rate of Return
Boom		
Slow Growth		
Zero Growth		
Recession		
	1.0	

Fig. 3.4   Form for Tabulating Probability Distribution
of Rates of Return for a Security

More or less than four economic conditions may be used for the form suggested in Fig. 3.4. In any event, an information sheet should accompany the form explaining in detail the nature of the various economic conditions.[7] This information would aid the security analyst in forecasting the rate of return that might occur under each state of nature. Using equations (2A.1'), (2A.3'), and (2A.4), the data from Fig. 3.4 can be converted into the statistical inputs needed for portfolio analysis.[8]

Conditional Estimates of the Rates of Return

The security analyst's task is to estimate the rates of return that may be expected to prevail over the planning horizon for each of the economic conditions the firm may experience. Historical data and/or subjective estimates may be used to derive these conditional estimates of the firm's various rates of return. The simplified models suggested by Markowitz[9] and Sharpe[10] are also quite useful in this work, they will be explained next.

---

[7] H. Markowitz, *Portfolio Selection* (New York: John Wiley & Sons, Inc., 1959), pp. 28–32.

[8] To calculate the covariances using equation (2A.4) the states of nature and their probabilities must be the same for all assets under consideration. However, this should present no problem—only one economic forecast need be prepared.

[9] Markowitz, *Portfolio Selection*, p. 100.

[10] William Sharpe, "A Simplified Model for Portfolio Analysis," *Management Science*, vol. 9, no. 2 (January 1963), pp. 277–293.

A Simple Econometric Forecasting Model

A third approach to generating the statistical inputs uses a regression line of the form shown in equation (3.4).

$$r_{it} = a + b(r_{It}) + e_t, \tag{3.4}$$

where r_i is the rate of return on asset i during some time period, r_I is the rate of change in some market index during the same period, the e's are random errors above and below the regression line, and a and b are the intercept and slope coefficient of the regression line.

One form that equation (3.4) may assume is represented graphically

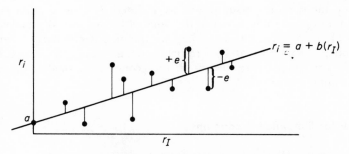

Fig. 3.5   One Possible Form for Equation (3.4)

in Fig. 3.5. Assuming the errors average out to zero, the conditional expectation is shown in equation (3.5).

$$E(r_i \mid r_I) = a + b(r_I). \tag{3.5}$$

Using this conditional expectation facilitates prediction. For example, if the economist predicts that the market index (r_I) assumes the value $r_I = \bar{r}_I$, then equation (3.5) implies that $\bar{r}_i$ is the expected value of the ith asset's rate of return. Figure 3.6 graphically depicts this process. Of

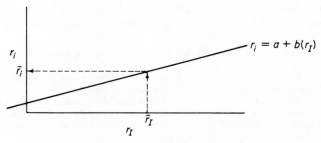

Fig. 3.6   One Possible Form of Equation (3.5)

course, this form of forecasting is dependent upon the constancy over time of the underlying regression model of equation (3.4).

Regression models such as (3.4) are stationary, unbiased, and efficient estimators only if the assumptions listed below are not violated:

1. e is a random variable with a mean of zero [that is, $E(e) = 0$].
2. e has a constant variance (that is, homoscedasticity).
3. e_t and e_{t+1} are not correlated [that is, cov $(e_t, e_{t+1}) = 0$].
4. e_t and r_{It} are not correlated [that is, cov $(r_{It}, e_t) = 0$].

If probability statements are to be made, e must also conform to a known probability distribution and be stochastically independent. Fama has shown that these assumptions may be violated.[11] Blume has conducted an investigation of models (3.4) and (3.5) to determine their adequacy and see if the assumptions are violated.[12] Blume concludes that the assumptions are not significantly violated in the post World War II period. Thus, models (3.4) and (3.5) are useful.[13] Particularly when the other independent estimates of return, risk, and covariance suggested earlier in this chapter are also used, the econometric models suggested here are appropriate.

Formulas for Simplified Predictions

In Appendix 4E the following formulas are derived from equation (3.4).

$$E(r_i) = a_i + b_{(i|I)}[E(r_I)], \tag{3.5}$$

$$\text{Var } (r_i) = b_{(i|I)}^2[\text{Var } (r_I)] + \sigma_{(i|I)}^2, \tag{3.6}$$

$$\text{Cov } (r_i, r_j) = [b_{(i|I)}][b_{(j|I)}][\text{Var } (r_I)], \tag{3.7}$$

where $E(r_i)$ is the expected return for asset i, a_i and $b_{(i|I)}$ are the regression parameters from equation (3.4) for the ith asset, $E(r_I)$ is the expected return on the market index, Var (r_I) is the variance of returns for the market index, $\sigma_{(i|I)}^2$ is the residual variance for regressing r_i onto r_I, and $b_{(j|I)}$ is the regression slope coefficient for asset j. The three formulas above may be used to estimate returns, risk, and covariances for various

---

[11] E. Fama, "The Behavior of Stock-Market Prices," *Journal of Business*, vol. XXXVIII, no. 1 (January 1965), pp. 34–100.

[12] Marshall E. Blume, "The Assessment of Portfolio Performance: An Application of Portfolio Theory," unpublished Ph.D. dissertation, University of Chicago, March 1968.

[13] Blume found that the returns conformed more closely to a non-normal stable Paretian Distribution than to a normal distribution. The problems presented by this finding are discussed later. See M. Blume, "Portfolio Theory: A Step Toward Its Practical Application," *Journal of Business*, April 1970, pp. 152–173.

assets.[14] The regression parameters a_i and b_i for each asset could be generated from historical data and perhaps adjusted subjectively. Then, an economist could predict the needed values of $E(r_I)$ and Var (r_I). It would then be a simple computation to generate all the statistical inputs needed for portfolio analysis.

Using this technique greatly simplifies forecasting the needed inputs. If n assets are under consideration, n returns, n variances, and $\frac{1}{2}(n^2 - n)$ covariances are required for portfolio analysis. Using equatons (3.5), (3.6), and (3.7) all these statistics may be generated from only the two economic estimates, $E(r_I)$ and Var (r_I), and the n values of a_i and b_i.

The regression parameters a_i and b_i may be generated by a computer. A canned regression program can be used to process historical data widely available on magnetic tapes. These regression parameters are sufficiently stationary over time that they need not be reestimated frequently for most securities. For example, consider the data in Fig. 3.7. The regression slope coefficients (that is, the beta coefficients) from some regressions in Blume's dissertation are shown.[15] Over the 33 years covered by the data

Firm	Time Period*	Beta	R^2†
Union Oil of California	1/27– 6/35	.55	.58
	7/35–12/43	.57	.49
	1/44– 6/51	.97	.45
	7/51–12/60	.98	.32
IBM	1/27– 6/35	.49	.49
	7/35–12/43	.25	.26
	1/44– 6/51	.56	.29
	7/51–12/60	.86	.23
May Dept. Stores	1/27– 6/35	.83	.74
	7/35–12/43	.64	.49
	1/44– 6/51	.72	.35
	7/51–12/60	.82	.32
Atlantic Coast Line RR	1/27– 6/35	1.2	.73
	7/35–12/43	1.26	.70
	1/44– 6/51	1.17	.43
	7/51–12/60	1.63	.57

* Date: month/year.
† R^2 = coefficient of determination
= (correlation coefficient)^2
= percent of variation explained

Fig. 3.7   Beta Coefficients

---

[14] K. J. Cohen and J. A. Pogue, "An Empirical Evaluation of Alternative Portfolio-Selection Models," *Journal of Business*, vol. XL, no. 2 (April 1967), pp. 166–193. Cohen and Pogue generate portfolios using unadjusted historical data. They also suggest more sophisticated econometric models which can be used to generate the input data.

[15] Blume, "The Assessment of Portfolio Performance: An Application of Portfolio Theory."

these regression coefficients are surprisingly consistent period after period·
And, the percentage of variation (R^2) explained by the regressions is high.
Clearly, these econometric relationships are useful.

A Consensus

It has been suggested that the ex ante statistical inputs necessary for
portfolio analysis be estimated independently by three procedures.
First, historical statistics may be tabulated and perhaps adjusted subjectively. Second, economic forecasters and fundamental security analysts
can work together to generate subjective probability distributions of
expected returns over various economic conditions. Finally, simple
econometric relationships were suggested which can be useful in generating the input statistics needed for portfolio analysis.

These three procedures can be used to generate three independent
estimates of return, risk and covariance for each asset under consideration.[16] The analysts compiling these estimates can meet together after
their estimates are finished. Then, these different estimates can be compared, argued, adjusted, and finalized. In this manner the portfolio
analyst will be assured of receiving a consensus of opinion about each
asset's expected return, risk, and covariance. Thus, the foundation is laid
for portfolio analysis.

---

[16] Unfortunately, the first and third techniques are not useful for new issues.

SECTION TWO

PORTFOLIO ANALYSIS

```
4444444444444444444444444444444444444444444444444444444444444444444444444444444444
4444444444444444444444444444444444444444444444444444444444444444444444444444444444
44444444444444444444444444444444    444    444444444444    444444444444444444444444444444444
44444444444444444444444444444444    4444    4444444444    44444444444444444444444444444444
44444444444444444444444444444444    44444    444444444    4444444444444444444444444444444444
44444444444444444444444444444444    444444    4444444    4444444444444444444444444444444444
44444444444444444444444444444444    4444444    44444    4444444444444444444444444444444444
44444444444444444444444444444444    44444444    444    44444444444444444444444444444444444444
44444444444444444444444444444444    444444444    4    44444444444444444444444444444444444444
44444444444444444444444444444444    4444444444    444444444444444444444444444444444444444
44444444444444444444444444444444    44444444444    444444444444444444444444444444444444444
4444444444444444444444444444444444444444444444444444444444444444444444444444444444
4444444444444444444444444444444444444444444444444444444444444444444444444444444444
```

Graphical Portfolio Analysis

Harry Markowitz conceived portfolio analysis.[1] *The objective of portfolio analysis* is to determine the set of efficient portfolios. In terms of Fig. 4.1, the objective is to find the efficient frontier—the heavy dark curve from *E* to *F*—for some given opportunity set generated by a group of assets.

Solution Techniques Available

Three methods of solving for the efficient set (that is, doing portfolio analysis) are available:

1. graphical,
2. with calculus, or
3. by quadratic programming (QP).[2]

For any given set of assets, any of the three algorithms will yield the same efficient set.

The graphical portfolio analysis will be presented in this chapter. The primary advantage of this technique is that it is easier to grasp conceptually. Most students internalize the analysis much more effectively if they

---

[1] The analysis was originally presented in an article: "Portfolio Analysis," *Journal of Finance*, March 1952, pp. 77–91. Later, Markowitz expanded his presentation in a book, *Portfolio Selection*—Cowles Foundation Monograph 16 (New York: John Wiley & Sons, Inc., 1959). Also, see Weston and Beranek, "Programming Investment Portfolio Construction," *The Analysts Journal*, May 1955, pp. 51–55.

[2] Also, Sharpe has written a linear programming algorithm which provides approximate solutions: William Sharpe, "A Linear Programming Algorithm for Mutual Fund Portfolio Selection," *Management Science*, March 1967, pp. 499–510. Furthermore, Sharpe and others have developed simplified solution methods—see Appendix 4E.

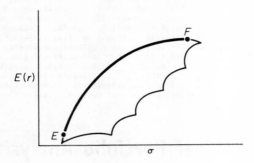

Fig. 4.1   The Opportunity Set in $[\sigma, E(r)]$Space

have a graphical analogue to which they may refer. Furthermore, leveraged portfolios may be represented graphically. The disadvantage of the graphical analysis is that it cannot handle portfolios containing more than four securities. Conceivably, four securities may be analyzed by treating one of them implicitly in three-dimensional graphs. No more than four securities may be analyzed graphically because the human mind cannot visualize more than three dimensions.

Two calculus algorithms will be presented in the appendices to Chapter 4. The primary advantage of the calculus methods lies in their ease of manipulation and their ability to handle portfolios containing a more realistic number of securities. Any number of securities may be analyzed, since mathematics can deal in n-dimensional space. As a result of these and other advantages the calculus solution can be useful to researchers. However, the calculus solution technique cannot handle inequality constraints.

Quadratic programming algorithms have been coded for computers. These programs are most useful in handling large-portfolio problems that are solved frequently. Like linear programming, quadratic programming (QP) can accommodate inequality constraints; thus, the portfolio may be optimized within constraints on the proportion of each security. For practical management of mutual funds or other large portfolios, the QP solution method is the most desirable. QP will be discussed further and references given in Appendix 4D. However, the mathematical programming algorithm (that is, the QP solution technique) itself will not be presented.

Inputs for Portfolio Analysis

Portfolio analysis requires certain data as inputs. The inputs to the portfolio analysis of a set of n assets are:

1. n expected returns,
2. n variances of returns, and
3. $(n^2 - n)/2$ covariances.

Thus, for a three-security portfolio the analysis requires the following statistics:

$E(r)$	σ_r^2	Cov (r_i, r_j)
$E(r_1)$	σ_1^2	Cov (r_1, r_2)
$E(r_2)$	σ_2^2	Cov (r_2, r_3)
$E(r_3)$	σ_3^2	Cov (r_1, r_3)

In the remainder of this chapter it will be shown how to solve a three-security portfolio graphically. The analysis is conducted upon the graphical plane representing two weights—as shown in Fig. 4.2. Point A

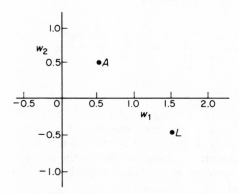

Fig. 4.2   Graph of Two Weight Variables—w_1 and w_2

represents a portfolio made up of 50 percent each of securities one and two. Point L represents a leveraged portfolio with 150 percent of the original capital invested in security one and -50 percent of the capital invested in security two. In other words, a security like security number two (for example, a bond with the same $E(r)$ and σ) is printed and sold in an amount equal to 50 percent of the net value of the portfolio. The short sale of security two, or leverage achieved by issuing a security like number two, is represented by a negative value for w_2.

For example, suppose the portfolio represented by point L in Fig. 4.2 had \$1,000 original equity invested. Then, the portfolio manager purchased \$1,500 of security one, so $w_1 = 1.5$. Then, to cover the \$500 shortage the portfolio manager issued \$500 worth of a security like number two, so $w_2 = -.5$. The total of the two weights is one (that is, $w_1 + w_2 = 1.5 - .5 = 1.0$)—this signifies that the net worth of the portfolio has all been accounted for.

The variables w_1 and w_2 are weights or percentages of the original capital of the portfolio invested in each security. The sum of the weights must be one or the analysis has no meaningful interpretation. Thus, throughout all portfolio analysis, either implicitly or explicitly, the following mathematical condition cannot be violated:

$$\sum_{i=1}^{n} w_i = 1.0,$$

where n represents the number of securities being analyzed. This does not mean that all the wealth must be invested. Cash can be one of the n assets.

Three-Security Numerical Example of Graphical Portfolio Analysis

In the interest of realism, real data will be used. Quarterly rates of return from 1957 to 1966 inclusively were calculated and the following input data derived.

Company	i	$E(r_i)$	$\sigma_{ii} = \sigma_i{}^2$	Cov $(r_i, r_j) = (r_{ij})(\sigma_i)(\sigma_j)$
U.S. Steel	1	.0167 = 1.67%	.24	$\sigma_{12} = .1497 = (.65)(.49)(.47)$
Olin-Mathieson	2	.0534 = 5.34%	.22	$\sigma_{23} = .0855 = (.34)(.47)(.52)$
Parke-Davis	3	.1314 = 13.14%	.27	$\sigma_{13} = .1631 = (.64)(.49)(.52)$

It would be possible for a good draftsman to find the set of efficient portfolios made from various proportions of three securities with a three-dimensional drawing. However, it is easier for most people to solve the problem in two-dimensional space—that is, the procedure followed here.

To solve the problem in two-dimensional space, the following steps will be performed:

1. Convert the formulas for the portfolio's expected return (that is, the isomean lines) and the portfolio's risk (that is, the isovariance ellipses) from three to two variables.
2. Find the minimum variance portfolio (MVP).
3. Graph the isomean lines.
4. Graph the isovariance ellipses.
5. Delineate the efficient set (that is, the critical line).
6. Calculate the expected return, $E(r_p)$, and risk, σ_p, for the efficient portfolios.
7. Graph the efficient frontier.

How to Solve for One Variable Implicitly

Conversion of the three-variable formulas for $E(r_p)$ and Var (r_p) to implicit formulas in two variables (w_1 and w_2) is possible due to the following identity:

$$\sum_{i=1}^{3} w_i = 1 = w_1 + w_2 + w_3.$$

This relation allows any one weight to be specified in terms of the other weights—for example,

$$w_3 = 1 - w_1 - w_2. \tag{4.1}$$

First, the conversion of $E(r_p)$ will be considered. This conversion is accomplished by substituting equation (4.1) into equation (2A.8) to yield:

$$E(r_p) = \sum_{i=1}^{3} w_i E(r_i) = w_1 E(r_1) + w_2 E(r_2) + w_3 E(r_3) \tag{2A.8}$$

$$= w_1 E(r_1) + w_2 E(r_2) + (1 - w_1 - w_2)E(r_3)$$
by substitution for w_3

$$= w_1 E(r_1) + w_2 E(r_2) + E(r_3) - w_1 E(r_3) - w_2 E(r_3)$$

$$= [E(r_1) - E(r_3)]w_1 + [E(r_2) - E(r_3)]w_2 + E(r_3). \tag{4.2}$$

Equation (4.2) is a linear equation in two variables (w_1 and w_2). Substitutions in the values for $E(r_i)$ in equation (4.2) yields:

$$E(r_p) = (.0167 - .1314)w_1 + (.0534 - .1314)w_2 + .1314$$

$$= -.1147w_1 - .0780w_2 + .1314. \tag{4.3}$$

Equation (4.3) gives the expected return of the three-security portfolio in terms of w_1 and w_2 explicitly and w_3 implicitly—it may be graphed in two variables, w_1 and w_2.

The three-security portfolio variance formula is similarly converted to two variables by substituting equation (4.1) into equation (2A.9) as follows.

$$\text{Var } (r_p) = \sum_{i=1}^{3} \sum_{j=1}^{3} w_i w_j \sigma_{ij}$$

$$= w_1^2 \sigma_{11} + w_2^2 \sigma_{22} + w_3^2 \sigma_{33} + 2w_1 w_2 \sigma_{12} + 2w_1 w_3 \sigma_{13} \tag{2A.9}$$
$$+ 2w_2 w_3 \sigma_{23}$$

$$= w_1^2 \sigma_{11} + w_2^2 \sigma_{22} + (1 - w_1 - w_2)^2 \sigma_{33} + 2w_1 w_2 \sigma_{12}$$
$$+ 2w_1(1 - w_1 - w_2)\sigma_{13} + 2w_2(1 - w_1 - w_2)\sigma_{23}$$

$$= w_1^2 \sigma_{11} + w_2^2 \sigma_{22} + (1 - 2w_1 - 2w_2 + 2w_1 w_2 + w_1^2$$
$$+ w_2^2)\sigma_{33} + 2w_1 w_2 \sigma_{12}$$
$$+ (2w_1 - 2w_1^2 - 2w_1 w_2)\sigma_{13} + (2w_2 - 2w_1 w_2$$
$$- 2w_2^2)\sigma_{23}$$

$$= w_1^2 \sigma_{11} + w_2^2 \sigma_{22} + \sigma_{33} - 2w_1 \sigma_{33} - 2w_2 \sigma_{33}$$
$$+ 2w_1 w_2 \sigma_{33} + w_1^2 \sigma_{33} + w_2^2 \sigma_{33}$$
$$+ 2w_1 w_2 \sigma_{12} + 2w_1 \sigma_{13} - 2w_1^2 \sigma_{13} - 2w_1 w_2 \sigma_{13}$$
$$+ 2w_2 \sigma_{23} - 2w_1 w_2 \sigma_{23} - 2w_2^2 \sigma_{23}$$

$$= (\sigma_{11} + \sigma_{33} - 2\sigma_{13})w_1^2 + (2\sigma_{33} + 2\sigma_{12} - 2\sigma_{13} - 2\sigma_{23})w_1 w_2$$
$$+ (\sigma_{22} + \sigma_{33} - 2\sigma_{23})w_2^2 + (-2\sigma_{33} + 2\sigma_{13})w_1$$
$$+ (-2\sigma_{33} + 2\sigma_{23})w_2 + \sigma_{33}. \tag{4.4}$$

Equation (4.4) is a second-degree equation in two variables. Recall that such equations have the general form:

$$Ax^2 + Bxy + Cy^2 + Dx + Ey + F = 0.$$

Appendix E at the back of the book is provided for those who need review in dealing with this type of expression.

Inserting the variances and covariances from the numerical example into equation (4.4) yields:

$$
\begin{aligned}
\text{Var } (r_p) &= [.24 + .27 - 2(.1631)]w_1{}^2 + [2(.27) + 2(.1497) - 2(.1631) \\
&\quad - 2(.0855)]w_1 w_2 + [.22 + .27 - 2(.0855)]w_2{}^2 \\
&\quad + [-2(.27) + 2(.1631)]w_1 + [-2(.27) + 2(.0855)]w_2 \\
&\quad + .27 \\
&= .1838 w_1{}^2 + .3422 w_1 w_2 + .3190 w_2{}^2 - .2138 w_1 \\
&\quad - .3690 w_2 + .27.
\end{aligned} \tag{4.5}
$$

Finding the Weights of the Minimum Variance Portfolio (MVP)

Before the graphing, it is desirable to find the minimum variance portfolio (MVP). Standard differential calculus techniques for finding maxima and minima are used on equation (4.4) or its numerical equivalent (4.5). Taking the partial derivatives of (4.4) with respect to w_1 and w_2 and setting the resulting equations equal to zero yields two linear equations (4.6) and (4.7).

$$
\begin{aligned}
\frac{\partial V}{\partial w_1} &= 2(\sigma_{11} + \sigma_{33} - 2\sigma_{13})w_1 + (2\sigma_{33} + 2\sigma_{12} - 2\sigma_{13} - 2\sigma_{23})w_2 \\
&\quad + (-2\sigma_{33} + 2\sigma_{13}) = 0, \quad (4.6) \\
\frac{\partial V}{\partial w_2} &= (2\sigma_{33} + 2\sigma_{12} - 2\sigma_{13} - 2\sigma_{23})w_1 + 2(\sigma_{22} + \sigma_{33} - 2\sigma_{23})w_2 \\
&\quad + (2\sigma_{23} + 2\sigma_{33}) = 0. \quad (4.7)
\end{aligned}
$$

Inserting the numerical values for the variances and covariances into equations (4.6) and (4.7) yields:

$$
\begin{aligned}
\frac{\partial V}{\partial w_1} &= 2[.24 + .27 - 2(.1631)]w_1 \\
&\quad + [2(.27) + 2(.1497) - 2(.1631) - 2(.0855)]w_2 \quad (4.8) \\
&\quad + [-2(.27) + 2(.1631)] \\
&= .3676 w_1 + .3422 w_2 - .2138 = 0.
\end{aligned}
$$

$$\frac{\partial V}{\partial w_2} = [2(.27) + 2(.1497) - 2(.1631) - 2(.0855)]w_1$$
$$+ 2[.22 + .27 - 2(.0855)]w_2$$
$$+ [-2(.27) + 2(.0855)]$$
$$= .3422w_1 + .6380w_2 - .3690 = 0.$$

(4.9)

To find the minimum variance portfolio (MVP) equations (4.8) and (4.9) are solved simultaneously. An appendix at the rear of the book discusses simultaneous solution of linear equations.[3] Solving (4.8) and (4.9) yields the weights of the MVP, which are graphed in Fig. 4.3. Equations (4.8) and (4.9) may be solved to obtain equations (4.8′) and (4.9′).

$$w_1 = \frac{-.3422w_2 + .2138}{.3676},$$

(4.8′)

$$w_2 = \frac{-.3422w_1 + .3690}{.6380}.$$

(4.9′)

Substitution yields the following weights for the MVP:

$$w_1 = \left(-.3422\left[\frac{.3422w_1 + .3690}{.6380}\right] + .2138\right)/.3676$$

$$= \frac{.1836w_1 - .1979 + .2138}{.3676}$$

$$= .4995w_1 + .0433$$

$$= .0863,$$

$$w_2 = \left(-.3422\left[\frac{-.3422w_2 + .2138}{.3676}\right] + .3690\right)/.6380$$

$$= \frac{.3186w_2 - .1990 + .3690}{.6380}$$

$$= .4994w_2 + .2665$$

$$= .5321,$$

$$w_3 = 1 - w_1 - w_2$$

$$= 1 - .0863 - .5321$$

$$= .3816.$$

---

[3] See Appendix D at the rear of the book for a brief review of simultaneous linear equation solution techniques.

Those who are performing a graphical portfolio analysis but are unfamiliar with the differential calculus may nevertheless find the MVP weights for any three-security portfolio by using equations (4.6) and (4.7). By substituting the values for the relevant variances and covariances into these equations and algebraically solving them for w_1 and w_2, the MVP weights may be determined as above. Thus, the calculus may be avoided.

Isomean Lines

After the formulas for the variance and expected return for the portfolio are reduced to two variables and the MVP weights are known, the graphing may begin. It makes little difference whether the graphing begins with the isovariance ellipses or isomean lines. Here the isomeans will be graphed first.

Since the word "iso" means equal, it follows that *isomean lines* must be lines which have equal mean returns—that is, equal $E(r_p)$—throughout their length. After arbitrarily selecting a few values of $E(r_p)$ in the neighborhood of the $E(r_i)$'s of the securities in the portfolio, the isomean lines may be determined. By selecting three arbitrary values (5, 10, and 20 percent) of $E(r_p)$ and using equation (4.2), the formulas for three isomean lines are derived:

$$E(r_p) = \ \ 5\% = .1314 - .1147w_1 - .078w_2,$$
$$E(r_p) = 10\% = .1314 - .1147w_1 - .078w_2,$$
$$E(r_p) = 20\% = .1314 - .1147w_1 - .078w_2.$$

The easiest way to graph these three linear equations in a cartesian plane as shown in Figs. 4.2 and 4.3 is to set one weight equal to zero and then solve the equation for the other weight. Since the isomean lines intersect the w_1 axis when w_2 is zero and vice versa, this process will yield points on the two axes. Connecting these points with a line yields the isomean lines.

For example, the 5 percent isomean line must have $w_1 = .7097$ when w_2 is set equal to zero:

$$.05 = .1314 - .1147w_1 - .078(0),$$
$$.1147w_1 = .1314 - .05 = .0814,$$
$$w_1 = .0814/.1147 = .7097.$$

When the 5 percent isomean has $w_1 = 0$, then $w_2 = 1.0436$:

$$.05 = .1314 - .1147(0) - .078w_2,$$
$$.078w_2 = .1314 - .05 = .0814,$$
$$w_2 = .0814/.078 = 1.0436.$$

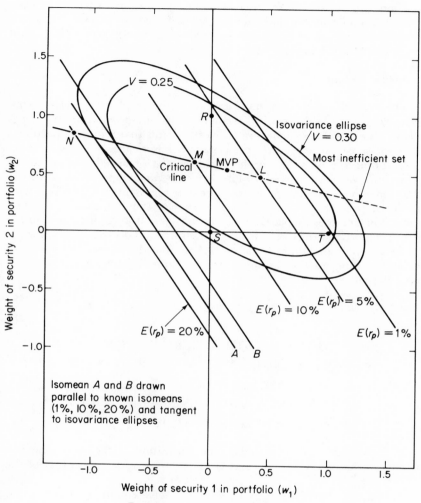

Fig. 4.3   Graphical Solution

Similarly, the following points are derived.

Isomean	w_1 axis intercept given $w_2 = 0$	w_2 axis intercept when $w_1 = 0$
5%	$w_1 = .7097$	$w_2 = 1.0436$
10%	$w_1 = .2738$	$w_2 = .4026$
20%	$w_1 = -.5981$	$w_2 = -.8795$

Plotting the three isomeans yields three parallel straight lines in Fig. 4.3.

There are an infinite number of isomeans, but only a few have been graphed. The primary characteristic of the isomeans is that they are all parallel to each other. Knowledge of this characteristic provides a good check when graphing the isomean lines.

Isovariance Ellipses

The next step of the graphical analysis is the graphing of isovariances. Isovariances are ellipses with a common center, orientation, and egg-shape. The *isovariance ellipses* are a locus of points that represent portfolios with the same variance. Isovariances are risk isoquants.

Graphing the isovariances should ideally be preceded by finding the minimum variance portfolio. The *minimum variance portfolio* (MVP) is the center point for all the isovariances—it represents the portfolio with the least (but not necessarily zero) variance. It is impossible to graph isovariance ellipses for variances less than the variance of the minimum variance portfolio (MVP). Thus, it is desirable to take the weights for the MVP and plug them into equation (4.4) to find the variance of the MVP before plotting any isovariances. In the numerical example, the computation yields:

$$\text{Var}\ (r_p) = w_1^2\sigma_{11} + w_2^2\sigma_{22} + w_3^2\sigma_{33} + 2w_1w_2\sigma_{12} + 2w_1w_3\sigma_{13}$$
$$\qquad\qquad + 2w_2w_3\sigma_{23} \qquad\qquad\qquad\qquad (2.9)$$
$$= (.0863)^2(.24) + (.5321)^2(.22) + (.3816)^2(.27)$$
$$\qquad + (2)(.0863)(.5324)(.1497) + (2)(.0863)(.3816)(.1631)$$
$$\qquad + (2)(.5321)(.3816)(.0855)$$
$$= .0018 + .0623 + .0392 + .0138 + .0108 + .0347$$
$$= .1626 = \text{the variance of the MVP.}$$

This step will save the analyst the frustration of trying to plot isovariances that do not exist (that is, with variances less than that of the MVP).

To graph isovariances, it is necessary to solve equation (4.4) or (4.5) in terms of one of the variables (that is, weights), while treating the remaining variables as constants. Arbitrarily selecting w_1 as the variable to be solved for, and treating w_2 as a constant, reduces equation (4.4) to a quadratic equation in one variable. An appendix at the rear of the book discusses the quadratic formula. The general form of a quadratic equation is: $aw^2 + bw + c = 0$, where the w is a variable and the other symbols are any constant values. Solution of such second-order equations in one variable may be obtained with the quadratic formula:

$$w = \frac{-b \pm \sqrt{b^2 - 4ac}}{2a}.$$

Let $w = w_1$ in equations (4.4) and (4.5) and treat w_2 as a constant. Then, let

$a =$ all coefficients of w^2—that is, all coefficients of w_1^2 in equations (4.4) and (4.5),

$b =$ all coefficients of w—that is, all coefficients of w_1 in equations (4.4) and (4.5),

$c =$ all values that are not coefficients of w_1^2 or w_1 [that is, all constants, which includes the w_2's and the Var (r_p)] in equations (4.4) and (4.5).

For equation (4.4) set the entire expression equal to zero as follows:

$$0 = (\sigma_{11} + \sigma_{33} - 2\sigma_{13})w_1^2 + (2\sigma_{33} + 2\sigma_{12} - 2\sigma_{13} - 2\sigma_{23})w_1 w_2$$
$$+ (\sigma_{22} + \sigma_{33} - 2\sigma_{23})w_2^2 + (-2\sigma_{33} + 2\sigma_{13})w_1$$
$$+ (-2\sigma_{33} + 2\sigma_{23})w_2 + \sigma_{33} - \text{Var } (r_p).$$

Then, the values of a, b, and c are

$$a = \sigma_{11} + \sigma_{33} - 2\sigma_{13},$$
$$b = (2\sigma_{33} + 2\sigma_{12} - 2\sigma_{13} - 2\sigma_{23})w_2 - 2\sigma_{33} + 2\sigma_{13},$$
$$c = (\sigma_{22} + \sigma_{33} - 2\sigma_{23})w_2^2 + (-2\sigma_{33} + 2\sigma_{23})w_2 + \sigma_{33} - \text{Var } (r_p).$$

The value of w_1 can be found by substituting these values of a, b, and c into the quadratic formula.

Following the procedure outlined above, equation (4.5) yields the following results:

$$\text{Var } (r_p) = .1838w_1^2 + .3422w_1 w_2 + .3190w_2^2 - .2138w_1 - .3690w_2$$
$$+ .27, \text{ or, in an implicit form,}$$
$$0 = .1838w_1^2 + .3422w_1 w_2 + .3190w_2^2 - .2138w_1 - .3690w_2$$
$$+ .27 - \text{Var } (r_p),$$
$$a = .1838,$$
$$b = .3422w_2 - .2138,$$
$$c = .3190w_2^2 - .3690w_2 + .27 - \text{Var } (r_p).$$

Inserting these values of a, b, and c into the quadratic formula yields:

$$w_1 = \frac{-b \pm \sqrt{b^2 - 4ac}}{2a}$$

$$w_1 = \frac{-(.3422w_2 - .2138) \pm \sqrt{\begin{array}{c}(.3422w_2 - .2138)^2 - (4)(.1838) \\ \times [.3190w_2^2 - .369w_2 + .27 - \text{Var } (r_p)]\end{array}}}{(2)(.1838)}$$

$$(4.10)$$

Equation (4.10) is the solution to equation (4.5) for w_1 while treating w_2 as a constant. It is necessary to solve the formula to graph the isovariances. To obtain points on the isovariance some arbitrary value for Var (r_p) and w_2 are selected and equation (4.10) is then solved for two values of w_1. It is easiest to select a value for Var (r_p) that is slightly larger than the variance of the MVP and select a value of w_2 at or near the MVP to get the first two values for w_1.

For example, for Var $(r_p) = .17433$ and $w_2 = .3$, equation (4.10) yields the following two values for w_1:

$$w_1 = \frac{-[3422(.3) - .2138] \pm \sqrt{\begin{array}{c}[.3422(.3) - .2138]^2 - (4)(.1838) \\ \times [.3190(.3)^2 - .3690(.3) + .27 - .17433]\end{array}}}{(2)(.1838)}$$

$$= \frac{-.10266 + .2138 \pm \sqrt{.012352 - .010057}}{.3076}$$

$$= \frac{.11114 \pm .04790}{.3676} = .4326 \text{ and } .1720.$$

The variance chosen in this example (.17433) is the variance of the portfolio when $E(r_p) = 5$ percent. This particular value was picked so that the reader may compare the analysis here with the computer program in an appendix at the back of the book. Of course, any value for Var (r_p) could have been chosen so long as it exceeded the variance of the MVP (that is, .1626).

Table   4.1   Isovariance   Points   In
(w_1, w_2) Space

w_2	Two Values of w_1		Variance
.3	.4326	.1720	.17433
.4	.4298	−.0113	.17433
.6	.2676	−.2214	.17433
.7	.1282	−.2682	.17433
.4	.3241	.0944	.16782
.6	.1791	−.1330	.16782
.7	−.0080	−.1321	.16782
.3	1.2892	−.6845	.35020
.4	1.2120	−.7935	.35020
.6	1.0314	−.9852	.35020
.7	.9280	−1.0681	.35020

It is left as an exercise for the reader to verify the points on the isovariance ellipses listed in Table 4.1.[4]

The Critical Line

After the isomeans and isovariances are graphed, it is a simple matter to determine the efficient set of portfolios. An efficient portfolio may be defined as the portfolio with the maximum return for any given risk class. Since each isovariance traces out a risk class, the point where the highest-valued isomean is just tangent to it is an efficient portfolio. The straight line starting from the MVP and connecting these points is the critical line. This critical line is the locus of points in (w_1, w_2) space representing the efficient set. In Fig. 4.3 the set of efficient portfolios starts at the MVP and runs upward to the left along points M and N.

Once the critical line is graphed, the efficient frontier may be graphed with ease. Reading weights (w_1, w_2) off the critical line at a few points (such as points L, M and N in Fig. 4.3), it is possible to calculate the $E(r)$ and σ of portfolios that have the highest rate of return for their risk class. Table 4.2 shows these values.

Table 4.2

Point	w_1	w_2	w_3	$E(r_p)$	Var (r_p)	σ
L	.3957	.4617	.1426	5%	.17433	.41753
M	−.1200	.5790	.5410	10%	.16782	.40966
N	−1.1514	.8137	1.3377	20%	.35020	.59178

The efficient frontier is found by plotting $E(r_p)$ and (σ_p) as done in Fig. 4.4. The graphical method is only approximate because of problems in drafting. This completes the graphical portfolio analysis.

The Most Inefficient Set of Portfolios

The inexperienced analyst must take care not to draw the critical line in the wrong direction away from the MVP. Such a line would be the locus of points representing the set of most inefficient portfolios. The dotted line in Fig. 4.3 is such a line; it is the locus of points representing the minimum return in each risk class.

---

[4] It is recommended that a computer program be used to evaluate the points necessary to plot the isovariances. The calculations are very exacting and tedious. The values in Table 4.1 are from Appendix F.

The Objective of Portfolio Analysis

Earlier in this chapter the objective of portfolio analysis was said to be the determination of the efficient set of portfolios. The efficient set is represented by the infinite number of portfolios whose weights lie along the critical line.

The reader who understands this and the preceding chapters will recognize that portfolio analysis utilizes Markowitz diversification. In fact, it could be said that the objective of portfolio analysis is to maximize the benefits from such diversification at each possible rate of return.

Legitimate Portfolios

Markowitz says an efficient portfolio must meet three conditions:

1. It must have the maximum return in its risk class;
2. it must have the minimum risk in its return class; and
3. it must be "legitimate."[5]

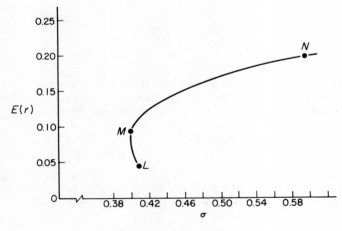

Fig. 4.4   Efficient Frontier

[5] Markowitz, *Portfolio Selection*, p. 140.

The third condition for efficiency has not been imposed in this book. By "legitimate," Markowitz means the portfolio can contain no negatively weighted securities. Graphically, this means the critical line may not leave the right triangle with R, S, and T at its corners in Fig. 4.3. Consequently, the "legitimate" efficient portfolios compose only part of the unconstrained critical line. Financially speaking, legitimate means no leverage or short sales are permitted.

Of course, negative weights are possible and have a rational interpretation. In this book the nonnegativity constraint will not be observed. Only public investment funds that are regulated need adhere to the legitimacy condition.

"Unusual" Graphical Solutions Do Not Exist

The authors typically assign each of their investments students a three-security portfolio-analysis term project. Many students are surprised to find their MVP has negative weights in it, or their isomeans are not tangent to their isovariances, or their entire set of efficient portfolios has negative weights, or their isomeans slope at an angle different than the previous examples they have seen, and so on. These occurrences are not unusual or abnormal. Figure 4.5 is an example containing all the characteristics that ordinarily surprise student analysts.

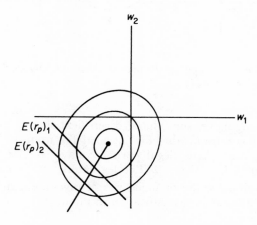

Fig. 4.5   An "Unusual" Solution

For examples of other graphical solutions, including a four-security portfolio, see Chapter VII of Markowitz's book.[6]

Graphical Representation of Constraints

Sometimes laws or corporate policies constrain portfolios. For example, law requires that open-end mutual funds may not borrow money to finance purchases—that is, leveraged portfolios are illegal. This is a portfolio constraint that allows formation of portfolios only within the triangle bounded by R, S, and T in Fig. 4.3 and 4.6. Further, assume some law made it illegal for portfolios to invest more than one-third of their total value in any given security. In terms of Fig. 4.6, the second law means that only the single portfolio at point L is legal.

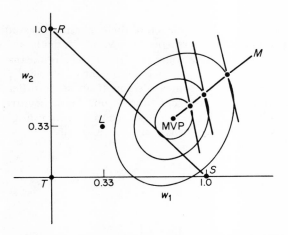

Fig. 4.6   Graphical Representation of Diversification
            Laws

Laws requiring naive, superfluous diversification can *increase* portfolio risk. With such constraints the efficient portfolios from the MVP to point M are illegal. And, these illegal portfolios have *less risk* than the legal portfolio at point L in Fig. 4.6. The legislators who imposed such laws (intended to minimize the financial risk of investment funds) obviously had a naive definition of diversification in mind.

---

[6] Markowitz, *Portfolio Selection*.

The "Interior-Decorator Fallacy"

Brealey explains the "interior-decorator concept" of portfolio management as follows:

> It is a commonly held view that the mix of common stocks maintained by an investor should depend on his willingness to bear risk. According to this view, a broker or investment counselor is a kind of financial interior decorator, skillfully designing portfolios to reflect his client's personality.[7]

According to the interior-decorator school an elderly widow should hold government bonds and utilities, for example, while a young aggressive investor should shun these assets.

The portfolio-analysis technique developed by Markowitz and explained in this chapter is at odds with the "financial interior-decorator" concept of portfolio management. For example, portfolio analysis may indicate that a person desiring to minimize risk should own a portfolio of only *two stocks that are very risky individually*. But, if the two risky stocks covary inversely, the portfolio will most likely have less risk (that is, variability of return) than any portfolio prepared by less analytical techniques.

Appendix 4A
The Baumol Criterion

It has been shown that rates of return on securities are roughly normally distributed[1] as shown in Fig. 4A.1. In the elementary course in classical statistics it is shown that about 68 percent of the occurrences of a normally distributed random variable occur in the range plus and minus one standard deviation (σ) from the mean. About 95 percent of the occurrences lie in the range $E(r) \pm 2\sigma$; and, over 99 percent of the outcomes will be in the range $E(r) \pm 3\sigma$ for a normal distribution. These ranges and their

---

[7] R. A. Brealey, *An Introduction to Risk and Return from Common Stocks* (Cambridge, Mass.: The M.I.T. Press, 1969), p. 115.

[1] Many empirical studies have suggested returns are only roughly normally distributed. Mandelbrot and Fama have shown they are distributed according to a stable Paretian distribution with parameters which cause the distribution to resemble a normal distribution with long tails. See Benoit Mandelbrot's "The Variation of Certain Speculative Prices," *Journal of Business*, October 1963, pp. 394–419. Also see Eugene Fama's "The Behavior of Stock Prices," *Journal of Business*, January 1965, pp. 34–99.

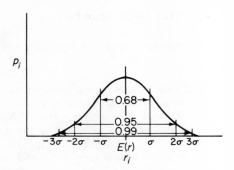

Fig. 4A.1   Unit Normal Probability Distribution

probabilities are shown graphically in Fig. 4A.1. Professor Baumol has used such relationships to develop a selection criterion for efficient portfolios that limits consideration to a subset of the Markowitz efficient set.[2]

Baumol suggests using a lower confidence limit (L) and $E(r)$ as a criterion in preference to Markowitz's σ and E criterion. He defines the lower confidence level (L) as follows:

$$L = E(r_p) - (k)(\sigma), \tag{4A.1}$$

where k is the maximum number of standard deviations below $E(r_p)$ which the portfolio can tolerate, $E(r_p)$ is expected return of the portfolio, and σ is the standard deviation of returns for the portfolio. k is selected by the investor or portfolio manager based on risk preferences—k and L vary inversely. For example, assuming returns are normally distributed, if the investors are willing to accept a .025 chance that the portfolio's return is below L (that is, $r_p < L = E(r) - k\sigma$), they should set $k = 2$. If less chance of a low return is desired, say, $P(r_p < L = E(r) - k\sigma) = .005$, this may be achieved by setting $k = 3$.

The rationale for Baumol's criterion may be seen in terms of Fig. 4A.2. The horizontal axis shows $E(r_p)$'s from the efficient set, the straight line from the origin has a 45° slope, and the vertical axis measures the lower confidence limits for efficient portfolios. The curve OL is the locus of $(E(r), L)$ pairs for portfolios in the efficient set. Portfolio B with $E(r_B)$ offers both a higher expected return *and* a more desirable lower confidence limit (L_B) than any portfolio to the left of B. For example, $E(r_A) < E(r_B)$ and $L_A < L_B$; therefore, A is completely dominated by B according to Baumol's criterion. Thus, all portfolios to the left of B should be eliminated according to Baumol. Baumol's criterion has an intuitive appeal—particularly to portfolio managers who cannot tolerate returns

[2] W. J. Baumol, "An Expected Gain-Confidence Limit Criterion for Portfolio Selection," *Management Science*, October 1963, pp. 174–182.

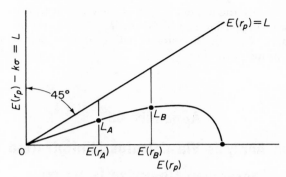

Fig. 4A.2   Baumol's $E(r)$, L Criterion

below L. The traditional Markowitz efficiency criterion would delineate both A and B as members of the efficient set. Baumol says:[3]

> The basic objection to the Markowitz criterion is that in the expression $L = E(r) - k\sigma$ an increasing $E(r)$ may more than counterbalance an increase in σ, so that despite greater variability in return from the portfolio with the larger $E(r_p)$, it may be considered relatively safe because the lower confidence limit L is relatively high.

Baumol's suggestion limits the set of portfolios under consideration to a subset of the curve from E to F in Fig. 4A.3. Baumol's criterion will limit

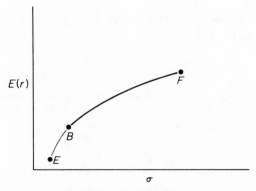

Fig. 4A.3   The Efficient Frontier

[3] Baumol, "An Expected Gain-Confidence Limit Criterion," p. 180.

consideration to only the upper portion of the efficient frontier, say, from B to F. Baumol's suggestion is well taken; however, it has been shown to be of little value when the investor is willing to consider inclusion of a risk-free asset in his portfolio.[4]

Appendix 4B

Portfolio Analysis Via Calculus Minimization of a Lagrangian Objective Function

Graphical portfolio analysis was presented in Chapter 4. As mentioned previously, graphical portfolio analysis cannot handle more than four securities. However, it serves well as an introduction to portfolio analysis. Hopefully, the graphical solution permits a better understanding of the analysis and of the solution obtained.

More efficient solution techniques are available for portfolio analysis. In this appendix a technique using differential calculus to minimize a Lagrangian objective function will be explained. A review of the basic formulas and symbols used is presented at the end of Appendix 2A.

In presenting the calculus solution numerical examples are provided in which a trivial two-security problem is solved. Hopefully, the simplicity of the arithmetic will make for easier reading. As in Chapter 4, a step-by-step "how-to-do-it" approach is followed in the numerical examples.

The General Formulation

Mathematically, the problem involves finding the minimum portfolio variance—that is, the minimum of

$$\text{Var } (r_p) = \sum_i \sum_j w_i w_j \sigma_{ij} \qquad (2\text{B}.9'')$$

subject to two Lagrangian constraints. The first constraint requires that the desired expected return (E^*) be achieved. This is equivalent to requiring the following difference be zero.

$$\sum_i w_i E(r_i) - E^*. \qquad (4\text{B}.1)$$

The second constraint requires that the weights sum to one. Of course,

---

[4] See W. R. Russell and P. E. Smith, "A Comment on Baumol's (E, L) Efficient Portfolios," *Management Science*, March 1966, pp. 619–621.

this constraint is equivalent to requiring the following difference be zero.

$$\sum_i w_i - 1. \tag{2B.7}$$

Combining these three quantities, the Lagrangian objective function of the risk-minimization problem with a desired return constraint is

$$z = \sum_i \sum_j w_i w_j \sigma_{ij} + \lambda_1 (\sum w_i E(r_i) - E^*) + \lambda_2 (\sum w_i - 1). \tag{4B.2}$$

The minimum-risk portfolio is found by setting $\partial z/\partial w_i = \partial z/\partial \lambda_j = 0$ for $i = 1, \ldots, n$ and $j = 1, 2$. The resulting system is composed of the $n + 2$ linear equations shown below.[1]

$$\frac{\partial z}{\partial w_1} = 2w_1\sigma_{11} + 2w_2\sigma_{12} + \cdots + 2w_n\sigma_{1n} + \lambda_2 E(r_1) + \lambda_1 = 0,$$

$$\frac{\partial z}{\partial w_2} = 2w_1\sigma_{21} + 2w_2\sigma_{22} + \cdots + 2w_n\sigma_{2n} + \lambda_2 E(r_2) + \lambda_1 = 0,$$

$$\cdot$$
$$\cdot$$
$$\cdot \tag{4B.3}$$

$$\frac{\partial z}{\partial w_n} = 2w_1\sigma_{n1} + 2w_2\sigma_{n2} + \cdots + 2w_n\sigma_{nn} + \lambda_2 E(r_n) + \lambda_1 = 0,$$

$$\frac{\partial z}{\partial \lambda_2} = w_1 + w_2 + \cdots + w_n - 1 = 0,$$

$$\frac{\partial z}{\partial \lambda_1} = w_1 E(r_1) + w_2 E(r_2) + \cdots + w_n E(r_n) - E^* = 0.$$

These $n + 2$ equations may be formulated as a Jacobian matrix.

$$
\overset{\displaystyle C}{
\begin{bmatrix}
2\sigma_{11} & 2\sigma_{12} & \cdots & 2\sigma_{1n} & E(r_1) & 1 \\
2\sigma_{21} & 2\sigma_{22} & \cdots & 2\sigma_{2n} & E(r_2) & 1 \\
\cdot & & & & & \\
\cdot & & & & & \\
\cdot & & & & & \\
2\sigma_{n1} & 2\sigma_{n2} & \cdots & 2\sigma_{nn} & E(r_n) & 1 \\
1 & 1 & \cdots & 1 & 0 & 0 \\
E(r_1) & E(r_2) & \cdots & E(r_n) & 0 & 0
\end{bmatrix}}
\cdot
\overset{\displaystyle w}{
\begin{bmatrix}
w_1 \\ w_2 \\ \\ \\ \cdot \\ w_n \\ \lambda_2 \\ \lambda_1
\end{bmatrix}}
=
\overset{\displaystyle k}{
\begin{bmatrix}
0 \\ 0 \\ 0 \\ \\ \cdot \\ \cdot \\ \cdot \\ 1 \\ E^*
\end{bmatrix}}, \tag{4B.4}
$$

---

[1] It can be shown that z is minimized rather than maximized. However, proof that these second-order conditions are met is omitted here.

where the coefficient matrix is denoted C, the weight vector is w, and k is the vector of constants. This system may be solved several different ways. Using matrix notation, the inverse of the coefficients matrix (C^{-1}) may be used to find the solution (weight) vector (w) as follows:

$$Cw = k,$$

$$C^{-1}Cw = C^{-1}k,$$

$$Iw = C^{-1}k,$$

$$w = C^{-1}k.$$

The solution will give the $n + 2$ variables in the weight vector in terms of E^*. The n weights will be in the form shown below.

$$w_1 = c_1 + d_1 E^*,$$

$$w_2 = c_2 + d_2 E^*,$$

$$\cdot$$
$$\cdot \qquad\qquad\qquad\qquad\qquad\qquad (4B.5)$$
$$\cdot$$

$$w_n = c_n + d_n E^*,$$

where $\sum_i w_i = 1$. The c_i and d_i are constants. For any desired value of E^* equations (4B.5) give the weights of the minimum variance portfolio. The weights of the portfolios in the efficient set are generated by varying E^* and evaluating the w_i's. Martin solved this problem and has shown the relationship between the solution and the graphical critical line solution in a readable article which the interested reader is invited to pursue.[2]

Calculus Minimization of Risk with Two Securities

For a two-security portfolio, the objective function to be minimized is

$$z = w_1{}^2\sigma_{11} + w_2{}^2\sigma_{22} + 2w_1 w_2 \sigma_{12} + \lambda_1(w_1 E(r_1)$$
$$+ w_2 E(r_2) - E^*) + \lambda_2(w_1 + w_2 - 1). \quad (4B.6)$$

---

[2] A. D. Martin, Jr., "Mathematical Programming of Portfolio Selections," *Management Science*, vol. 1, no. 2 (January 1955), pp. 152–166. Reprinted in E. B. Fredrickson, *Frontiers of Investment Analysis* (Scranton, Penn.: International Textbook Co., 1965), pp. 367–381. For an interpretation of shadow prices represented by the Lagrangian multipliers, λ_1 and λ_2, see Martin's footnote 9. Martin's presentation shows how to delineate legitimate portfolios—that is, portfolios with nonnegative weights.

The partial derivatives are set equal to zero to yield:

$$\frac{\partial z}{\partial w_1} = 2w_1\sigma_{11} + 2w_2\sigma_{12} + \lambda_1 E(r_1) + \lambda_2 = 0,$$

$$\frac{\partial z}{\partial w_2} = 2w_2\sigma_{22} + 2w_1\sigma_{12} + \lambda_1 E(r_2) + \lambda_2 = 0,$$

$$\frac{\partial z}{\partial \lambda_2} = w_1 + w_2 - 1 = 0,$$

$$\frac{\partial z}{\partial \lambda_1} = w_1 E(r_1) + w_2 E(r_2) - E^* = 0.$$

(4B.7)

This system is linear, since the weights (w_i's) are the variables and they are all of degree one. Thus, the system may be solved as a system of linear equations. The matrix representation of this system of linear equations is shown below.

$$\begin{bmatrix} 2\sigma_{11} & 2\sigma_{12} & E_1 & 1 \\ 2\sigma_{21} & 2\sigma_{22} & E_2 & 1 \\ 1 & 1 & 0 & 0 \\ E_1 & E_2 & 0 & 0 \end{bmatrix} \begin{bmatrix} w_1 \\ w_2 \\ \lambda_2 \\ \lambda_1 \end{bmatrix} = \begin{bmatrix} 0 \\ 0 \\ 1 \\ E^* \end{bmatrix}.$$

(4B.8)

$$C \qquad\qquad w \;=\; k$$

This system may be solved several different ways. Using matrix notation, the inverse of the coefficients matrix (C^{-1}) may be used to find the solution (weight) vector (w).

$$Cw = k, \qquad w = C^{-1}k.$$

The solution will give the n (that is, $n = 2$ in this case) weights in terms of E^*.

$$w_1 = c_1 + d_1 E^*, \qquad w_2 = c_2 + d_2 E^*$$

where the c_i and d_i are constants. For any desired E^* the equations give the weights of the minimum variance portfolio. A numerical example follows that is solved via Cramer's rule.

Numerical Example with Two Assets

Using the values $E(r_1) = .05$, $E(r_2) = .15$, $\sigma_1 = .02$, $\sigma_{11} = .04$, $\sigma_2 = .4$, $\sigma_{22} = .16$, $r_{12} = 0$, $\sigma_{12} = 0$ yields the following coefficients' matrix.

$$\begin{bmatrix} 2\sigma_{11} & 2\sigma_{12} & E_1 & 1 \\ 2\sigma_{21} & 2\sigma_{22} & E_2 & 1 \\ 1 & 1 & 0 & 0 \\ E_1 & E_2 & 0 & 0 \end{bmatrix} = \begin{bmatrix} 2(.04) & 2(0) & .05 & 1 \\ 2(0) & 2(.16) & .15 & 1 \\ 1 & 1 & 0 & 0 \\ .05 & .15 & 0 & 0 \end{bmatrix} = C.$$

Solving this system for the first weight (w_1) using Cramer's rule proceeds as shown below. Using column one of the top matrix to expand on yields the following:[3]

$$
w_1 = \frac{\begin{bmatrix} 0 & 2\sigma_{12} & E_1 & 1 \\ 0 & 2\sigma_{22} & E_2 & 1 \\ 1 & 1 & 0 & 0 \\ E^* & E_2 & 0 & 0 \end{bmatrix}}{\begin{bmatrix} 2\sigma_{11} & 2\sigma_{12} & E_1 & 1 \\ 2\sigma_{21} & 2\sigma_{22} & E_2 & 1 \\ 1 & 1 & 0 & 0 \\ E_1 & E_2 & 0 & 0 \end{bmatrix}}
\begin{aligned}
&= 0(-1)^{1+1}C_{11} + 0(-1)^{2+1}C_{21} \\
&\quad + 1(-1)^{3+1}C_{31} \\
&\quad + E^*(-1)^{4+1}C_{41} \\
&= -.015 + .1E^*,
\end{aligned}
$$

$$
\begin{aligned}
&= 1(-1)^{1+4}C_{14} + 1(-1)^{2+4}C_{24} \\
&\quad + 0(-1)^{3+4}C_{34} \\
&\quad + 0(-1)^{4+4}C_{44} = -.01,
\end{aligned}
$$

where C_{ij} is the minor of the element in the ith row and jth column. Evaluating w_1 yields

$$
w_1 = \frac{-(E(r_2))^2 + E(r_1) \cdot E(r_2) - E^*(E(r_1) - E(r_2))}{E(r_1) \cdot E(r_2) - (E(r_2))^2 - (E(r_1))^2 + E(r_1) \cdot E(r_2)}
$$

$$
= \frac{-.015 + .1E^*}{-.01} = 1.5 - 10E^*.
$$

Using Cramer's rule to solve for the second weight (w_2) yields the following computations when expanding on column four of the top matrix.

$$
w_2 = \frac{\begin{bmatrix} 2\sigma_{11} & 0 & E_1 & 1 \\ 2\sigma_{21} & 0 & E_2 & 1 \\ 1 & 1 & 0 & 0 \\ E_1 & E^* & 0 & 0 \end{bmatrix}}{\begin{bmatrix} 2\sigma_{11} & 2\sigma_{12} & E_1 & 1 \\ 2\sigma_{21} & 2\sigma_{22} & E_2 & 1 \\ 1 & 1 & 0 & 0 \\ E_1 & E_2 & 0 & 0 \end{bmatrix}}
\begin{aligned}
&= 1(-1)^{1+4}C_{14} + 1(-1)^{2+4}C_{24} \\
&\quad + 0(-1)^{3+4}C_{34} + 0(-1)^{4+4}C_{44},
\end{aligned}
$$

$$
= \text{same denominator.}
$$

[3] See Taro Yamane's, *Mathematics for Economists: An Elementary Survey* (Englewood Cliffs, N.J.: Prentice-Hall, Inc., 1962), pp. 262–275, for a discussion of the matrix algebra. Or see the appendix at the rear of this book.

Evaluating w_2 yields

$$w_2 = \frac{-(E(r_1))^2 + E(r_1) \cdot E(r_2) - E^*(E(r_1) - E(r_2))}{E(r_1) \cdot E(r_2) - (E(r_2))^2 - (E(r_1))^2 + E(r_1) \cdot E(r_2)}$$

$$= \frac{-.1E^* + .005}{-.01} = 10E^* - .5.$$

Thus, the minimum-risk weights are a linear function of E^*, which sums to one.

$$w_1 = 1.5 - 10E^*, \qquad w_2 = -.5 + 10E^*.$$

When $E^* = .07 = 7$ percent is desired, the weights of the minimum variance portfolio are:

$$w_1 = 1.5 - 10(.07) = 1.5 - .7 = .8$$
$$w_2 = -.5 + 10(.07) = -.5 + .7 = \frac{.2}{1.0}$$

By varying E^* other portfolios in the efficient set will be generated. Of course, the solutions are identical whether the solution is obtained graphically or with calculus.

This calculus optimization solution may be interpreted as shown in Figs. 4B.1 and 4B.2. The curve passing through points 1 and 2 in Fig. 4B.1 shows that as E^* is increased from $E^* = 5$ percent to $E^* = 20$ percent, the portfolio variance increases from $\sigma_p = 20$ percent to $\sigma_p = 40$ percent, and the efficient frontier is generated.

In Fig. 4B.2 the weight of security one, given some E^*, that is, $(w_1 \mid E^*)$ is shown on the left vertical axis. On the right vertical axis the weight of security two required to achieve the desired E^* is shown. Each dotted horizontal line represents a locus of expected returns for the portfolio

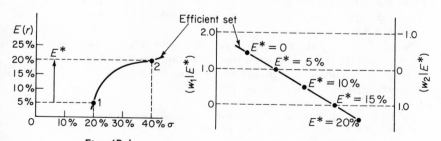

Fig. 4B.1
Graphical Representation of Portfolio Selected as E^* Varies

Fig. 4B.2
Graphical Representation of Weights as E^* Varies

[that is, $E(r_p)$]. Thus, Fig. 4B.2 shows that for, say, $E(r_p) = 5$ percent the minimum-risk portfolio would have $w_1 = 1$, and $w_2 = 0$. The diagonal solid line is the locus of all weights for the most efficient portfolio attainable from the two securities for the E^* shown on the horizontal lines. Figure 4B.2 covers only the range $0 \leq E^* \leq 20$ percent. However, it could be extended to either negative values of E^* (that is, a portfolio with unfavorable financial leverage) or to values of E^* above 20 percent (that is, a high degree of favorable leverage).

Figure 4B.2 shows that the weights change from $w_1 = 1$, $w_2 = 0$ when $E^* = 5$ percent to $w_1 = 0$ and $w_2 = 1$ when $E^* = 15$ percent—these are both simply one-security portfolios. Numerous combinations of weights that sum to one may be generated by varying E^*. For values of E^* below 5 percent or above 15 percent one of the weights will be negative, although they will still sum to one. These negative weights represent the issuance (leverage or short sale) of a security possessing the characteristics (that is, return and risk) of the security to which the negative weights refer.

Caveat

As Fig. 4B.2 shows, the weights of the efficient portfolio become negative for $E^* < 5$ percent and $E^* > 15$ percent. Such solutions lack realism. Some large public portfolios are legally forbidden to use leverage. And, securities having the same risk and return as the security with the negative weight may not be easy to draw up and issue.

It is possible to extend this algorithm so it does not produce negative weights. At the point where the first weight reaches zero (before becoming negative), stop the analysis. Remove the row and column in the bordered covariance matrix (4B.4) corresponding to the security that is at zero weight. The solution now has one less asset from which to select. Invert the new smaller matrix and solve for a new vector of efficient weights. This set of efficient portfolios will intersect the original efficient set where the eliminated asset's weight went to zero. Thus, the analysis proceeds. Each time another asset's weight reaches zero, that asset is eliminated, the new smaller matrix is inverted, and the efficient set is extended further. Martin provides a numerical example and a graphical representation of this process.[4]

For student projects, research, and other work where negative weights are permissible, this calculus solution is recommended. But, for realistic portfolio problems, either quadratic programming must be used or the process described above must be used to eliminate negative weights.

---

[4] A. D. Martin, Jr., "Mathematical Programming of Portfolio Selections," *Management Science*, vol. 1, no. 2 (January 1955), pp. 160–165.

Appendix 4C

Portfolio Analysis Via Calculus Maximization of a Lagrangian Objective Function[1]

Graphical portfolio analysis was presented in Chapter 4. As mentioned previously, graphical portfolio analysis cannot handle more than four securities. However, it serves well as an introduction to portfolio analysis. Hopefully, the graphical solution permits a better understanding of the analysis and of the solution obtained.

Other, more efficient solution techniques are available for portfolio analysis. In this appendix a solution algorithm using differential calculus to maximize a Lagrangian objective function will be explained. Of course, this technique generates the same set of efficient portfolios as the other calculus technique or the graphical technique. A review of the basic formulas and symbols used is presented at the end of Appendix 2A.

In presenting this calculus solution a numerical example is provided, in which a trivial two-security problem is solved. Hopefully, the simplicity of the arithmetic will make for easier reading. As in Chapter 4, a step-by-step "how-to-do-it" approach is followed in the numerical examples.

A Calculus Maximization Solution—General Formulation[2]

The objective of portfolio analysis is to delineate the efficient *set* of portfolios. This problem may be solved mathematically by maximizing a linear combination of the following two equations:

$$E(r_p) = \sum_{i=1}^{n} w_i E(r_i), \tag{2A.8}$$

$$-\text{Var}(r_p) = -\sum_{i=1}^{n} \sum_{j=1}^{n} w_i w_j \sigma_{ij}, \qquad \text{negative of} \tag{2A.9}$$

subject to the following constraint equation:

$$\sum_{i=1}^{n} w_i = 1. \tag{2A.7}$$

Maximizing Var (r_p) times -1 is equivalent to minimizing Var (r_p).

---

[1] This appendix uses mathematics that are not essential to a basic grasp of portfolio analysis.

[2] The authors learned this calculus maximization solution technique from Professor William F. Sharpe in a seminar presented at the University of Washington during 1968.

Let ϕ represent the portfolio managers' preferences for return relative to risk. ϕ may be thought of as the reciprocal of the slope of an indifference line in $(E(r), \sigma^2)$ space.[3] ϕ is the weight attached to a unit of $E(r_p)$ relative to a unit of Var (r_p). A Lagrangian expression may be formed. As in the graphical portfolio analysis, the weights are variables to be optimized.

$$z = \phi E(r_p) - \text{Var}(r_p) + \lambda(1 - \sum w_i) \qquad (4\text{C}.1)$$

$$= \phi \left(\sum_{i=1}^{n} w_i E(r_i)\right) - \sum_{i=1}^{n} w_i w_j \sigma_{ij} + \lambda(1 - \sum w_i), \qquad (4\text{C}.2)$$

The value of the Lagrangian expression is arbitrarily designated z.[4] The value of z is an index of investor satisfaction that has only ordinal significance. Maximizing z subject to the Lagrangian constraint determines the set of weights (w_i's) that are Markowitz efficient for some value of ϕ. Varying ϕ delineates the efficient frontier (EF). As shown in Fig. 4C.1,

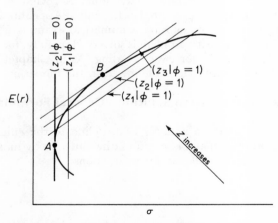

Fig. 4C.1   Efficient Frontier Traced by Varying ϕ

when $\phi = 0$ the maximum value of z is z_2 and point A represents the appropriate Markowitz efficient portfolio. When $\phi = 1$, the maximum value of z is z_3 and point B is the appropriate Markowitz efficient portfolio for this investor's preferences.

---

[3] The use of indifference lines in $(E(r), \sigma^2)$ space is not meant to imply any investor actually has such preferences—it is merely a mathematical convenience. Later, it will be shown that the widely observed phenomena of diversification implies that most investors' indifference curves are concave to the $E(r)$ axis.

[4] For a discussion of similar formulations see D. E. Farrar, *The Investment Decision Under Uncertainty* (Englewood Cliffs, N.J.: Prentice-Hall, Inc., 1962), chap. II.

The Lagrangian expression (4C.2) may be maximized by setting the partial derivative of z with respect to the w_i's and λ equal to zero as below.[5]

$$\frac{\partial z}{\partial w_1} = \phi E(r_1) - 2w_1\sigma_{11} - 2w_2\sigma_{12} - \cdots - \quad 2w_n\sigma_{1n} \quad - \lambda = 0,$$

$$\frac{\partial z}{\partial w_2} = \phi E(r_2) - 2w_2\sigma_{22} - 2w_1\sigma_{21} - \cdots - \quad 2w_n\sigma_{2n} \quad - \lambda = 0,$$

$$\vdots \qquad \qquad \vdots \qquad \vdots \qquad \vdots \qquad\qquad \vdots \qquad\qquad\qquad \text{(4C.3)}$$

$$\frac{\partial z}{\partial w_n} = \phi E(r_n) - 2w_n\sigma_{nn} - 2w_1\sigma_{n1} - \cdots - 2w_{n-1}\sigma_{n.n-1} - \lambda = 0,$$

$$\frac{\partial z}{\partial \lambda} = 1 - w_1 - w_2 - \cdots - w_n = 0.$$

Since the variances, covariances, and the portfolio managers' attitude coefficient (ϕ) can be treated as constants, the system of equations is linear. Forming the Jacobian matrix (that is, the matrix of first partial derivatives), the above system may be restated as follows:

$$
\begin{array}{ccc}
C & w & k
\end{array}
$$

$$
\begin{bmatrix}
2\sigma_{11} & 2\sigma_{12} & \cdots & 2\sigma_{1n} & 1 \\
2\sigma_{21} & 2\sigma_{22} & \cdots & 2\sigma_{2n} & 1 \\
\vdots & \vdots & & \vdots & \vdots \\
2\sigma_{n1} & 2\sigma_{n2} & \cdots & 2\sigma_{nn} & 1 \\
1 & 1 & \cdots & 1 & 0
\end{bmatrix}
\cdot
\begin{bmatrix}
w_1 \\ w_2 \\ \vdots \\ w_n \\ \lambda
\end{bmatrix}
=
\begin{bmatrix}
\phi E(r_1) \\ \phi E(r_2) \\ \vdots \\ \phi E(r_n) \\ 1
\end{bmatrix}. \quad \text{(4C.4)}
$$

Let the coefficient matrix be denoted by C, the weight vector by w, and the constant vector by k. Such simultaneous linear equations may be solved several different ways.

This system of $n + 1$ equations may be represented in matrix notation by writing $Cw = k$. Solving for the vector of w_i's by matrix inversion:

$$Cw = k, \qquad C^{-1}Cw = C^{-1}k, \qquad w = C^{-1}k.$$

In evaluating the weights' vector (w), it will be found that the weights are a linear function of the portfolio manager's attitude coefficient (ϕ). The system of $n + 1$ separate equations with the w_i's as a linear function of ϕ

---

[5] It may be shown that the second-order conditions to ensure a maximum exist. However, such proof will not be given here.

is of the following form:

$$w_1 = c_1 + d_1(\phi),$$
$$w_2 = c_2 + d_2(\phi),$$
$$\vdots$$
$$w_n = c_n + d_n(\phi),$$
$$\lambda = c_\lambda + d_\lambda(\phi),$$

(4C.5)

where the c's and the d's are some constants. By letting ϕ vary from zero to infinity, the set of weights that is optimum for each value of ϕ is generated.[6]

If the Jacobian matrix is small or a computer program to invert C is not available, the system of equations in matrix form may be solved using Cramer's rule.

Some of the w_i's may be negative for extreme values of ϕ. These negative w_i's represent short sales or a leveraged portfolio. Consider a simple two-security numerical example of this solution technique which can be represented graphically.

Calculus Maximization—A Numerical Example

For a two-asset portfolio the Lagrangian objective function is:

$$\text{Max } z = \phi w_1 E(r_1) + \phi w_2 E(r_2) - w_1{}^2\sigma_{11}$$
$$- w_2{}^2\sigma_{22} - 2w_1 w_2 \sigma_{12} + \lambda(1 - w_1 - w_2), \quad (4C.6)$$

which is equivalent to the equations (4C.1) and (4C.2).
Taking the partial derivative with respect to all variables yields the three linear equations (4C.7)

$$\frac{\partial z}{\partial w_1} = \phi E(r_1) - 2w_1 \sigma_{11} - 2w_2 \sigma_{12} - \lambda = 0,$$

$$\frac{\partial z}{\partial w_2} = \phi E(r_2) - 2w_2 \sigma_{22} - 2w_1 \sigma_{21} - \lambda = 0, \quad (4C.7)$$

$$\frac{\partial z}{\partial \lambda} = 1 - w_1 - w_2 = 0,$$

which is equivalent to the system of equations (4C.3). The matrix representation of the above is: $Cw = k$.

$$\begin{matrix} C & w & k \end{matrix}$$
$$\begin{bmatrix} 2\sigma_{11} & 2\sigma_{12} & 1 \\ 2\sigma_{12} & 2\sigma_{22} & 1 \\ 1 & 1 & 0 \end{bmatrix} \cdot \begin{bmatrix} w_1 \\ w_2 \\ \lambda \end{bmatrix} = \begin{bmatrix} \phi E(r_1) \\ \phi E(r_2) \\ 1 \end{bmatrix}. \quad (4C.8)$$

---

[6] Negative values of ϕ represent irrational behavior—that is, risk-loving.

Using the values $E(r_1) = .05$, $E(r_2) = .15$, $\sigma_1 = .2$, $\sigma_{11} = .04$, $\sigma_2 = .4$, $\sigma_{22} = .16$, $r_{12} = 0$, $\sigma_{12} = 0$ yields

$$
\begin{matrix} C & w & k \end{matrix}
$$

$$
\begin{bmatrix} .08 & 0 & 1 \\ 0 & .32 & 1 \\ 1 & 1 & 0 \end{bmatrix} \cdot \begin{bmatrix} w_1 \\ w_2 \\ \lambda \end{bmatrix} = \begin{bmatrix} .05\phi \\ .15\phi \\ 1.0 \end{bmatrix}, \tag{4C.9}
$$

which is equivalent to the system of equations (4C.4). Finding the inverse[7] of C, the system may be solved for the weight vector (w)—that is, $w = C^{-1}k$.

$$
\begin{matrix} w & & C^{-1} & & k \end{matrix}
$$

$$
\begin{bmatrix} w_1 \\ w_2 \\ \lambda \end{bmatrix} = \begin{bmatrix} 2.5 & -2.5 & .8 \\ -2.5 & 2.5 & .2 \\ .8 & .2 & .064 \end{bmatrix} \cdot \begin{bmatrix} .05\phi \\ .15\phi \\ 1 \end{bmatrix}. \tag{4C.9}
$$

Writing out the three linear equations in w_i and ϕ,

$$
w_1 = 2.5(.05\phi) - 2.5(.15\phi) + .8(1.) = .8 - .25\phi,
$$

$$
w_2 = -2.5(.05\phi) + 2.5(.15\phi) + .2(1.) = .2 + .25\phi, \tag{4C.10}
$$

$$
\lambda = .8(.05\phi) + .2(.15\phi) + .064(1.) = .064 + .07\phi,
$$

which is equivalent to the system of equations (4C.5). Alternately, solving the matrix for w_1 and w_2 using Cramer's rule yields

$$
w_1 = \frac{\begin{bmatrix} \phi E(r_1) & 2\sigma_{12} & 1 \\ \phi E(r_2) & 2\sigma_{22} & 1 \\ 1 & 1 & 0 \end{bmatrix}}{\begin{bmatrix} 2\sigma_{11} & 2\sigma_{12} & 1 \\ 2\sigma_{21} & 2\sigma_{22} & 1 \\ 1 & 1 & 0 \end{bmatrix}} = \frac{\phi E(r_2) - \phi E(r_1) + 2\sigma_{12} - 2\sigma_{22}}{4\sigma_{12} - 2\sigma_{11} - 2\sigma_{22}}
$$

$$
= \frac{.1\phi - .32}{-.4} = .8 - .25\phi = w_1. \tag{4C.11}
$$

---

[7] Matrix inversion is discussed very briefly in an appendix at the rear of this book. Or, see T. Yamane, *Mathematics for Economics* (Englewood Cliffs, N.J.: Prentice-Hall, Inc., 1962), pp. 255–275.

Omitting the matrices, the solution for w_2 follows.

$$w_2 = \frac{\phi E(r_1) - \phi E(r_2) - 2\sigma_{11} + 2\sigma_{12}}{4\sigma_{12} - 2\sigma_{11} - 2\sigma_{22}} = \frac{-.1\phi - .08}{-.4}$$

$$= .2 + .25\phi = w_2. \quad (4C.12)$$

Of course, equations (4C.11) and (4C.12) are identical to the two equations for w_1 and w_2 in the system of equations (4C.10). Obviously, the correct solution does not vary with the technique used to solve the system of linear equations.

Solving for w_1 and w_2 as ϕ varies from zero to ten yields the following portfolio returns and pairs of weights which in each case sum to unity.

$$\phi = 0 \begin{cases} w_1 = .8 \\ w_2 = .2 \end{cases} E(r_p) = 7.0\%,$$

$$\phi = \tfrac{1}{2} \begin{cases} w_1 = .675 \\ w_2 = .325 \end{cases} E(r_p) = 8.25\%,$$

$$\phi = 1 \begin{cases} w_1 = .55 \\ w_2 = .45 \end{cases} E(r_p) = 9.5\%,$$

$$\phi = 2 \begin{cases} w_1 = .3 \\ w_2 = .7 \end{cases} E(r_p) = 11.5\%,$$

$$\phi = 5 \begin{cases} w_1 = -.45 \\ w_2 = 1.45 \end{cases} E(r_p) = 19.5\%,$$

$$\phi = 10 \begin{cases} w_1 = -1.7 \\ w_2 = 2.7 \end{cases} E(r_p) = 32.0\%.$$

These portfolios may be represented graphically several different ways. Figure 4C.2 shows that as the portfolio manager's attitude coefficient (ϕ) ranges from $\phi = 0$ to $\phi = 10$ the portfolio's proportion invested in both securities varies. The dotted line represents the weights of security two (w_2). The weights for security two, the more risky security which offers a higher return, ranges from .2 when $\phi = 0$ up to 2.7 when $\phi = 10$ and the portfolio manager is more aggressive. The 2.7 value of w_2 may be interpreted as a portfolio with 270 percent of its total amount invested in security two. To finance this aggressive portfolio, securities with $E(r) = 5$ percent and $\sigma = 20$ percent were issued. That is, the portfolio manager sold securities like security one in an amount equal to 170 percent of the total portfolio to form a leveraged portfolio. But, the budget constraint

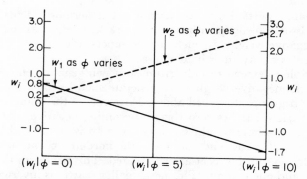

Fig. 4C.2   Graphical Representation of Weights as ϕ Varies

is not violated—specifically, $w_1 + w_2 = -1.7 + 2.7 = 1.0$. Figure 4C.2 could be extended to cover any values for ϕ.

Figure 4C.3 shows how the indifference line shifts as its slope ϕ varies. Higher values of ϕ represent more aggressive attitudes for the portfolio manager. Correspondingly, higher values of ϕ lead to riskier portfolios— that is, higher tangency points with the efficient frontier. The opportunity

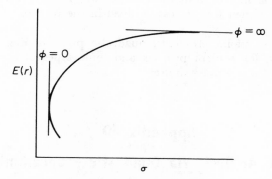

Fig. 4C.3   Graphical Representation of Portfolio Selected from Efficient Frontier as ϕ Varies

locus comprised of the $[E(r_p), \sigma_p]$ pairs representing the infinite number of possible efficient portfolios that can be formed from the two securities does not change as ϕ is varied. Rather, the indifference line becomes tangent to the opportunity locus at different points as ϕ is varied.

Caveat

As Fig. 4C.2 shows, the weights of some assets in the efficient set can become negative—representing leveraged portfolios. It is against the law for some public portfolios to use leverage. Furthermore, it may not be possible to issue a security with the same risk and return as the security with the negative weight. In such circumstances, the solution generated by this calculus algorithm is inadequate.

It is possible to extend this algorithm so it will generate efficient portfolios with nonnegative weights. To generate such legitimate portfolios, the analysis begins as described above. However, at the point where the first asset's weight reaches zero (before becoming negative) the analysis stops. The asset whose weight has attained zero is eliminated from the matrix. That is, the row and column in the bordered covariance matrix (4C.4) pertaining to this asset are eliminated. This decreases the matrix by one row and one column. This new smaller matrix is inverted, and a new efficient vector of weights is attained. The process repeats again. Where the next asset's weight becomes zero, it is eliminated. Then a new, smaller matrix is inverted and a new efficient vector of weights obtained. The series of successive efficient sets generated by this process are connected at the points where the successive assets go out of solution (that is, weights go to zero).

In the case where the entire efficient set contains negative weights over all ranges of expected return for the portfolio, the first solution is unacceptable. At least one asset (different ones may be tried) must be cast out of the initial matrix until the efficient weights all start with nonnegative values. Then the process outlined in the preceding paragraph is used.

For realistic portfolio problems, quadratic programming should be used. However, for student projects and some types of research, this calculus algorithm is simpler to use.

Appendix 4D
Portfolio Analysis Via Quadratic Programming— Some Comments

Markowitz has written an algorithm to solve the mathematical portfolio problem.[1] Markowitz's solution is by quadratic programming rather than calculus. Operational computer codes are available to the public to

---

[1] H. Markowitz, "The Optimization of a Quadratic Function Subject to Linear Constraints," *Naval Research Logistics Quarterly*, vol. 3 (March–June 1956); also see P. Wolfe, "The Simplex Method of Quadratic Programming," *Econometrica*, June 1959, pp. 382–398. Or, see Appendix A of H. Markowitz, *Portfolio Selection* (New York: John Wiley & Sons, Inc., 1959).

perform the quadratic programming algorithm.[2] The input data require-ments are the same for either the calculus solution or the quadratic programming technique.

The quadratic programming code lends itself to the solution of prob-lems with upper and/or lower bounds and nonnegativity constraints on the securities weights. For example, suppose the portfolio manager of a mutual fund is trying to determine his optimum portfolio of securities. But, owing to some regulation he is required to diversify by holding no more than 5 percent of the portfolio in any given security. The portfolio manager can obtain such a constrained optimum solution with the quad-ratic programming algorithm. By putting an upper bound of 5 percent on any security entering the optimum solution, the portfolio will contain at least 20 securities. The quadratic programming algorithm also handles lower-bound constraints on any or all securities weights. Of course, the unconstrained solution will yield a more efficient portfolio unless none of the constraints are binding.

The QP Algorithm

The QP algorithm iteratively minimizes the quadratic objective func-tion Var (r_p) subject to different values of a linear constraint $E(r_p)$. The tangency points of the minimum values of the quadratic function for each $E(r_p)$, or, what is the same thing, the tangency points of the maximum $E(r_p)$ for each Var (r_p) from a straight line—the critical line. The critical line was shown graphically in Fig. 4.3 for the three-security case. The critical line represents the weights of the efficient port-folios in $(w_1, w_2, \ldots, w_n)$ space for an n-security portfolio.

Generating the Efficient Frontier with QP

In terms of the efficient frontier, the QP algorithm begins by finding the portfolio with maximum $E(r_p)$. This is usually a one-security port-folio. It is located at point E in Fig. 4D.1. Point E is the first *corner port-folio*. Corner portfolios are portfolios where a security either enters or leaves the portfolio. The QP algorithm delineates the set of corner port-folios rather than the infinite number of points along the efficient frontier.

After finding the first corner portfolio at E, the algorithm finds the second corner portfolio. The second corner portfolio will lie below E on the efficient frontier (EF) at, say, point S in Fig. 4D.1. The second

<hr>

[2] Programs are available to the general public. The programs are titled, "Portfolio Selection Program." For the IBM 1401 computer, program number 1401-Fl-04X, de-scribed in an IBM manual entitled *Portfolio Selection for the IBM 1401*, is available. For the IBM 7090 the program number is 7090-Fl-03X. The Rand Corporation also has a code titled "Product Form Quadratic Programming Code (RS QPF4)" available under SHARE General Program Library. The latter two programs are quadratic programming algorithms, while the first program uses a simplified model discussed in the next appendix.

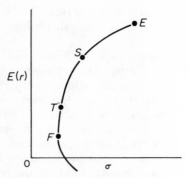

Fig. 4D.1   Efficient Frontier

corner portfolio is the efficient portfolio where a second security comes into solution. The computer program calculates the weights in these corner portfolios and prints out their weights and perhaps their $E(r_p)$ and Var (r_p), depending on the particular program. The algorithm proceeds down the efficient frontier finding the corner portfolios. The number of securities in the corner portfolios typically increases at first and reaches a maximum in the neighborhood of point T in Fig. 4D.1. Then, as the algorithm moves on down toward point F, the number of securities in the successive corner portfolios may or may not change. Point F is the minimum variance portfolio.

The actual number of assets entering into any given efficient portfolio is largely determined by the upper-bound constraints on the weights of the assets. If the weights are free to assume large values (for example, $w_i = 2.0$), the efficient frontier may contain one- or two-asset portfolios at the low- or high-risk extremes.[3] The slope of the efficient frontier, $\phi = dE(r_p)/d\sigma$, at each point, is the trade-off between risk and return at that point.

Technically, the efficient frontier (ESTF) is not a continuous line like the solid line in Fig. 4D.1; rather, it is a series of curves connected at the corner portfolios. A glance back at Fig. 2.10 should explain why the efficient frontier assumes this shape.

Capability for Constraints

Using the quadratic programming algorithm, it is possible to produce a leveraged portfolio. Like linear programming, the quadratic programming algorithm cannot handle negative variables (that is, short sales or leverage), so artificial variables must be used.

---

[3] K. J. Cohen and J. A. Pogue, "An Empirical Evaluation of Alternative Portfolio Selection Models," *Journal of Business*, vol. XL, no. 2 (April 1967), pp. 166–193. Cohen and Pogue show the number of assets entering efficient portfolios with constraints of $w_i \leq .05$ and $w_i \leq .025$. See Tables 6 and 7 on pages 183 and 184.

On the other hand, the optimum solutions with calculus allow negative weights (that is, short sales or leverage) but cannot handle inequality constraints such as upper and lower bounds on the securities weights. However, equality constraints can be included as additional Lagrangian constraints when using one of the calculus methods. The matrix increases one row and one column for each Lagrangian constraint added. The calculus solution seems most advantageous for solving small portfolios without bounds, such as research applications, student projects, and so on.

Appendix 4E
Simplified Models for Portfolio Analysis*

Markowitz suggested certain sophistications that might be used with his model.[1] Following his suggestion, Sharpe developed an ingenious simplified model of portfolio analysis.[2] Sharpe called his model the diagonal model. Sharpe's diagonal model, or the single-index model, as it is alternatively referred to, is presented first. Then, multi-index models will be considered.

Inputs to Simplified Models

The simplified models discussed in this appendix derive their name from the fact they require less input data, the data can be tabulated more simply, and the solution process simplifies certain necessary calculations. As a result, the computer running time for solving the simplified models is a small fraction of the time required to solve the same problem using the full Markowitz technique. As might be expected, the solutions obtained using these simplifications are only approximately efficient—more on this later.

The simplified models assume that the individual covariances between all securities are zero. Thus, the covariances per se are not used in these models. To allow for interrelationships, the models assume securities returns are related only through their individual relations with one or more indices of business activity. By reducing the number of covariances needed, both the security-analysis job and the portfolio-analysis computations are made easier.

---

* This appendix contains mathematics and intricacies that are not essential to grasp the basic analysis.

[1] See Markowitz, *Portfolio Selection*, especially pp. 97–101, including the footnotes.

[2] W. F. Sharpe, "A Simplified Model for Portfolio Analysis," *Management Science*, January 1963, pp. 277–293.

However, some additional inputs are required, too. To use the simplified models, estimates are required of the expected value and variance of the one or more indices of market activity. Markowitz suggested how the forecasts of the index and the security itself may be tabulated for inputting into the algorithm.[3]

Sharpe's Diagonal Model: Assumptions and Relations

Sharpe suggests the return on any security may be related to the performance of some index of business activity. He says:[4]

> The major characteristic of the diagonal model is the assumption that the returns of various securities are related only through common relationships with some basic underlying factor. The return from any security is determined solely by random factors and this single outside element, more explicitly:
>
> $$r_{jt} = a_j + b_j r_{It} + e_{jt}, \tag{5.1}$$

where a_j and b_j are regression parameters for the jth firm, r_{It} is the tth return on some market index, r_{jt} is the tth return on security j, and e_{jt} is the tth random-error term for the jth firm. This model is based on several assumptions about the random-error term. Assuming:

1. the e_{jt}'s average is zero—that is, $E(e) = 0$;
2. the var (e) is constant—that is, homoscedasticity;
3. the e's are uncorrelated with r_I—that is, cov $(e, r_I) = 0$;
4. the e's are not serially correlated—that is, cov $(e_{jt}, e_{j_1 t+n}) = 0$; and
5. the jth firm's e's are uncorrelated with any other firm's, e's,

then the regression parameters a_j and b_j are unbiased, minimum variance linear estimates of the true regression parameters.[5]

Graphically, Sharpe suggests a regression line such as shown in Fig. 4E.1.[6] Such a model allows considerable simplifications in portfolio analysis. First of all, it is possible to estimate the inputs for the regular portfolio analysis—that is, $E(r)$, Var (r), and Cov $(r_i r_j)$—using the following simple formulas:

$$E(r_i) = a_i + b_i(a_{n+1}), \tag{4E.1}$$

$$\text{Var }(r_i) = (b_{i|I})^2 \,(\text{Var }(r_I)) + \sigma^2_{(r_i|r_I)}, \tag{4E.2}$$

$$\text{Cov }(r_i r_j) = (b_{i|I}) \cdot (b_{j|I}) \cdot (\text{Var }(r_I)), \tag{4E.3}$$

---

[3] See Figures 6 and 7 at pp. 29 and 30 of Markowitz's *Portfolio Selection*.

[4] Sharpe, "A Simplified Model for Portfolio Analysis," sec. IV.

[5] According to the Gauss-Markov theorem.

[6] Equations (5.1) and (5.2), Figs. 5.5 and 5.4, and their discussion in Chapter 5 are relevant to equation (4E.1) and Fig. 4E.1 in this appendix.

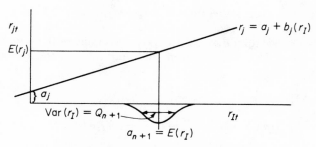

Fig. 4E.1   Sharpe's Diagonal Model

where $a_{n+1} = E(r_I)$, $b_{(i|I)}$ is the regression coefficient of r_i onto r_I, and $\sigma^2(r_i/r_I) = E(e_{it}^2)$ is the residual variance about the regression line.

Note that the parameters for equations (4E.1), (4E.2), and (4E.3) can be estimated several ways. For example, the regression coefficients can be fitted using historical data; they can be estimated intuitively; or, using both approaches, historically derived parameters may be adjusted intuitively. A future expected return for index $E(r_I) = a_{n+1}$ and a future variance for the index, Var (r_I), must also be estimated.[7]

The derivation of equations (4E.1), (4E.2), and (4E.3) follows. The expected value of equation (5.1) is the conditional expectation, equation (4E.1).

$$r_i = a_i + b_i r_I + e_i, \tag{5.1}$$

$$E(r_i) = E(a_i + b_i r_I + e_i) \qquad \text{[expectation of (5.1)]},$$

$$= E(a_i) + E(b_i)E(r_I) + E(e_i)$$

$$= a_i + b_i a_{n+1} + 0 = E(r_i \,|\, a_{n+1}). \tag{4E.1}$$

Equation (4E.2) is derived from the definition of the variance (equation 2A.2′) and the assumptions underlying equation (5.1).

$$\text{Var }(r_i) = \sigma_{ii} = E[r_i - E(r_i)]^2 \tag{2A.2′}$$

$$= E[(a_i + b_i r_I + e_i) - E(a_i + b_i r_I + e_i)]^2$$

$$\text{by substitution for } r_i$$

$$= E(a_i + b_i r_I + e_i - E(a_i) - E(b_i)a_{n+1} + E(e_i))^2$$

$$= E[b_i^2(r_I - a_{n+1})^2 + (e_i)^2 + 2b_i(r_I - a_{n+1})(e_i)]$$

$$= b_i^2 E(r_I - a_{n+1})^2 + E(e_i^2) + 0$$

$$= b_i^2 \text{ Var }(r_I) + \sigma^2(r_i \,|\, r_I) \tag{4E.2}$$

$$= \text{systematic risk} + \text{unsystematic risk}.$$

---

[7] K. V. Smith, "Stock Price and Economic Indexes for Generating Efficient Portfolios," *Journal of Business*, July 1969, pp. 326–336.

In equation (4E.2), the first term [that is, $b_i^2 \cdot \text{Var}'(r_I)$] measures systematic risk. The second term [that is, $\sigma^2_{r_i|r_I}$] measures unsystematic risk. This relation may clarify the partitioning of the total variance.

Equation (4E.3) is derived from the definition of the covariance as follows:

$$\text{Cov}\,(r_i r_j) = \sigma_{ij} = E[(r_i - E(r_i))(r_j - E(r_j))] \qquad (2A.5)$$

$$= E\langle([a_i + b_i r_I + e_i] - E[a_i + b_i r_I + e_i]) \cdot ([a_j + b_j r_I + e_j]$$

$$- E[a_j + b_j r_I + e_j])\rangle$$

$$= E\{([b_i r_I - b_i a_{n+1}] + e_i) \cdot ([b_j r_I - b_j a_{n+1}] + e_j)\}$$

$$= b_i b_j E(r_I - a_{n+1})^2 + 0 + 0 + 0$$

$$= b_i b_j \,\text{Var}\,(r_I). \qquad (4E.3)$$

When using the full covariance portfolio-analysis techniques and n is large, equations (4E.1), (4E.2), and (4E.3) greatly simplify the security analyst's job. For example, if $n = 100$, then $(n^2 - n)/2 = 4,950$ covariances that are required for the conventional Markowitz analysis. Covariances do not readily yield to intuitive estimation as easily as expected return and standard deviation of returns. But, using equation (4E.3), only 100 regression coefficients and the Var (r_I) must be estimated to derive the 4,950 covariances necessary for the full covariance model. The use of the two printed forms suggested by Markowitz[8] and the formulas (4E.1), (4E.2), and (4E.3) is highly recommended for large commercial portfolio applications.

In addition to the three equations for deriving the regular input data easily, a second benefit can be obtained by using Sharpe's simplified model. The actual portfolio-analysis problem itself may be reformulated in terms of equation (4E.1), $a_{n+1} = E(r_I)$, and Var (r_I). This simplified model offers computational shortcuts; it is explained in the next section.

Sharpe's Single-Index Model

The formulation of the simplified model is analogous to the regular Markowitz formulation. The return of the portfolio is defined as before.

$$E(r_p) = \sum_{i=1} w_i E(r_i). \qquad (2A.8)$$

However, using equation (5.1), the return on the portfolio is redefined as

---

[8] Figures 6 and 7 at pp. 29 and 30 of Markowitz's book, *Portfolio Selection*, could be very useful for tabulating the information to input into the portfolio-analysis algorithm.

follows:

$$E(r_p) = \sum w_i E(r_i) = \sum_{i=1}^{n} w_i E(a_i + b_i r_I + e_i)$$

$$= \sum_{i=1}^{n} w_i(a_i + e_i) + \sum_{i=1}^{n} w_i(b_i r_I).$$

Sharpe suggests that the portion of the portfolio placed in the ith security can be viewed as two components:

1. an investment in the "basic characteristics" of the ith security—that is, $w_i(a_i + e_i)$; and
2. an "investment" in the index—that is, $w_i(b_i r_I)$.

Thus, the portfolio return is a combination of n "basic securities" and an investment in the index:

$$r_p = \sum_{i=1}^{n} w_i(a_i + e_i) + \left[\sum_{i=1}^{n} w_i b_i \right] r_I. \qquad (4E.4)$$

Denoting the weighted average of the n b_i terms in equation (4E.4) as

$$w_{n+1} = \sum_{i=1}^{n} w_i b_i \qquad (4E.5)$$

and substituting (4E.5) into (4E.4) yields

$$r_p = \sum_{i=1}^{n} w_i(a_i + e_i) + w_{n+1}(a_{n+1} + e_{n+1}) \qquad (4E.6)$$

$$= \sum_{i=1}^{n+1} w_i(a_i + e_i).$$

Since $E(e_i) = 0$, the expected value of (4E.6) is

$$E(r_p)' = \sum_{i=1}^{n} w_i a_i + w_{n+1} E(r_I) = \sum_{i=1}^{n+1} w_i a_i. \qquad (4E.7)$$

Examination of the algebraic simplifications leading to equation (4E.7) will reveal why the notation $a_{n+1} = E(r_I)$ was used—it facilitates compact notation in equation (4E.7) and the remainder of the discussion.

Owing to simplifying assumption 5, equation (2A.9) must be modified to measure the variance of the portfolio. Setting all covariance terms in (2A.9) to zero, the variance of the portfolio in the simplified model is given by equation (4E.8).

$$\text{Var}\,(r_p)' = \sum_{i=1}^{n} w_i^2\,\text{Var}\,(r_i) + w_{n+1}^2\,\text{Var}\,(r_I)$$

$$= \sum_{i=1}^{n+1} w_i^2\,\text{Var}\,(r_i). \qquad (4E.8)$$

The significance of the name "diagonal model" can be seen from equation (4E.8). The variance-covariance matrix has zeros in all positions other than the diagonal—as shown below.

$$
\begin{bmatrix}
\sigma_{11}^2 & 0 & 0 & \cdots & 0 \\
0 & \sigma_{22}^2 & 0 & \cdots & 0 \\
0 & 0 & \sigma_{33}^2 & \cdots & 0 \\
\cdot & \cdot & \cdot & \cdot & \cdot \\
\cdot & \cdot & \cdot & \cdot & \cdot \\
\cdot & \cdot & \cdot & \cdot & \cdot \\
0 & 0 & 0 & \cdots & \sigma_I^2
\end{bmatrix}.
$$

This diagonal matrix can be inverted with less computation than a full matrix. This computational ease leads to considerable savings, particularly in large-portfolio problems.

Using the above relations, Sharpe's simplified model may be solved by formulating it as a Lagrangian objective function.

Maximize:

$$
Z = \phi E(r_p)' - \text{Var }(r_p)' + \lambda_1(\sum w - 1) + \lambda_2(\sum^n w_i b_i - w_{n+1}),
$$

$$(4E.9)$$

where $E(r_p)'$ is defined by equation (4E.7), ϕ is the investor's risk preference coefficient as explained in Appendix 4C. Larger values of ϕ represent more aggressiveness—that is, a flatter indifference line in Fig. 4C.1. Var $(r_p)'$ is defined by equation (4E.8); the first Lagrangian constraint (λ_1) assures equation (2A.7) is not violated; and the second Lagrangian (λ_2) constraint assures equation (4E.5) holds. Expanding the objective function (4E.9) yields equation (4E.9').

Maximize:

$$
Z = \phi \sum^{n+1} w_i a_i - \sum^{n+1} w_i^2 \text{ Var }(r_i) + \lambda_1(\sum^n w_i - 1) + \lambda_2(\sum^n w_i b_i - w_{n+1}).
$$

$$(4E.9')$$

Equations (4E.9) and (4E.9') are analogous to equations (4C.1) and (4C.2) in the full covariance model solved by the calculus method shown in Appendix 4C.

Numerical Example for Single-Index Model

Consider a simplified solution to the two-security portfolio problem solved with the full variance-covariance matrix. Using Sharpe's single-index model for comparison, the objective function for $n = 2$ is shown as equation (4E.10).

Maximize:

$$Z = \phi w_1 a_1 + \phi w_2 a_2 + \phi w_3 a_3 - w_1{}^2 \operatorname{Var}(r_1) - w_2{}^2 \operatorname{Var}(r_2)$$
$$- w_3{}^2 \operatorname{Var}(r_3) + \lambda_1 w_1 + \lambda_1 w_2 - \lambda_1 + \lambda_2 w_1 b_1$$
$$+ \lambda_2 w_2 b_2 - \lambda_2 w_3. \tag{4E.10}$$

Notice the terms containing a_3 and $\operatorname{Var}(r_3)$ in equation (4E.10). The simplified model is able to omit all the covariance terms in the full Markowitz model by substituting the relationship with the index instead. The optimal portfolio using the simplified model depends on the forecasted expected value and variance of the index. As the forecasted index changes, the optimum portfolio will change. This feature provides valuable opportunities for sensitivity analysis, which will be discussed later.[9]

There are five variables in equation (4E.10), the three weights and the two Lagrangian multipliers. All other quantities are parameters (that is, constants). Taking the first-order partial derivatives with respect to the five variables in equation (4E.10) yields the following five equations, which are linear in the five variables.

$$\frac{\partial Z}{\partial w_1} = \phi a_1 - 2w_1 \operatorname{Var}(r_1) + \lambda_1 + \lambda_2 b_1 = 0,$$

$$\frac{\partial Z}{\partial w_2} = \phi a_2 - 2w_2 \operatorname{Var}(r_2) + \lambda_1 + \lambda_2 b_2 = 0,$$

$$\frac{\partial Z}{\partial w_3} = \phi a_3 - 2w_3 \operatorname{Var}(r_3) + \lambda_1 + \lambda_2 b_3 = 0,$$

$$\frac{\partial Z}{\partial \lambda_1} = w_1 + w_2 - 1 = 0,$$

$$\frac{\partial z}{\partial \lambda_2} = w_1 b_1 + w_2 b_2 - w_3 = 0.$$

---

[9] Later in this appendix it is shown how the optimum weights in the simplied model can be made a function of the index. In the appendix to Chapter 6 it is similarly shown how the Markowitz efficient-weight formulas from the full covariance model may be made functions of the index. These formulations allow the portfolio analyst to see how the optimum weights vary with the expectations about the index of market activity.

The five linear equations yields the system below:

$$
\begin{bmatrix}
-2\,\mathrm{Var}\,(r_1) & 0 & 0 & 1 & b_1 \\
0 & -2\,\mathrm{Var}\,(r_2) & 0 & 1 & b_2 \\
0 & 0 & -2\,\mathrm{Var}\,(r_3) & 0 & -1 \\
1 & 1 & 0 & 0 & 0 \\
b_1 & b_2 & -1 & 0 & 0
\end{bmatrix}
\cdot
\begin{bmatrix}
w_1 \\ w_2 \\ w_3 \\ \lambda_1 \\ \lambda_2
\end{bmatrix}
=
\begin{bmatrix}
-\phi a_1 \\ -\phi a_2 \\ -\phi a_3 \\ 1 \\ 0
\end{bmatrix}.
$$

Using Cramer's rule to solve for w_1 proceeds as shown below.

$$
w_1 = \frac{
\begin{bmatrix}
-\phi a_1 & 0 & 0 & 1 & b_1 \\
-\phi a_2 & -2\,\mathrm{Var}\,(r_2) & 0 & 1 & b_2 \\
-\phi a_3 & 0 & -2\,\mathrm{Var}\,(r_3) & 0 & -1 \\
1 & 1 & 0 & 0 & 0 \\
0 & b_2 & -1 & 0 & 0
\end{bmatrix}
}{
\begin{bmatrix}
-2\,\mathrm{Var}\,(r_1) & 0 & 0 & 1 & b_1 \\
0 & -2\,\mathrm{Var}\,(r_2) & 0 & 1 & b_2 \\
0 & 0 & -2\,\mathrm{Var}\,(r_3) & 0 & -1 \\
1 & 1 & 0 & 0 & 0 \\
b_1 & b_2 & -1 & 0 & 0
\end{bmatrix}
},
$$

$$
w_1 = \frac{
\begin{aligned}
&-2b_2^2\,\mathrm{Var}\,(r_3) - 2\,\mathrm{Var}\,(r_2) + \phi a_2 + b_2\phi a_3 \\
&\quad + 2b_1 b_2\,\mathrm{Var}\,(r_3) - \phi a_1 - b_1\phi a_3
\end{aligned}
}{
\begin{aligned}
&-2b_2^2\,\mathrm{Var}\,(r_3) - 2\,\mathrm{Var}\,(r_2) + 4b_1 b_2\,\mathrm{Var}\,(r_3) \\
&\quad - 2b_1^2\,\mathrm{Var}\,(r_3) - 2\,\mathrm{Var}\,(r_1)
\end{aligned}
}.
$$

$$(4E.11)$$

Similarly, w_2 is found:

$$
w_2 = \frac{
\begin{aligned}
&b_1\phi a_3 - \phi a_2 + \phi a_1 - b_2\phi a_3 + b_1 b_2^2\,\mathrm{Var}\,(r_3) \\
&\quad - b_1^2\,2\,\mathrm{Var}\,(r_3) - 2\,\mathrm{Var}\,(r_1)
\end{aligned}
}{
\begin{aligned}
&-2b_2^2\,\mathrm{Var}\,(r_3) - 2\,\mathrm{Var}\,(r_2) + 4b_1 b_2\,\mathrm{Var}\,(r_3) \\
&\quad - 2b_1^2\,\mathrm{Var}\,(r_3) - 2\,\mathrm{Var}\,(r_1)
\end{aligned}
}.
$$

$$(4E.12)$$

In order to compare the solution attained with Sharpe's simplified model and the solution attained in Appendices 4B and 4C, using the full variance-covariance matrix, the same data will be used here. Assuming $b_1 = b_2 = 0$ and substituting $a_1 = E(r_1) = .05$, $a_2 = E(r_2) = .15$, $\sigma_{11} = .04$, $\sigma_{22} = .16$, $a_3 = E(r_I) = .1$, Var $(r_I) = .1 =$ Var (r_3), into equations (4E.11) and (4E.12) yields equations (4E.13) and (4E.14).

$$w_1 = .8 - .25\phi, \qquad (4E.13)$$

$$w_2 = \frac{.2 + .25\phi}{1.0 + 0}. \qquad (4E.14)$$

Equations (4E.13) and (4E.14) are identical to the formulas for the weights found in Appendices 4B and 4C. As long as $b_1 = b_2 = 0$, equations (4E.13) and (4E.14) will continue to equal the weight formulas attained in Appendices 4B and 4C. However, if the parameters are changed so $b_1 \neq b_2$, the weight formulas will differ from those of Appendices 4B and 4C. For example, if $b_2 = 1$, instead of zero, equations (4E.13) and (4E.14) would change to give more weight to lower-risk asset one as shown below:

$$w_1 = \tfrac{13}{15} - \phi/3, \qquad (4E.15)$$

$$w_2 = \frac{\tfrac{2}{15} + \phi/3}{1.0 + 0}. \qquad (4E.16)$$

The weights' formulas in equations (4E.13) and (4E.14) sum to one as do the weights in (4E.15) and (4E.16). The weight of the security with the higher return increases with ϕ. And, equations (4E.13) and (4E.14) are identical to those attained in Appendices 4B and 4C. It appears that Sharpe's simplified model yields identical solutions to the full covariance model—but this is not true. Only because of the trivial nature of this numerical example did the solutions work out identically. However, the simplified solution doesn't differ a great deal from the solutions using the full variance-covariance matrix. Comparisons are made later in this chapter.

Sensitivity Analysis with the Index as the Variable

Equations (4E.11) and (4E.12) or the weights' formulas from the full covariance model could be solved with ϕ set to some value and treating $a_3 = E(r_I)$ and Var $(r_3) =$ Var (r_I) as variables. Then, by varying the forecasted parameters of the index, it is possible to see precisely how sensitive the optimum portfolio is to these forecasted parameters. If the solution is very sensitive to the index forecast, it might be desirable to devote additional effort to insure the accuracy of the forecast.

For example, setting $\phi = 1$, $b_1 = 1$, $b_2 = 2$, $a_1 = E(r_1) = .05$, $a_2 = E(r_2) = .15$, $\sigma_{11} = .04$, $\sigma_{22} = .16$ in equations (4E.11) and (4E.12) results in equations (4E.17) and (4E.18).

$$w_1 = \frac{-4 \text{ Var } (r_3) - .22 + a_3}{-2 \text{ Var } (r_3) - .4}, \qquad (4E.17)$$

$$w_2 = \frac{+2 \text{ Var } (r_3) - .18 - a_3}{-2 \text{ Var } (r_3) - .4}. \qquad (4E.18)$$

Equations (4E.17) and (4E.18) sum to one; they are like the other weights' formulas derived above except the expected value, $E(r_I) = a_3$, and the variance of the index, Var $(r_3) = $ Var (r_I), are treated as variables rather than treating ϕ as a variable. If Var (r_3) is set at .1 and a_3 is varied from .1 to .2, the optimum weights shift toward more of security two (that is, w_2)—the high-risk, high-return security. The values of equations (4E.17) and (4E.18) are shown in Table 4E.1 as a_3 varies. Clearly, when the index is expected to rise, the resulting portfolio will reflect these expectations appropriately.

Table 4E.1

	Low a_{n+1}	High a_{n+1}
Given parameters:	$a_3 = .1$, $V_3 = .1$	$a_3 = .2$, $V_3 = .1$
Resulting portfolio:	$w_1 = 26/30$	$w_1 = 21/30$
	$w_2 = \quad 4/30$	$w_2 = \quad 9/30$
$w_1 + w_2$ totals:	1.0	1.0

Multi-Index Models

Between the simplicity of Sharpe's single-index model and the comprehensive full covariance model of Markowitz lies a spectrum of possible models. Two, three, four, or more indices can be used. In effect, the Markowitz model using the full variance-covariance matrix without any simplifications uses each security as an index. Of course, the more indices used, the less simple the model and the less the computational savings that can be achieved.

Intuitively, it seems as if a multi-index model should generate a more efficient set of portfolios than a single-index model, since it utilizes more information about the interrelationships. In this case, the loss of computational savings may be more than offset by the gain in the Markowitz efficiency of the solution. The research to date is not clear as to the point at which this balance is in fact achieved. One study showed that the single-index model produced more efficient portfolios than a multi-index model.[10]

Although multi-index models use several indices, the performance of each security in the portfolio is assumed to be related to only one of the indices. The index that is most highly correlated with an asset is usually the best index with which to functionally relate that security to the rest of the portfolio. Thus, in portfolios considering different types of assets (such as common stocks, bonds, commodities, real estate, and others) that are not all highly correlated with each other or with a common index the multi-index models are particularly appropriate.

In order to reveal the construction of a multi-index model, a two-index model is presented below. Models using more indices are direct extensions of the two-index model.

Two-Index Model

Consider a two-index simplified portfolio-analysis model with N securities to be analyzed. Denote the first index I_1 and the second index I_2. These two indices might be GNP in dollars (I_1) and rates of return on the Standard and Poor's 500 Stocks Average (I_2) or anything else that has a significant correlation with the securities' returns. Assume the first M securities numbered $1, 2, \ldots, M$, where $M < N$, correlate most highly with index one (I_1). Assume the remaining ($N - M$) securities numbered $M + 1, M + 2, \ldots, N$ are correlated most highly with index two (I_2). Then the return on the ith security can be written as

$$r_i = a_{i1} + b_{i1}I_1 + e_{i1} \qquad \text{if } 0 < i \le M, \qquad (4E.19)$$

$$r_i = a_{i2} + b_{i2}I_2 + e_{i2} \qquad \text{if } M < i \le N, \qquad (4E.20)$$

where a_{i1} and b_{i1} are the regression parameters for the ith security which is correlated with I_1 and e_{i1} is a random-error term (with the five assumptions pertaining to the error term listed earlier in this chapter still applicable). Equation (4E.20) is the similar regression model for I_2 and securities $M + 1, M + 2, \ldots, N$. Both (4E.19) and (4E.20) are analogous to equation (5.1).

The variance of the ith security is defined below in equations (4E.21) and (4E.22).

$$\text{Var } (r_i) = (b_{i1})^2 \text{ Var } (r_{I1}) + \sigma^2_{(r_i|I_1)} \qquad \text{if } i \le M, \qquad (4E.21)$$

$$\text{Var } (r_i) = (b_{i2})^2 \text{ Var } (r_{I2}) + \sigma^2_{(r_i|I_2)} \qquad \text{if } i > M. \qquad (4E.22)$$

---

[10] K. J. Cohen and J. A. Pogue, "An Empirical Evaluation of Alternative Selection Models," *Journal of Business*, vol. XL, no. 2 (April 1967), pp. 166–193. Cohen and Pogue concluded that this result was due to the homogeneity of their sample—that is, all common stocks. For more heterogeneous samples they suggested multi-index models.

The covariance terms are defined as:

$$\text{Cov } (r_i, r_j) = (b_{i1})(b_{j1}) \text{ Var } (r_{I_1}) \qquad \text{if } i \text{ and } j \leq M \qquad (4\text{E}.23)$$

$$\text{Cov } (r_i, r_j) = (b_{i1})(b_{j2}) \text{ Cov } (I_1, I_2) \quad \text{if } \begin{cases} i \leq M \text{ and } j > M \\ \text{or } j \leq M \text{ and } i > M, \end{cases} \qquad (4\text{E}.24)$$

$$\text{Cov } (r_i, r_j) = (b_{i2})(b_{j2}) \text{ Var } (r_{I2}) \qquad \text{if } i \text{ and } j \geq M, \qquad (4\text{E}.25)$$

where Cov (I_1, I_2) is the covariance of the rates of change in the two indices. In the simple case that the two indices aren't correlated with each other, the following simplifications are possible:

$$w_{n+1} = \sum_{i=1}^{M} w_i b_{i1}, \qquad (4\text{E}.26)$$

$$w_{n+2} = \sum_{i=M+1}^{N} w_i b_{i2}. \qquad (4\text{E}.27)$$

Using equations (4E.26) and (4E.27), the return and variance of the portfolio can be expressed as

$$E(r_p)'' = \sum_{i=1}^{N+2} a_i w_i, \qquad (4\text{E}.28)$$

$$\text{Var } (r_p)'' = \sum_{i=1}^{N+2} w_i^2 \text{ Var } (r_i), \qquad (4\text{E}.29)$$

where $a_{n+1} = E(r_{I1})$ and $a_{n+2} = E(r_{I2})$ denote expected returns on the indices and Var (r_{n+1}) and Var (r_{n+2}) measure the uncertainty surrounding the estimates of the indices.

The Lagrangian objective function to be maximized is

$$Z = \phi E(r_p)'' - \text{Var } (r_p)'' + \lambda_1 (\sum w_1 - 1) + \lambda_2 \left(\sum_1^M w_i b_i - w_{n+1} \right)$$

$$+ \lambda_3 \left(\sum_{m+1}^{N} w_i b_i - w_{n+2} \right) \qquad (4\text{E}.30)$$

$$= \phi \sum^{n+2} w_i a_i - \sum^{n+2} w_i^2 \text{ Var } (r_i) + \lambda_1 \left(\sum^N w_i - 1 \right)$$

$$+ \lambda_2 \left(\sum^M w_i b_i - w_{n+1} \right) + \lambda_3 \left(\sum_{m+1}^{N} w_i b_i - w_{n+2} \right). \qquad (4\text{E}.31)$$

Comparing the Efficiency of One- and Two-Index Models' Portfolios

Limited work has been done to determine whether the loss of computational efficiency resulting from introducing additional indices is offset by an increase in the efficiency of the portfolios generated. As mentioned above, Cohen and Pogue found that the single-index model outperformed a two-index model—a rather surprising conclusion.

Wallingford, on the other hand, found that two-index models generated more efficient portfolios than single-index models.[11] Wallingford's sample was only 20 securities; he experimented with simulated data and actual historical data. In view of their larger sample and the various models they tested, Cohen and Pogue's results will be reviewed here.[12]

Figure 4E.2 shows efficient frontiers that they generated with Sharpe's single-index model, a multi-index model, and the Markowitz full-covariance model for two universes. In one universe, 150 randomly

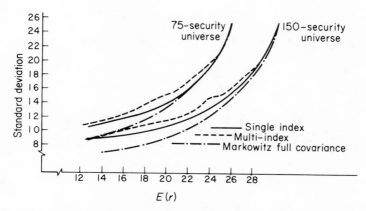

Fig. 4E.2   Different Efficient Frontiers Generated by
Cohen and Pogue (their Fig. 2)

selected common stocks were analyzed for possible inclusion in the efficient set. In the other universe, a randomly selected subset of 75 securities from the 150-security universe was used.

Cohen and Pogue, like Wallingford, find that the Markowitz full-covariance model generates the dominant efficient frontier. Unlike Wallingford, Cohen and Pogue find that Sharpe's single-index model outperforms or matches the efficiency attained with the multi-index model. However, Cohen and Pogue point out that their sample is homogeneous (that is, all common stocks) enough that it is amenable to the single-index type of assumptions.

Considering the contradictory evidence uncovered by Cohen and Pogue, it is not possible to generalize about the relative efficiency of various simplified models. In another vein, Cohen and Pogue's data show that the efficient frontier generated by any method is quite sensitive to the number of securities in the universe under analysis.

[11] B. A. Wallingford, "A Survey and Comparison of Portfolio Selection Models," *Journal of Finance and Quant. Anal.*, June 1967, pp. 85–106.
[12] K. J. Cohen and J. A. Pogue, "An Empirical Evaluation of Alternative Selection Models," fig. 2, pp. 178–181.

SECTION THREE

IMPLICATIONS OF PORTFOLIO ANALYSIS

```
555555555555555555555555555555555555555555555555555555555555555555555555555555555
555555555555555555555555555555555555555555555555555555555555555555555555555555555
5555555555555555555555555555555555555    5555555555    55555555555555555555555555555
5555555555555555555555555555555555555    5555555555    55555555555555555555555555555
5555555555555555555555555555555555555    555555555    55555555555555555555555555555
5555555555555555555555555555555555555    5555555    55555555555555555555555555555
5555555555555555555555555555555555555    55555    55555555555555555555555555555
5555555555555555555555555555555555555    555    55555555555555555555555555555
5555555555555555555555555555555555555    5    55555555555555555555555555555
5555555555555555555555555555555555555        55555555555555555555555555555
5555555555555555555555555555555555555      55555555555555555555555555555
555555555555555555555555555555555555555555555555555555555555555555555555555555555
555555555555555555555555555555555555555555555555555555555555555555555555555555555
```

Capital Market Theory

AFTER Markowitz developed the two-parameter portfolio analysis model, analysts began to wonder what were the stock-market implications if all investors were to use the two-parameter model.[1] As a result, what shall be referred to here as *capital market theory* was developed. The capital market theory set out here is not the only theory which could be called a "capital market theory." Such notions as the Dow theory and many others could be accurately called capital market theories too. Perhaps a more descriptive title for this chapter would have been "The Capital Market Theory of the Two-Parameter Model." However, for the sake of brevity, it will simply be called capital market theory.

---

[1] The reader who wishes to follow the original development of capital market theory is directed to the following four articles, especially the second. This list is not exhaustive.

W. F. Sharpe, "A Simplified Model for Portfolio Analysis," *Management Science*, vol. 9. no. 2 (January 1963), pp. 277–293, especially see part 4 on the Diagonal Model. Reprinted in Cohen and Hammer, *Analytical Methods in Banking* (Homewood, Ill. : Richard D. Irwin, Inc., 1966), chap. 12.

William Sharpe, "Capital Asset Prices: A Theory of Market Equilibrium Under Conditions of Risk," *The Journal of Finance*, September 1964, pp. 425–442. Reprinted in Archer and D'Ambrosio, *The Theory of Business Finance* (New York : The Macmillan Company, 1967), reading #42.

John Lintner, "Security Prices, Risk, and the Maximal Gains from Diversification," *The Journal of Finance*, December 1965, pp. 587–615.

Eugene F. Fama, "Risk, Return and Equilibrium: Some Clarifying Comments," *The Journal of Finance*, March 1968, pp. 29–40.

Assumptions Underlying the Theory

Capital market theory is based on the assumptions underlying portfolio analysis, since the theory is essentially a description of the logical (that is, mathematical and economic) implications of portfolio analysis. These assumptions, listed in Chapter 1, are repeated below.

1. The rate of return from an investment adequately summarizes the outcome from the investment, and investors see the various possible rates of return in a probabilistic fashion—that is, a probability distribution of rates of return.
2. Investors' risk estimates are proportional to the variability of return they visualize.
3. Investors are willing to base their decisions on only two parameters of the probability distribution of returns: the expected return and the variance (or its square root, the standard deviation) of returns. Symbolically, $U = f(E(r), \sigma)$ where U denotes the investor's utility.
4. For any risk class, investors prefer a higher to a lower rate of return. Symbolically, $\partial U / \partial E(r) > 0$. Or, conversely, among all securities with the same rate of return, investors prefer less, rather than more, risk. Symbolically, $\partial U / \partial \sigma < 0$.

The reader should reflect upon Chapter 4 until he has convinced himself that these assumptions do form the basis for portfolio analysis.

An investor who conforms to the preceding assumptions will prefer Markowitz efficient portfolios over other portfolios. Such investors will be referred to as *Markowitz efficient investors*. With this background, it is possible to begin to discuss capital market theory. A fairly exhaustive list of the assumptions necessary to generate the theory is given below.

1. All investors are Markowitz efficient diversifiers who delineate and seek to attain the efficient frontier.
2. Any amount of money can be borrowed or lent at the risk-free rate of interest (R). The return on short-term U.S. government bonds may be used as a proxy for R. Money may not be borrowed at any other rate.
3. "Idealized uncertainty" prevails. That is, all investors visualize identical probability distributions for future rates of return—or "homogeneous expectations."
4. All investors have the same one-period time horizon.
5. All investments are infinitely divisible: fractional shares may be purchased in any portfolio or any individual asset.
6. No taxes and no transactions cost for buying and selling securities exist.
7. No inflation and no change in the level of interest rates exist—or all changes are fully anticipated.
8. The capital markets are in equilibrium.

The reader who is unaccustomed to economic analysis is probably confused and discouraged by a theory that begins with a list of unrealistic assumptions. Such should not be the case. These assumptions are only

necessary to get started and will be relaxed later. The assumptions provide a concrete foundation upon which a theory can be derived by applying
the forces of logic, intuition, and mathematics. Without these assumptions, the analysis would degenerate into a polemic discussion. Discussions
of which historical facts, what folklore, and which institutions were
significant, which were insignificant, what their relationships were, and
what conclusions might be reached by a "reasonable man" are not very
productive. Such thinking usually gets bogged down short of the objective.

Traditionally, economists have based their analysis on as few and as
simple assumptions as possible. Then a theory is derived with conclusions
and implications that are incontestable, given the assumptions. Then the
assumptions are relaxed, usually one at a time, to determine what can be
expected in more realistic circumstances.

The Capital Market Line

With little loss of realism, an opportunity set such as the one shown in
Fig. 5.1 can be assumed.[2] This opportunity set is composed of the individual investments found in the capital markets plus the infinite number
of portfolios that can be formed from these individual investments.[3]

---

[2] In some of the financial literature the reader will find Fig. 5.1 as produced here in
Fig. 5.1 Alternate. Of course, the two figures represent identical situations,
merely having their axes switched. Fig. 5.1 reflects the custom of placing the independent
variable on the horizontal axis and the dependent variable on the vertical axis.

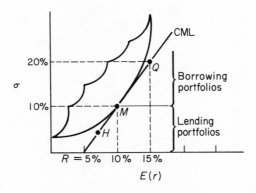

FIG. 5.1 (ALTERNATE)

[3] If the CML is thought of as representing the community's indifference line between
risk and return, an interesting interpretation of R is possible. The risk-free asset R can be
thought of as the *certainty equivalent* of the risky assets along the CML, such as H,
M, and Q.

As was shown earlier (see Fig. 2.10), owing to the effects of diversification the opportunity set will be composed of curves that are convex to the $E(r)$ axis. According to the assumption of idealized uncertainty (assumption 3), all investors will envision opportunity sets that are exactly identical. Thus, the following discussion can treat Fig. 5.1 as if it were clearly implanted in each investor's mind. This allows moot questions of investors' ignorance, different tax brackets, and so on to be postponed. The $E(r)$ is the cost of capital for the assets in the graph—it varies directly with the risk class of the asset in this model.

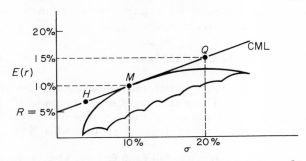

Fig. 5.1   The Opportunity Set in Risk-Return Space

Assuming any amount of money may be borrowed and lent by anyone at rate R (that is, assumption 2), the CML follows. The CML is generated by drawing a straight line out from the riskless rate (R) into $(E(r), \sigma)$ space. This line is then swung down as far as possible until it is just tangent to the opportunity set as shown in Fig. 5.1. If R or the opportunity set moves, the resulting CML would move too. The point where the CML is tangent to the efficient frontier of the opportunity set is denoted point M.

Points between R and M on Fig. 5.1 represent *lending portfolios*. The portfolios are comprised of varying proportions of R (for example, short-term U.S. government bonds held to maturity) and M. A point like H, located halfway between R and M, represents a portfolio of half R and half M.

Points on the CML that lie above M represent *borrowing portfolios* (that is, leveraged portfolios), since their creation requires borrowing at rate R to increase total investable capital. The total investable capital is then invested in M, and the return on equity and its variability (that is, risk) are increased. Consider a numerical example of how a leveraged portfolio's expected return and risk is determined to lie above M on the CML.

Numerical Example of a Leveraged Portfolio

Suppose one share of investment M cost \$1,000 and offered a fifty-fifty chance of returning either \$1,000 or \$1,200. The expected return for the holding period is 10 percent as shown below.

$$E(r) = \sum_{i=1}^{2} p_i r_i = (.5) \left(\frac{1,000 - 1,000}{1,000} \right) + (.5) \left(\frac{1,200 - 1,000}{1,000} \right)$$

$$= (.5)0 + (.5)(20\%) = 0 + 10\% = 10 \text{ percent.}$$

The standard deviation of returns is 10 percent for M.

$$\sigma = \sqrt{\sum p_i (r_i - E(r))^2} = \sqrt{(.5)(0 - .1)^2 + (.5)(.2 - .1)^2}$$

$$= \sqrt{(.5)(.01) + (.5)(.01)} = \sqrt{.01} = .1 = 10 \text{ percent.}$$

Now, if an investor borrows \$1,000 at $R = 5$ percent and buys a second share of M, he has a fifty-fifty chance of receiving \$950 or \$1,350 on his \$1,000 of original equity. This is shown below.

	Two Alternative Outcomes	
	one	two
Original equity	\$1,000	\$1,000
Principal amount borrowed at 5%	1,000	1,000
Total amount invested in M	\$2,000	\$2,000
Return on two shares of M	\$2,000	\$2,400
Repayment of loan principal	⟨1,000⟩	⟨1,000⟩
Payment of interest at 5%	⟨50⟩	⟨50⟩
Net return on original equity	\$950	\$1,350
Probability of outcome	50%	50%

The expected return on M leveraged is 15 percent. The calculations follow.

$$E(r) = \sum_{i=1}^{2} pr = (.5) \left(\frac{950 - 1,000}{1,000} \right) + (.5) \left(\frac{1,350 - 1,000}{1,000} \right)$$

$$= (.5)(-.05\%) + (.5)(35\%) = -2.5\% + 17.5\% = 15 \text{ percent.}$$

The standard deviation of returns on the leveraged portfolio is 20 percent as shown on p. 116.

$$\sigma = \sqrt{\sum p_i(r_i - E(r_i))^2} = \sqrt{(.5)(-5\% - 15\%)^2 + (.5)(35\% - 15\%)^2}$$
$$= \sqrt{(.5)(-20\%)^2 + (.5)(20\%)^2} = \sqrt{(.5)(.04) + (.5)(.04)}$$
$$= \sqrt{(.02) + (.02)} = \sqrt{.04} = .2 = 20 \text{ percent.}$$

These results are shown graphically in Fig. 5.1 as point Q.

The CML is Linear

It is simple to prove the CML is linear in $(E(r), \sigma)$ space for all possible portfolios of M and R. The expected return is obviously a linear function:

$$E(r) = w_R R + (1 - w_R)E(r_M).$$

Since investment in R has zero risk, $\sigma_R = 0$, the formula for the variance of a portfolio of R and M is a special case of equations (2A.9) and (2A.10).

$$\sigma = \sqrt{w_R^2 \sigma_R^2 + (1 - w_R)^2 \sigma_M^2 + 2w_R(1 - w_R)\sigma_{RM}},$$

which reduces to

$$\sigma = \sqrt{(1 - w_R)^2 \sigma_M^2} = (1 - w_R)\sigma_M \qquad \text{when } \sigma_R = 0.$$

Thus, the risk and expected return of any two-security portfolio containing one riskless asset (R) is a linear function. So, the CML must be linear in $(E(r), \sigma)$ space.[4]

Unanimous Investment Decision

Since the CML dominates the opportunity set and the assumptions assure all investors are rational and Markowitz efficient, all investors will buy security M in some combination (that is, they will seek to be on the CML). No other investment or combination of investments available are as efficient as M or portfolios made of M. The decision to purchase M, the *investment decision*, will be unanimous among investors under the present assumptions.

After completing the investment decision, the investor will determine how to finance his purchase of M based on his personal risk-return prefer-

---

[4] The slope of the CML is $dE(r)/d\sigma$. This slope is the constant:

$$\frac{dE(r)}{d\sigma} = \frac{dE(r)}{dW_R} \cdot \frac{dW_R}{d\sigma}$$

See the appendix of this chapter for completion of this proof that the CML is linear.

ences. An aggressive investor, whose utility isoquants are graphed in the upper part of Fig. 5.2, will reach his highest level of utility (U_3) by borrowing at R to buy portfolio B. A conservative investor will prefer dividing his funds between R and M to form a lending portfolio: his highest indifference curve is just tangent to the CML at a point like L in Fig. 5.2. The above observation is the basis for the separability theorem.

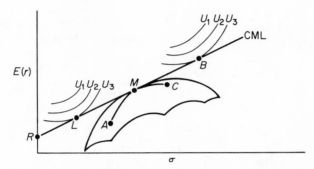

Fig. 5.2   Risk-Return Indifference Curves Determine Financing

Separability Theorem

The investment decision (to buy M) is independent of the financing decision (to buy some R or leverage the portfolio).

Given the situation and assumptions above, the theorem follows directly. The *separability theorem* implies that all investors, timid and aggressive, should hold the same mix of stocks in their portfolio. They should then use borrowing or lending to attain their preferred risk class. This conclusion is diametrically opposed to the popular "financial interior decorator" concept of portfolio management. The "financial interior decorator" school of portfolio management teaches that the portfolio manager should skillfully design a portfolio to match his client's personality. Thus, a timid investor's portfolio would contain a completely different set of securities than an aggressive investor's portfolio. This analysis shows that they should both own the same portfolio and differ only in financing it.

The Market Portfolio[5]

Imagine a capital market such as the one graphed in Fig. 5.2, which is in equilibrium. By the definition of equilibrium in a market, excess

[5] For a discussion of the market portfolio, see E. Fama, "Risk, Return and Equilibrium: Some Clarifying Comments," *Journal of Finance*, March 1968, pp. 32–33.

demand is zero for all goods.[6] That is, all securities in the market must belong to some owner. Since all investors unanimously want M, it follows that in equilibrium M must be a huge portfolio containing *all* marketable assets in the proportions w_i, where

$$w_i = \frac{\text{total value of the }i\text{th asset}}{\text{total value of all assets in the market}}.$$

And, in equilibrium, R must be the interest rate that equates the supply of, and demand for, loanable funds. Let M be designated as the *market portfolio*. The market portfolio is the unanimously desirable portfolio containing all securities in exactly the proportions they are supplied in equilibrium.[7] The return on the market portfolio is the weighted average return of all securities in the market. The market portfolio is a risky portfolio—its risk is σ_M.

---

[6] Excess demand = demand less supply. Thus, when supply and demand are equal, excess demand is zero.

[7] Sharpe envisioned in his paper ("Capital Asset Prices," *Journal of Finance*, September 1964) a different equilibrium picture. Fama ("Risk, Return and Equilibrium," *Journal of Finance*, March 1968) comments on this in his footnote 11 (p. 33).

Sharpe's equilibrium does not appear as the one graphed in Fig. 5.2. In Sharpe's case M (the point of tangency between the ray from the return on the riskless asset and the efficient frontier—Sharpe calls it ϕ) is just one "optimal combination of risky assets" (Sharpe, "Capital Asset Prices," p. 433). In the "beginning," as Sharpe sees it, only portfolio M will be in demand. Consequently, prices of assets in M will rise and their expected returns will fall. Prices of assets not in M will fall and their expected returns will rise.

Thus, a condition represented in the Fig. 5.3 emerges. Several portfolios lie along the CML—all those along the line segment AMB. Any of these combinations could be combined with borrowing or lending at R. Equilibrium is attained when all assets are included in combinations lying along AMB and they are included in such proportions as they are supplied to the market.

Consider the implications of diversification theory for the equilibrium shown in Fig. 5.3. It was shown (in Fig. 2.10) that when two or more assets plot in a straight line in $(E(r), \sigma)$ space they must be perfectly, positively correlated. Thus, assets like A, M, B and all other combinations along AMB must be perfectly, positively correlated.

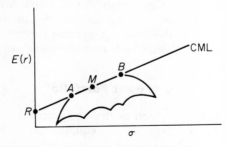

Fig. 5.3   The CML with Multiple Tangencies

(*Footnote*[7] *continued on page* 119)

Of course, there is no real-life market portfolio. However, it is a useful theoretical construct, since the return on M is the return the Dow Jones Average, Standard & Poor's, the New York Stock Exchange Index, and other market indices are estimating.

Systematic and Unsystematic Risk

Sharpe has designated that portion of assets' variability of returns which is attributable to a common source as *systematic risk*.[8] Systematic risk is the minimum level of risk that may be achieved via diversification across a large group of randomly selected assets. The independent variations in the returns of the individual assets in such a portfolio average out to zero, and only systematic variability of return is left. This remaining common or systematic variability among all assets is due to changes in the economic, psychological, and political environment that affect all assets.

The independent or unsystematic variability of return in an asset has been called *unsystematic risk* by Sharpe[9] and *residual variance* by Lintner.[10] The two terms may be used interchangeably. Unsystematic risk is caused by events that are unique to the firm, such as strikes, inventions, management errors, and so on. Unsystematic risk and systematic risk sum to total risk as measured by the variance of returns of a security. See the appendix at the end of this chapter for a statistical division of the total risk into these two mutually exclusive pieces.

A Linear Relation with the Market

The nature of systematic and unsystematic risk is seen most graphically in terms of the following simple linear regression model which Sharpe

---

The risky combinations of assets along AMB vary due to some common cause—variation in the overall economic, psychological, and market situation. The returns on combinations A, M, and B will vary together systematically. All other variability of return (that is, risk) due to causes unrelated to movements in market conditions has been reduced by diversification.

An equilibrium where many assets were tangent to the CML could be expected to emerge if most investors could not delineate the true efficient frontier or used naive diversification. And, if most investors were naive diversifiers, the SML, defined later in this chapter, could not be expected to give significant correlation coefficients. Sharpe's multiple-tangency model is realistic, but it violates our first assumption for capital market theory.

[8] W. Sharpe, "Capital Asset Prices."
[9] Sharpe, "Capital Asset Prices." In his diagonal model, Sharpe designates the unsystematic risk Q.
[10] Lintner, "Security Prices, Risk and Maximal Gains," op. cit.

has referred to as the "diagonal model."[11] Treynor would call (5.1) the "characteristic line" for the ith asset.[12]

$$r_{it} = a_i + b_i r_{It} + e_{it},\qquad(5.1)$$

where r_{it} is the tth observation of the ith firm's rate of return, r_{It} is the tth rate of return for some market index, e_{it} is the tth random-error term which has an expected value of zero, constant finite variance, and is independent of other e_{it}'s, and a_i and b_i are least-squares regression coefficients.[13]

In equation (5.1) variation in r_i is introduced from two sources: variation in r_I and variation in e_i. In fact, it is shown in Appendix 4E that

$$\text{Var}\ (r_i) = \text{Var}\ (a + b_i r_I + e_i)$$

$$= \text{Var}\ (b_i r_I) + \text{Var}\ (e_i)\qquad(4E.3)$$

$$\text{Total risk} = \text{systematic risk} + \text{unsystematic risk.}$$

Equation (4E.3) above shows clearly the two sources of variability in r_i.

For prediction of r_i the conditional expectation of equation (5.1), which is shown below, may be used.[14]

$$r_i = E(r_i \mid r_I) = a_i + b_i r_I.\qquad(5.2)$$

Two possible forms equation (5.2) may assume are shown in Figs. 5.4 and 5.5. Figure 5.4 is a graph of equation (5.2) fit to a firm that has returns

---

[11] W. F. Sharpe, "A Simplified Model for Portfolio Analysis," *Management Science*, January 1963, pp. 277–293; see sec. 4 on the "Diagonal Model."

The index which the ith security's returns are regressed onto should not be the same stock price index containing the ith security, or the model will be overspecified. For example, consider the following least-squares model $r_{it} = a + b r_{Mt} + e_{it}$. This model has cov $(e_i, r_M) \neq 0$ and cov $(r_M, r_i) \neq 0$ because M contains the ith security (by definition of M). As a result the regression statistics are not minimum variance, unbiased estimators of the parameters a and b. To simply assume cov $(e_i, r_M) = 0$ and/or cov $(r_M, r_i) = 0$ would result in overspecification of the model. In this particular case, the above caveat is to ensure correct application of mathematical regression theory and shouldn't be interpreted to mean the least-squares model above is worthless. Fama discusses this problem and its significance: E. Fama, "Risk, Return and Equilibrium: Some Clarifying Comments," *Journal of Finance*, March 1968, pp. 37–39. Fama reaches the correct conclusion that the error introduced by the least-squares model above is infinitesimally small.

[12] Jack L. Treynor, "How to Rate Management of Investment Funds," *Harvard Business Review*, January-February 1965, pp. 63-75.

[13] According to the Gauss-Markov theorem, equation (5.2) is a minimum variance, linear, unbiased estimator if the assumptions beneath (5.1) are met.

[14] Blume has shown that the conditional expectation (5.2) is fairly stationary over time and may be used for prediction. M. E. Blume, "The Assessment of Portfolio Performance—An Application to Portfolio Theory," unpublished Ph.D. dissertation, University of Chicago, 1968.

that are positively correlated with the returns on some market index (r_I). Figure 5.5 is the graph of equation (5.2) fit to a firm that has returns that are negatively correlated with the market.

In terms of capital-market-theory language, the firm in Fig. 5.4 has more systematic risk than the firm in Fig. 5.5. The firm in Fig. 5.4 has a positive slope coefficient [b_i in equations (5.1) and (5.2)], positive covariance of returns with the returns on M, and positive correlation of returns with returns on M. The firm in Fig. 5.5, on the other hand, has returns that move countercyclically. The firm in Fig. 5.5 has a negative regression coefficient (b_i), negative covariance, and a negative correlation with M. Thus, adding the firm in Fig. 5.5 to a portfolio will decrease

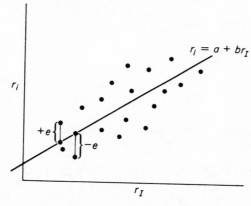

Fig. 5.4   Regression Line for a Firm with Cyclical Returns

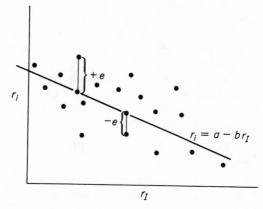

Fig. 5.5   Regression Line for a Firm with Countercyclical Returns

the risk of a portfolio that is correlated with M—as most portfolios are—more than adding the firm in Fig. 5.4 to the portfolio. Most simply, the firm in Fig. 5.5 is the better candidate for Markowitz diversification purposes. The b_i coefficient is an index of systematic risk. It is sometimes called *Sharpe's beta coefficient* or a measure of volatility.

Whenever equation (5.1) produces a correlation coefficient below one, the observations will not all lie on the regression line—of course, this is the typical case graphed in Figs. 5.4 and 5.5. The vertical deviations of the observations from the regression line are called residual errors and are denoted e in equation (5.1) and Figs. 5.4 and 5.5. Although the least-squares regression technique used to derive equation (5.2) minimizes the sum of the squared errors $\left(\text{that is, } \sum_{t=1}^{n} e_{it}^2 \right)$ over all n observations, the sum is still a nonnegative value. The term $\sigma^2(r_i \mid r_M)$ is called the residual variance around the regression line in statistical terms or unsystematic risk in capital-market-theory language.

$$\sigma^2(r_i \mid r_M) = \frac{\sum\limits^{N} e^2}{N} = \frac{\sum\limits^{N}[r_i - (a_i + b_i r_M)]^2}{N}. \tag{5.3}$$

The residual variance is the squared standard error in regression language; it is a measure of unsystematic variance.

Only Portfolios Efficient Enough for CML

Only *combinations* of risk assets (that is, portfolios) are efficient enough to lie on the CML in equilibrium. An individual security's risk will consist not only of the systematic risk of portfolios along the CML, but, in addition, an individual security's risk will contain unsystematic risk. Thus, all individual assets must be more risky than points on the CML. Empirical evidence bears this out. King concluded "that the typical stock has about half of its variance explained by an element of price change that affects the whole market."[15] That is, systematic risk comprises half the risk in the typical stock.

Individual securities (as opposed to portfolios) will be located *within* the opportunity set instead of *on* the CML. In terms of Fig. 5.2 individual securities will be located at points like A and C. Only through the benefits of successful diversification can A and C be held in efficient portfolios like M.

The Security Market Line

Thus far in this chapter the analysis has determined that in the type of equilibrium situation assumed, the expected return of *portfolios* is a

---

[15] B. F. King, "Market and Industry Factors in Stock Price Behavior," *The Journal of Business*, January 1966, *Security Prices: A Supplement*, pp. 139–190.

linear function of the portfolios' standard deviation of returns. This linear relation has been denoted the CML. Next, consider a model for the determination of the equilibrium rate of return of an *individual security* or a portfolio.

For an n-security portfolio the variance is

$$\text{Var}\,(r_p) = \sum_{i=1}^{n} w_i^2\,\text{Var}\,(r_i) + \sum_{i=1}^{n} \sum_{j=1}^{n} w_i w_j \sigma_{ij} \qquad \text{for } i \neq j. \qquad (2\text{A}.9')$$

Note that within the expression for the risk of a portfolio of any size are covariance terms between all possible pairs of securities in the portfolio. The essence of effective diversification is to combine securities with either low or negative covariances. Therefore, demand for securities that have low or negative covariance of returns with most other securities will be high. Those securities whose returns covary inversely or are independent of the returns from the market portfolio will have their prices bid up. And, securities that have high covariance with M—that is, high systematic risk—will experience low demand. As a result, the prices of securities with high systematic risk will fall, and securities with low systematic risk will have their prices bid up. Since equilibrium rates of return move inversely with the price of the security, securities with high covariance with the market will have relatively low prices and high average or expected returns. Conversely, securities with low or negative covariances will have relatively high prices and, therefore, experience low expected rates of return in equilibrium. This relationship is depicted in Fig. 5.6. The $E(r_i)$ is the appropriate discount rate to use in valuing the ith asset's income—it is the cost of capital.

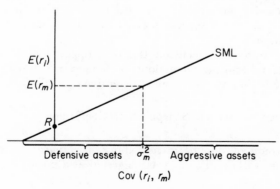

Fig. 5.6   The Security Market Line

In words, Fig. 5.6 says that in equilibrium an *asset's expected return is a positive linear function of its covariance* of returns with the market. That is, the expected return from a security is an increasing function of its systematic risk as measured by its covariance with the market. Since systematic risk is the portion of a security's total risk that hinders rather than helps diversification, this relationship is intuitively appealing. The more risk a security has that cannot be eliminated by diversification, the more return investors will require to induce them to hold that security in their portfolios. The locus of equilibrium points in Fig. 5.6 will be called the *security market line* (SML)—a separate and distinct relation from the CML.[16]

In equilibrium, every individual security's expected return and risk observation will lie *on* the SML and *off* the CML. But, in equilibrium, portfolios $E(r)$ and σ will lie on the CML *and* on the SML. Thus, even under idealistic assumptions and at static equilibrium, the CML will not include all points if portfolios and individual securities are plotted together on one graph. However, all assets should lie on the SML in equilibrium. Both portfolios' and individual securities' returns are determined by systematic risk.

Defensive and Aggressive Securities

In Fig. 5.6 the portion of the vertical axis representing low or negative covariances is marked as including "*defensive securities*"—defensive in the sense that they offer the opportunity to reduce portfolio risk by including them in a portfolio that is correlated with M, as nearly all portfolios will be. This definition is similar but not identical to the term "defensive security" as used by security salesmen, financial analysts, and others. Traditionally, when speaking of defensive securities, financial analysts gave examples of firms that are unlikely to experience decreases in earning power. Since these people tend to define risk ambiguously—if at all—their definitions of a defensive security are hard to pin down. In any event, the definition of defensive securities given here is similar to the more common definition.

The *aggressive securities* are securities that offer opportunities for speculation; their dividend and price reactions to changes in market conditions are more dramatic than the reactions of defensive securities.

The SML Restated in Terms of Sharpe's Beta Coefficient

In the discussion of systematic risk above, the regression coefficient b_i from equations (5.1) and (5.2) was suggested as a possible measure of

---

[16] The name *security market line* can be attributed to William Sharpe.

systematic risk. The covariance of returns with M was also suggested as a measure of systematic risk. Two methods of defining the SML are possible. Fig. 5.7 defines the SML in terms of the regression coefficient b_i. In terms of b_i, defensive and aggressive securities can be delineated more easily. It is intuitively appealing to think of securities with $b_i < 1$ as being defensive and aggressive securities as having $b_i > 1$.

The SML defined in terms of Cov (r_i, r_M) is shown in Fig. 5.8. It is equivalent to Fig. 5.7. The only difference between Figs. 5.7 and 5.8 is

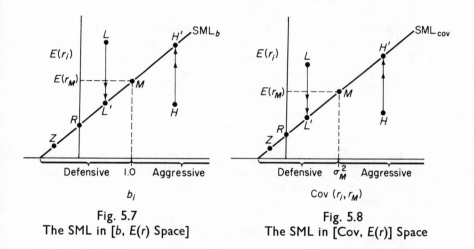

Fig. 5.7
The SML in [b, E(r) Space]

Fig. 5.8
The SML in [Cov, E(r)] Space

that the horizontal scale of Fig. 5.7 is $(1/\sigma_M^2)$ times the length of the horizontal scale of 5.8. This is due to the definition of the regression slope coefficient—that is, Sharpe's beta coefficient.

$$b_{(i|M)} = \frac{\text{Cov } (r_i, r_M)}{\sigma_M^2} = \text{Cov } (r_i, r_M) \cdot \left(\frac{1}{\sigma_M^2}\right) \tag{5.4}$$

$$= \frac{r_{iM}\sigma_i\sigma_M}{\sigma_M^2}$$

$$= \frac{r_{iM}\sigma_i}{\sigma_M},$$

where r_{iM} is the correlation coefficient of r_i and r_M, and σ_i and σ_M are the standard deviations of returns for asset i and the market portfolio, respectively. Since σ_M^2 is a constant for all assets in the market, b_i is simply a linear transformation of cov (r_i, r_M). Note that when $b_{(i|M)} = 1$, then Cov $(r_i, r_M) = \sigma_M^2$. This relation reveals why the divisions between defensive and aggressive securities in Figs. 5.6, 5.7, and 5.8 are comparable.

Over- and Underpriced Securities

Figures 5.7 and 5.8 and the SML have security-price implications. Points between the SML and the $E(r)$ axis, such as point L in Figs. 5.8 and 5.7, represent securities whose prices are lower than they would be in equilibrium. Since points such as L represent securities with unusually high returns for the amount of systematic risk they bear, they will enjoy strong demand which will bid their prices up until their equilibrium rate of return is driven back onto the SML at point L'.

Likewise, securities represented by points between the SML and the systematic risk axis represent securities whose prices are too high. Securities such as point H in Figs. 5.7 and 5.8 do not offer sufficient return to induce rational investors to accept the amount of systematic risk they bear. As a result, their prices will fall owing to lack of demand. Their prices will continue to fall until the denominator of the expected return formula

$$E(r) = \frac{\text{capital gains or losses} + \text{dividends}}{\text{purchase price}}$$

is low enough to allow the return to reach the SML at a point such as H'. Then the capital loss will cease and an equilibrium will emerge until a change in the firm's systematic risk, a change in R, or some other change causes another disequilibrium.

Negative Correlation with M

Consider point Z in Figs. 5.7 and 5.8. Point Z represents a defensive security that has an equilibrium rate of return below the return on riskless assets (R). Upon observing rates of return that were consistently below R, the traditional financial analyst would typically attribute the low return to a high price for the security which was bid up in expectation of growth. But, capital market theory provides a second rationalization of points like Z: their prices are maintained at high levels due to the Markowitz diversification benefits they offer.

Relaxing the Assumptions

As promised, the assumptions underlying the derivation of capital market theory will now be aligned more to conditions existing in the "real world." First, assumption two (that is, one interest rate—R) will be relaxed.

Multiple Interest Rates

In more realistic capital markets, the borrowing rate (B) is higher than the lending rate (L). In Fig. 5.9, this is represented by two lines emerging from points L and B. The dotted portions of these two lines do not

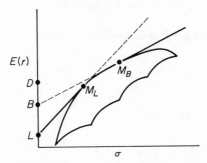

Fig. 5.9   The CML When Borrowing and Lending Rates
            Differ

represent actual opportunities and are included merely to indicate the
construction of the figure. The line formed by the solid sections of the two
lines and a section of the opportunity locus is the relevant efficient frontier
when the borrowing and lending rates differ. As a result, the CML has a
curved section between M_L and M_B in Fig. 5.9. The curved section is the
front of the opportunity locus.

Of course, not all investors can borrow at rate B. Investors with poor
credit ratings must pay a higher borrowing rate than investors with good
credit ratings. Thus, the proverbial "deadbeat" might be able to borrow
money only by paying rate D in Fig. 5.9. Obviously, the more difference
between the lending and the various borrowing rates, the more curved
the CML will become. And, the CML will change for each individual as
his credit rating changes. Likewise, the CML for the market in general
will change with credit conditions. These complications would reduce the
stability and the commonality of the CML. The reader may graph these
complications as an exercise.[17]

In Fig. 5.9, points M_L and M_B are two separate tangency portfolios
for lending and borrowing, respectively, if only one lending and one
borrowing rate is recognized. The existence of two tangency portfolios
creates problems.

The formulas[18] for the SML is given in equation (5.5):

$$E(r_i) = R + (E(r_M) - R) \cdot \left(\frac{\text{Cov}(r_i, r_M)}{\sigma_M{}^2} \right)$$

$$= R + [E(r_M) - R] \cdot \left(\frac{r_{iM}\sigma_i}{\sigma_M} \right)$$

$$= R + [E(r_M) - R] \cdot b_{(i|M)}, \qquad (5.5)$$

[17] K. L. Hastie, "The Determination of Optimal Investment Policy," *Management
Science*, August 1967, pp. B-757 through B-774.

[18] Equation (5.5) is derived formally in the appendix to this chapter, which deals
explicitly with the mathematical foundations of capital market theory.

where $[E(r_M) - R]$ may be referred to as the risk premium for the market portfolio.

If separate borrowing (B) and lending (L) rates are assumed to exist, two SML's emerge:

$$E(r_i) = B + (E(r_{MB}) - B) \cdot \left(\frac{\text{Cov } (r_i, r_{MB})}{\sigma_{MB}{}^2}\right) \qquad (5.5B)$$

for $E(r_i) \geq E(r_{MB})$, and

$$E(r_i) = L + (E(r_{ML}) - L) \cdot \left(\frac{\text{Cov } (r_i, r_{ML})}{\sigma_{ML}{}^2}\right) \qquad (5.5L)$$

for $E(r_i) \leq E(r_{ML})$.

These two SML's will not only have different horizontal axis intercepts; they will have different slopes, since $[E(r_M) - R]$ will be different. Also, since the covariances are with two different tangency portfolios (that is, M_L and M_B), even the covariances differ. As a result, it is impossible to specify the relation between the two SML's without adding to, rather than reducing, the number of assumptions. In Fig. 5.10, one possible relationship between SML_L and SML_B is shown.

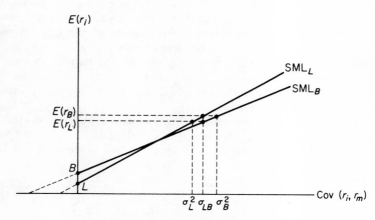

Fig. 5.10   Two SML's When Borrowing and Lending
Rates Differ

As a result of divergent borrowing and lending rates, no equilibrium prices are possible for all individual securities. Since further relaxation of assumption two would clutter Figs. 5.9 and 5.10 without yielding any additional insights, this task is left to the reader's imagination.

Transaction Costs

If assumption six (that is, no transactions costs) were dropped, the CML and SML would have "bands" on their sides as shown in Figs. 5.11 and 5.12. Within these bands, it wouldn't be profitable for investors to buy and sell securities and generate the price revisions necessary to attain equilibrium—transactions costs would consume the profit that induces such trading. As a result, the markets would never reach the theoretical equilibrium as described here, even if the other assumptions were retained.

In Chapter 7, empirical evidence will be examined showing that investors need not diversify over many securities to obtain portfolios near

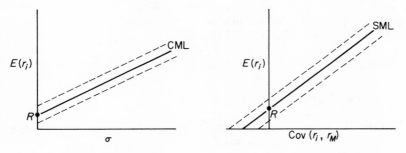

Fig. 5.11
Transactions Costs Obscure CML

Fig. 5.12
Transactions Costs Obscure SML

the CML. Thus, the effects of transactions costs need not be particularly detrimental to the equilibrium picture derived in theory.

Indivisibilities

If all assets weren't infinitely divisible—that is, if assumption five were discontinued—the SML would degenerate into a dotted line: each dot would represent an opportunity attainable with an integral number of shares. Little profit is to be gained from further examination of this trivial situation.

General Uncertainty

To jettison assumption three (that is, idealized uncertainty) would require drawing an opportunity locus and CML composed of "fuzzy" curves and lines. The more investors' expectations differed, the "fuzzier" all lines and curves would become. As a result of general uncertainty the analysis becomes determinate only within limits. Only major disequilibriums will be corrected. Similarly, the picture of the SML becomes blurred. Statements cannot be made with certainty, and predictions must contain a margin for error.

Different Tax Brackets

To recognize the existence of different tax rates on ordinary income and capital gains would blur the picture more. Equation (1.1') for the after-tax rate of return (r_{AT}) is

$$r_{AT} = \frac{\text{(capital gains)} \cdot (1 - T_G) + \text{(dividends)} \cdot (1 - T_O)}{\text{price at beginning of the holding period}},$$

where T_G is the capital gains tax rate and T_O is the tax rate applicable to ordinary income. In terms of after-tax returns, every investor would see a slightly different CML and SML depending on his particular tax situation. Thus, a static equilibrium could never emerge under existing tax laws, even if all the other assumptions were rigorously maintained.

Inflation and Varying Productivity of Capital

The interest rates observed in reality are nominal interest rates rather than real interest rates. Symbolically,

$$R_N = \text{mpk} + \frac{\Delta P}{P} + f(\text{risk}) + \text{transactions costs}, \qquad (5.6)$$

where R_N is the nominal rate of interest per period seen in the news media, mpk the marginal productivity of capital or real rate of interest per period, and $\Delta P/P$ is the expected percentage change in the general price level per period—that is, the expected rate of inflation or deflation.[19] This discussion will omit the impact of risk premiums, transactions costs, and the term structure of interest rates in determining R_N. The marginal productivity of capital and the rate of inflation fluctuate with technology, the level of investment, monetary policy, fiscal policy and consumers' tastes; it follows that R_N fluctuates too.

Relaxing assumption seven means that even if R_N is the interest rate of U.S. short-term government bonds, it must, nevertheless, vary. Thus, there is no true riskless asset: even default-free securities will experience

---

[19] Δ is used to mean "change." Thus, technically speaking,

$$\frac{\Delta P}{P} = \frac{\text{change in price level per period}}{\text{price level at the beginning of the period}} = \text{rate of inflation or deflation}.$$

The mpk is the rate at which capital reproduces itself.

systematic variability of return.[20] Graphically, this means point R in Fig. 5.13 ceases to exist as a lending possibility and is replaced by a point like R_N. The efficient frontier is now the curve from S to Z or from S' to Z, assuming all money is borrowed at rate R_N. Portfolio S or S' is the minimum-risk portfolio—it may or may not contain default-free securities and it

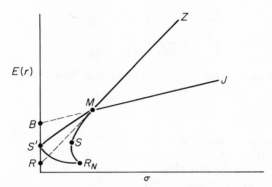

Fig. 5.13   Lack of Riskless Rate Obscures CML

may or may not have zero risk as S' does. A point like S' will emerge if returns on R_N and M are perfectly negatively correlated. A point like S will be the minimum variance portfolio if returns on R_N and M are uncorrelated but not perfectly negatively correlated.[21] If borrowing at rate B, rather than at rate R, is considered, the efficient frontier becomes SMJ or $S'MJ$, depending on whether S or S' is the minimum variance portfolio.

Lack of a riskless interest rate makes the lower section of the SML indeterminate. Above $E(r_{MB})$ the formula for the SML is given by equation (5.7):

$$E(r) = B + \left(\frac{E(r_{MB}) - B}{\sigma_{MB}^{2}}\right) \cdot (\text{Cov}\,(r_i, r_{MB})). \qquad (5.7)$$

Fig. 5.14 shows the SML, assuming B does not vary. Below $E(r_{MB})$ the locus of equilibrium returns lies in the neighborhood of the dotted segment of the SML. However, since a riskless rate and a market portfolio of maximum efficiency for lending are not defined when $\sigma_R > 0$, it is impossible to specify the SML below $E(r_{MB})$.

---

[20] K. L. Hastie, "The Determination of Optimal Investment Policy," *Management Science*, August 1967, pp. B-771 through B-772.

[21] See Figure 2.10 and the accompanying discussion of how the correlation coefficient determines the degree of convexity.

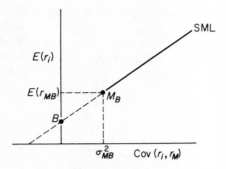

Fig. 5.14   SML Obscured by Lack of Risk-Free Rate

Equilibrium

The assumption of equilibrium (assumption eight) is, of course, heroic. Information arrives to various investors at different times. Thus, investors' expectations do not change in unison. As a result, there is no reason to expect assets' prices to adjust so that all investors are satisfied with their holdings (that is, excess demand is zero for all assets) at any given point in time. Instead, assets' prices are in a continuous, dynamic disequilibrium. Hopefully, most of the time this disequilibrium is minor.

Concluding Remarks on Capital Market Theory Assumptions

Thus far, all except the first assumption underlying capital market theory have been relaxed one at a time, and it was observed in each case that the previous analysis was somewhat obscured. If all were relaxed simultaneously, the result would be even less determinate. However, the fact that the analysis is not exactly determinate under realistic assumptions does not mean it has no value. The analysis still rationalizes much observed behavior, explains such hitherto unexplained practices as diversification, and offers realistic suggestions about directions prices and returns should follow when they deviate significantly from equilibrium.

If the first assumption—that all investors were efficient Markowitz diversifiers—was partially relaxed, the SML would be obscured correspondingly. A market of naively diversified investors would most likely adjust asset prices until returns were proportional to the total risk in an asset. In such a market the CML would have multiple tangencies as shown in Fig. 5.3 and yield higher correlation coefficients than the SML. This seems to be the situation in capital markets today. Of course, if assumption one were discarded completely, there would be no capital market theory other than the previously existing assortment of descriptive theories.

Expectations, Ex Ante, and Ex Post

This analysis implies equilibrium *expected* returns are determined by *expected* risk. Or, as economists say, ex ante returns are a function of expected risk. Historical, or ex post, returns are not what investors use as a basis for their decisions about the future, although their expectations can be affected by ex post behavior. Thus, it should be noted that a "jump" is made in going from the ex ante theory to the ex post data. If the probability distribution of historical returns has remained fairly stationary over time, then the historical expected returns and variances can be used to estimate future returns. However, historical data play no role in the theory itself.

To test capital market theory, expectations must be observed—an obviously impossible task if conducted on a meaningful scale. Of course, expectations may be formed from historical observations.[22] But, unless historical investors were clairvoyant, historical data will not be satisfactory to completely validate the theory.[23]

Empirical Tests of Capital Market Theory

Capital market theory offers a number of clear-cut hypotheses in a (mathematical) form suitable for empirical testing. However, empirical data cannot be expected to verify every phase of capital market theory for the following reasons:

1. Since investors' expectations sometimes differ from the ex post results, empirical data cannot furnish an entirely satisfactory vehicle for tests. Unfortunately, investors' expectations cannot be measured directly.
2. As pointed out above, capital market theory is based on certain simplifying assumptions. To the extent that these assumptions oversimplify, the theory is simply inadequate.
3. Although some portions of the theory are supported with the empirical data, other portions of the theory may not be so well supported empirically.[24] For example, if most investors operated under the naive definition of diversification instead of Markowitz diversification techniques, then the CML might be supported empirically while the SML might not be supported by the data.

---

[22] See Chapter 8, Table 8.1, Fig. 8.1 and the related discussion for a test of the CML using historical data.

[23] This does not mean a surrogate for expectations can't be used to validate the theory. After numerous attempts by other economists, Meiselman found a surrogate for expectations of interest rates and made a major step toward validating the expectations hypothesis concerning the term structure of interest rates. See Meiselman, *The Term Structure of Interest Rates* (Englewood Cliffs, N.J.: Prentice-Hall, Inc., 1962). Perhaps capital market theory will lend itself to such subtle analysis and testing someday.

[24] William Sharpe, "Risk Aversion in the Stock Market: Some Empirical Evidence," *Journal of Finance*, September 1965, pp. 416–422.

4. Variability-of-return measures are only risk *surrogates*. Although the variability-of-return measures are used widely by academic researchers, it is not difficult to imagine that better risk surrogates may be developed.
5. The regression coefficients and correlation coefficients found by the usual least-squares techniques are biased downward owing to errors that enter into both the expected-return estimates and the expected-risk estimates. More sophisticated techniques than are commonly employed in regression and correlation work must be employed to test capital market theory adequately.[25]

Appendix 5A

The Mathematical Foundations of Capital Market Theory*

At the beginning of Chapter 5 the assumptions underlying capital market theory were listed. These assumptions insure that the capital markets will maintain an equilibrium as graphed in Fig. 5.1.[1] As long as these assumptions are not violated, several important propositions about capital market theory may be proven mathematically. Throughout the rest of this chapter, reference will be made to Fig. 5A.1 as some propositions are proved.

---

[25] To test the CML, suppose the true relation is

$$E(R) = A + B\,(\Sigma). \tag{5.8}$$

Suppose only $E(r)$ and σ can be observed empirically where

$$E(r) = E(R) + v, \tag{5.9}$$

$$\sigma = \Sigma + u, \tag{5.10}$$

and u and v are random errors. Substituting (5.9) and (5.10) into (5.8) gives (5.11):

$$E(r) = a + b(\sigma) + w. \tag{5.11}$$

where $w = v - Bu$. This model (5.11) violates the assumptions of the commonly employed least-squares techniques, since Cov $(\sigma, w) = -B$ Var (u) even if u and v are independent. J. Johnston, *Econometric Methods* (New York: McGraw-Hill, Inc., 1963); see Chapter Six for an analysis of this common problem.

* This appendix takes up mathematics that is not necessary for a basic understanding.
[1] Actually, the assumptions may also represent an equilibrium where more portfolios than just M are tangent to the CML—as shown in Fig. 5A.1 alternate. The propositions developed in this chapter are not altered by using this approach.

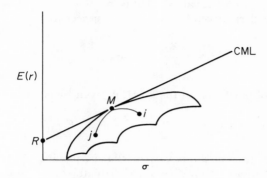

Fig. 5A.1   Opportunities in Risk-Return Space

PROPOSITION I :   *The capital market line is linear in $(E(r), \sigma)$ space.*

Proof: Every point on the CML is some combination of R and M. Thus, the measure of risk for points on the CML is given by the formula for σ_h, where h stands for the "hypothetical portfolio" containing two assets, R and M.

$$\sigma_h = \sqrt{w_R{}^2\sigma_R{}^2 + (1 - w_R)^2\sigma_M{}^2 + 2w_R(1 - w_R)r_{RM}\sigma_R\sigma_M}. \quad (5A.1)$$

By definition, R is the riskless asset and must have $\sigma_R = 0$. Thus, equation (5A.1) may be rewritten as (5A.1') by substituting zero for σ_R.

$$\sigma_h = \sqrt{0 + (1 - w_R)^2\sigma_M{}^2 + 0}$$
$$= (1 - w_R)\sigma_M = \sigma_M - \sigma_M w_R. \quad (5A.1')$$

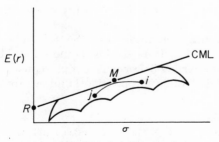

Fig. 5A.1 (alternate)

The change in σ_h as w_R is varied (that is, moving up and down the CML) is given by the derivative of (5A.1') with respect to w_R.

$$\frac{d\sigma_h}{dw_R} = -\sigma_M. \tag{5A.2}$$

The return of portfolios on the CML is given by equation (5A.3).

$$E(r_h) = w_R R + (1 - w_R) \cdot E(r_M) \tag{5A.3}$$

The change in $E(r_h)$ as w_R is varied (that is, moving up and down the CML) is given by the derivative of (5A.3) with respect to w_R.

$$\frac{dE(r_h)}{dw_R} = R - E(r_M). \tag{5A.4}$$

The slope of the CML is represented by the differential equation $dE(r_h)/d\sigma_h$. This differential may be evaluated by applying the chain rule to equations (5A.4) and (5A.2) as shown in equation (5A.5) below.

$$\frac{dE(r_h)}{d\sigma_h} = \frac{dE(r_h)}{dw_R} \cdot \frac{dw_R}{d\sigma_h} = \frac{E(r_M) - R}{\sigma_M}. \tag{5A.5}$$

Since (5A.5) is a constant and it is the formula for the slope of the CML, the CML is linear in $(E(r), \sigma)$ space.   QED.

Sharpe's Beta Coefficient

In a 1964 article Sharpe hypothesized the CML and therefrom derived the SML[2]. He derived the SML using the regression coefficient from equation (5.2) as a measure of systematic risk.

$$E(r_i \,|\, r_I) = a + b_i r_I. \tag{5.2}$$

As discussed in Chapter 5, the b_i is a measure of systematic risk. The b_i is sometimes called *Sharpe's beta coefficient*.

Sharpe's mathematical derivation of the SML is to be found in a footnote of his original 1964 article—see his footnote 22. The derivation of the SML in terms of Sharpe's beta coefficient presented below is identical to Sharpe's original derivation. Proposition II follows from the derivation of the SML in terms of b_i.

---

[2] Sharpe, "Capital Asset Prices: A Theory of Market Equilibrium Under Conditions of Risk," *Journal of Finance*, September 1964, pp. 425–442. Reprinted at pp. 653–670 of Archer and D'Ambrosio, *The Theory of Business Finance: A Book of Readings* (New York: The Macmillan Company, 1967).

PROPOSITION II: *The expected return from the ith asset is a positive linear function of Sharpe's beta coefficient for that security.*

Proof: Recall that point M in Fig. 5A.1 is the market portfolio. Also recall that every point on the CML is some combination of M and the risk-free security represented by point R. Let α be the weight of security i in any hypothetical portfolio composed of i (or j) and M. The hypothetical portfolio will move along the curve iM in Fig. 5A.1 as α varies. And, let $(1 - \alpha)$ be the weight of M in the hypothetical portfolio. In equilibrium, the price of any security like i must adjust so excess demand for it is zero. When excess demand for securities like i is zero, the market portfolio will contain all securities in the proportions they exist. And, the curve iM must be tangent to the CML, reflecting the equality of the rate of exchange available in the market (that is, the slope of CML) and investor's marginal rate of transformation of risk for return (that is, the slope of iM at $\alpha = 0$). These tangency conditions imply: (1) the appropriate risk measure for individual securities, and, (2) equilibrium security prices.

The risk of the hypothetical (h) portfolio is given as σ_h below:

$$\sigma_h = \sqrt{\alpha^2\sigma_i{}^2 + (1 - \alpha)^2\sigma_M{}^2 + 2r_{iM}\alpha(1 - \alpha)\sigma_i\sigma_M}, \qquad (5A.6)$$

where i is the portfolio represented by point i in Fig. 5A.1. Of course, equation (5A.6) is the square root of equation (2A.9) for the two-security case.

Moving from i to M along the curve in Fig. 5A.1, α approaches zero at M where the curve is tangent to the CML. The concomitant change in σ_h with respect to the change in α is shown by differentiating equation (5A.6) with respect to α.

$$\frac{d\sigma_h}{d\alpha} = \frac{2\alpha\sigma_i{}^2 - 2\sigma_M{}^2 + 2\alpha\sigma_M{}^2 + 2r_{iM}\sigma_i\sigma_M(1 - 2\alpha)}{2\sigma_h}, \qquad (5A.7)$$

which simplifies to (5A.7') at $\alpha = 0$:

$$\frac{d\sigma_h}{d\alpha}\bigg|_{\alpha=0} = \frac{-1}{\sigma_h}[\sigma_M{}^2 - r_{iM}\sigma_i\sigma_M]. \qquad (5A.7')$$

But, at $\alpha = 0$, the hypothetical portfolio is identical to the market portfolio. So, $\sigma_h = \sigma_M$ at $\alpha = 0$. This equality means equation (5A.7) simplifies to (5A.8) by substituting σ_M for σ_h.

$$\frac{d\sigma_h}{d\alpha}\bigg|_{\alpha=0} = -[\sigma_M - r_{iM}\sigma_i]. \qquad (5A.8)$$

The expected return of the hypothetical portfolio is given by equation (5A.9).

$$E(r_h) = \alpha E(r_i) + (1 - \alpha)E(r_M). \qquad (5A.9)$$

The change in $E(r_h)$ with respect to a change in α is

$$\frac{dE(r_h)}{d\alpha} = -[E(r_M) - E(r_i)]. \qquad (5A.10)$$

Applying the chain rule to equations (5A.10) and (5A.7) yields the slope of the curve from i to M.

$$\frac{dE(r_h)}{d\sigma_h}\bigg|_{\alpha=0} = \frac{dE(r_h)}{d\alpha} \cdot \frac{d\alpha}{d\sigma_h}\bigg|_{\alpha=0} = \frac{-[E(r_M) - E(r_i)]}{-[\sigma_M - r_{iM}\sigma_i]}. \quad (5A.11)$$

Since equation (5A.11) is tangent to the CML where $\alpha = 0$, the slopes of the curve from i to M (that is, the marginal rate of substitution available to investors) is equal to the slope of the CML (that is, the rate of substitution available in the market). This condition of market equilibrium means equation (5A.11) and (5A.5) must be equal at $\alpha = 0$. Specifically:

$$\frac{dE(r_h)}{d\sigma_h}\bigg|_{\alpha=0} = \frac{E(r_M) - E(r_i)}{\sigma_M - r_{iM}\sigma_i} = \frac{E(r_M) - R}{\sigma_M}, \quad (5A.12)$$

where the right side of (5A.12) is (5A.5). It is well known that the b_i, slope parameter, in (5.2) is variously defined as follows:

$$b_i = \frac{\text{cov}\,(r_i, r_M)}{\sigma_M{}^2} = \frac{r_{iM}\sigma_i\sigma_M}{\sigma_M{}^2} = \frac{r_{iM}\sigma_i}{\sigma_M}. \quad (5A.13)$$

Equation (5A.12) may be solved in terms of $b_i = (r_{iM}\sigma_i/\sigma_M)$ to find $E(r_i)$ as shown below.

$$\frac{E(r_M) - E(r_i)}{\sigma_M{}^2 - r_{iM}\sigma_i\sigma_M} = \frac{E(r_M) - R}{\sigma_M{}^2} = \left(\frac{1}{\sigma_M} \text{ multiplied by } (5A.12)\right),$$

$$(\sigma_M{}^2 - r_{iM}\sigma_i\sigma_M)(E(r_M) - R) = (\sigma_M{}^2)(E(r_M) - E(r_i)),$$

$$E(r_M)\sigma_M{}^2 - E(r_M)r_{iM}\sigma_i\sigma_M - R\sigma_M{}^2 + Rr_{iM}\sigma_i\sigma_M$$
$$= E(r_M)(\sigma_M{}^2) - E(r_i)(\sigma_M{}^2),$$

$$[R - E(r_M)] \cdot [r_{iM}\sigma_i\sigma_M] = [-E(r_i) - E(r_M)]\sigma_M{}^2$$
$$+ [E(r_M) + R]\sigma_M{}^2;$$

$$\frac{r_{iM}\sigma_i}{\sigma_M} = \frac{[-E(r_i) - E(r_M)]\sigma_M{}^2 + [E(r_M) + R]\sigma_M{}^2}{[R - E(r_M)]\sigma_M{}^2},$$

$$\frac{r_{iM}\sigma_i}{\sigma_M} = \frac{-E(r_i) - E(r_M) + E(r_M) + R}{R - E(r_M)};$$

$$-E(r_i) + R = \left(\frac{r_{iM}\sigma_i}{\sigma_M}\right)[R - E(r_M)],$$

$$E(r_i) = R + \left(\frac{r_{iM}\sigma_i}{\sigma_M}\right)(E(r_M) - R),$$

$$E(r_i) = R + (b_i)(E(r_M) - R). \quad (5A.14)$$

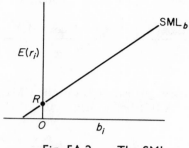

Fig. 5A.2   The SML

In words, equation (5A.14) says the expected return on the ith security is equal to the riskless rate of return (R) plus the product of b_i times the risk premium on the market portfolio. Equation (5A.14) is graphed in Fig. 5A.2 QED.

Fama's Derivation of the SML in Terms of Cov (i, M)

Professor Fama showed a different approach to deriving the SML.[3] Fama formulates the SML in terms of the covariance of the ith security's returns with the returns of the market portfolio—cov (r_i, r_M), referred to below as simply Cov (iM). Fama's derivation proves proposition III.

PROPOSITION III: *The expected return from the ith security is a positive linear function of the covariance of that security's returns with the market.*

Proof: Again using Fig. 5A.1 as a graphical reference, Fama's derivation is presented below. Like Sharpe, Fama differentiates the curve from i to M with respect to a change in α—the proportion of the hypothetical portfolio invested in i. He then sets $\alpha = 0$ and solves the equation for the slopes of the CML and the curve iM at their tangency point, M, for the SML formula.

Taking the change in $E(r_h) = \alpha E(r_i) + (1 - \alpha)E(r_M)$ with respect to a change in α, Fama finds

$$\frac{dE(r_h)}{d\alpha} = -[E(r_M) - E(r_i)], \tag{5A.15}$$

which is equation (5A.10) above. Then, differentiating

$$\sigma_h = \sqrt{\alpha^2\sigma_i + (1 - \alpha)^2\sigma_M{}^2 + 2\alpha(1 - \alpha)\,\text{cov}\,(iM)}$$

[3] E. F. Fama, "Risk, Return, and Equilibrium: Some Clarifying Comments," *Journal of Finance*, 1968, pp. 29–39.

with respect to the change in α, Fama finds equation (5A.16):

$$\frac{d\sigma_h}{d\alpha} = \frac{[-2\sigma_M{}^2 + 2\alpha\sigma_M{}^2 + 2\alpha\sigma_i{}^2 + 2 \text{ cov } (iM) - 4\alpha \text{ cov } (iM)]}{2\sigma_h}.$$

(5A.16)

Where $\alpha = 0$ and the curve iM is tangent to the CML, equation (5A.16) simplifies to equation (5A.16') below at $\alpha = 0$.

$$\frac{d\sigma_h}{d\alpha}\bigg|_{\alpha=0} = \left(\frac{1}{2\sigma_h}\right) [-2\sigma_M{}^2 + 2 \text{ cov } (iM)] = \frac{\text{cov } (iM) - \sigma_M{}^2}{\sigma_h}.$$

(5A.16')

Applying the chain rule to equations (5A.15) and (5A.16') yields

$$\frac{dE(r_h)}{d\sigma_h}\bigg|_{\alpha=0} = \frac{dE(r_h)}{d\alpha} \cdot \frac{d\alpha}{d\sigma_h}\bigg|_{\alpha=0} = \frac{E(r_i) - E(r_M)}{(\text{Cov } (i, M) - \sigma_M{}^2)/\sigma_h}.$$

(5A.17)

Setting the slope of the CML [equation (5A.5)] equal to the slope of the curve iM at point M [equation (5A.17)] yields the following equality.

$$\underbrace{\frac{E(r_M) - R}{\sigma_M}}_{\text{Eq. (5A.5)}} = \underbrace{\frac{E(r_i) - E(r_M)}{(\text{Cov } (i, M) - \sigma_M{}^2/\sigma_h}}_{\text{Eq. (5A.17)}} = \frac{d\sigma_h}{dE(r_h)}\bigg|_{\alpha=0}.$$

(5A.18)

At the tangency point M, where $\alpha = 0$, the fact that $\sigma_M = \sigma_h$ facilitates algebraic manipulation. Solving equation (5A.18) for $E(r_i)$ yields the SML. The algebra is shown below.

$$\frac{E(r_M) - R}{\sigma_M} = \frac{E(r_i) - E(r_M),}{(\text{Cov } (iM) - \sigma_M{}^2)/\sigma_h},$$

(5A.18)

$$\sigma_M{}^2[E(r_i) - E(r_M)] = [E(r_M) - R] \cdot [\text{cov } (iM) - \sigma_M{}^2],$$

$$\sigma_M{}^2[E(r_i) + E(r_M) - R - E(r_M)] = [E(r_M) - R] \text{ cov } (iM),$$

$$E(r_i) = R + \left[\frac{E(r_M) - R}{\sigma_M{}^2}\right] \text{ cov } (iM).$$

(5A.19)

In words, equation (5A.19) says the expected return on the ith security equals the riskless return (R) plus the product of the slope coefficient

$$\left[\frac{E(r_M) - R}{\sigma_M{}^2}\right]$$

times the covariance of returns for security i with the market. More simply, expected return on the ith security is a linear function of its systematic risk as measured by cov (iM). QED.

Equation (5A.19) is graphed in Fig. 5A.3. Fama's equation for the SML [that is, (5A.19)] is identical to a scale factor to Sharpe's equation

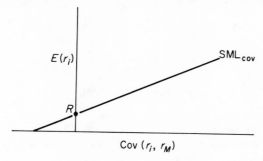

Fig. 5A.3   The SML

[that is, (5A.14)] for the SML. The scale factor is $(1/\sigma_M{}^2)$. More specifically,

$$b_i = \frac{\text{cov } (iM)}{\sigma_M{}^2}.\tag{5A.13}$$

Equation (5A.13) shows that Figs. 5A.2 and 5A.3 are identical except that 5A.2 has a scaled-down horizontal axis.

The preceding paragraph proves Proposition IV.

PROPOSITION IV: *Figures 5A.2 and 5A.3 are equivalent.* That is, Sharpe's and Fama's derivations of the SML are equivalent.

A Third Form of the SML

It is possible to restate equation (5A.19) (using the relation shown in equation (2A.6)) as equation (5A.20).

$$E(r_i) = R + \left[\frac{E(r_M) - R}{\sigma_M{}^2}\right] \text{cov } (r_i, r_M)\tag{5A.19}$$

$$= R + \left[\frac{E(r_M) - R}{\sigma_M{}^2}\right] (r_{iM})(\sigma_i)(\sigma_M)$$

$$= R + \left[\frac{E(r_M) - R}{\sigma_M}\right] (r_{iM})(\sigma_i).\tag{5A.20}$$

Equation (5A.20) is graphed as Fig. 5A.4. This third statement of the SML highlights the facts that (1) the individual security's total

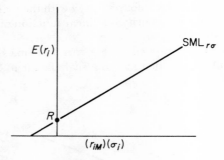

Fig. 5A.4   The SML

variability as measured by σ_i, and (2) its correlation with the market (r_{iM}), are the essential determinants of the security's systematic risk. Fig. 5A.4 is equivalent to Figs. 5A.2 and 5A.3.

Lintner's Derivation Leads to the SML

Taking a different approach than the others, Lintner sought to determine the conditions for a stock-market equilibrium by studing the relationships within the market portfolio (M).[4] To find the asset most desired by Markowitz efficient investors (that is, M) Lintner used standard calculus techniques to maximize θ. θ is the slope of a line from R to an asset in risk-return space as measured from the horizontal dotted line out of R. As shown in Fig. 5A.5, point 2 is more desirable than point 1, since $\theta_1 < \theta_2$.[5]

$$\theta = \frac{E(r_p) - R}{\sigma_{r_p}} = \frac{\text{risk premium of the portfolio}}{\text{risk of the portfolio}} \qquad (5A.21)$$

$$= \frac{\sum w_i E(r_i) - R}{\sqrt{\sum_i \sum_j w_i w_j \sigma_{ij}}} = \frac{\text{Eq. (2.8) less } R}{\text{Eq. (2.9)}}. \qquad (5A.21')$$

For an n-security case, the securities weights in the maximum-θ portfolio are found by simultaneously solving the first partial derivatives for the

[4] Lintner didn't use the terminology "market portfolio"—however, that is what he was studying. Lintner's article attempted to find a more general equilibrium than that of Sharpe's 1964 article, "Capital Asset Prices . . . ." See John Lintner, "Security Prices, Risk and Maximal Gains from Diversification," *Journal of Finance*, December 1965, pp. 587–615. Fama clarified the issue and removed the seeming disparity between Lintner and Sharpe. E. Fama, "Risk, Return and Equilibrium: Some Clarifying Comments," *Journal of Finance*, March 1968, pp. 29–40, especially pp. 35–36.

[5] Equations (5A.21) and (5A.21') are Lintner's equation (7) on p. 595; Lintner, *ibid*.

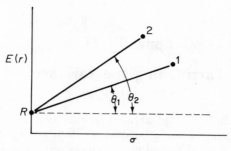

Fig. 5A.5   Lintner's θ

weight vector:[6]

$$\frac{\partial \theta}{\partial w_1} = \frac{(E(r_1) - R) - (E(r_p) - R)(1/\sigma_p^2)\left(\sum_i w_i \sigma_{i1}\right)}{\sigma_{r_p}} = 0,$$

$$\frac{\partial \theta}{\partial w_2} = \frac{(E(r_2) - R) - (E(r_p) - R)(1/\sigma_p^2)\left(\sum_i w_i \sigma_{i2}\right)}{\sigma_{r_p}} = 0, \quad (5A.22)$$

$$\vdots$$

$$\frac{\partial \theta}{\partial w_n} = \frac{(E(r_n) - R) - (E(r_p) - R)(1/\sigma_p^2)\left(\sum_i w_i \sigma_{in}\right)}{\sigma_{r_p}} = 0.$$

The partial derivative of the ith security from the system of equations (5A.22) may be restated as follows.

$$\frac{\partial \theta}{\partial w_i} = \frac{(E(r_i) - R) - (E(r_p) - R)(1/\sigma_p^2)(\sum_i w_i \sigma_{ij})}{\sigma_{r_p}} = 0. \quad (5A.22')$$

$$E(r_i) - R = \left(\frac{E(r_p) - R}{\sigma_p^2}\right)\left(\sum_i w_i \sigma_{ij}\right)$$

$$= \lambda \operatorname{cov}(r_i, r_M), \quad (5A.19)$$

where $\lambda = [E(r_p) - R]/\sigma_p^2$ and $\sum_i w_i \sigma_{ij} = \operatorname{cov}(r_i, r_M)$ if the portfolio in (5A.21) contains all assets in the market. Note that (5A.22') has been reduced to (5A.19)—the SML in terms of $\operatorname{cov}(r_i, r_M)$. Thus, Lintner's approach also yields the SML just as Sharpe's and Fama's methods did.

---

[6] This system comprises Lintner's equations (11) on p. 596; Lintner, *ibid.*

Appendix 5B

Partitioning the Variance

Partition is a technical word as used in statistics. It means to divide something into mutually exclusive pieces. Partitioning the variance is usually discussed under the heading *analysis of variance* in statistics literature. It is desirable that the variance of a security's returns (that is, its risk) be partitioned and analyzed so that the various sources of the variance (that is, risk) may be determined.

Students of analysis of variance will understand that the variance in an asset's returns (σ_r^2) may be partially explained by the simple linear regression model of equation (5.2), where $E(r_i \mid r_I) = \hat{r}_i$ is the return predicted for the ith asset when r_I is the return on some index of market activity. Total variance $(\hat{\sigma}^2)$ can be partitioned into "explained" risk (MSSQ_R) and "unexplained" risk (MSSQ_E) by standard analysis-of-variance techniques.

Source	SSQ	degrees of freedom	MSQ
Variance explained by the regression equation (5.2)	$\sum\limits^{N} (\hat{r}_i - E(r_i))^2 = \mathrm{SSQ}_R$	1	$\dfrac{\mathrm{SSQ}_R}{1} = \mathrm{MSSQ}_R$
Residual error	$\sum\limits^{N} (r_i - \hat{r}_i)^2 = \mathrm{SSQ}_E$	$N-2$	$\dfrac{\mathrm{SSQ}_E}{N-2} = \mathrm{MSSQ}_E$
Total variance	$\sum\limits^{N} (r_i - E(r_i))^2 = \mathrm{SSQ}_T$	$N-1$	$\sigma^2 = $ total variance

The MSSQ_E term is the mean sum of the squared errors around the regression line. In regression language MSSQ_E is an unbiased estimator of the residual variance; it is a measure of unsystematic risk. Total risk is measured by the total variance, σ^2.

```
6666666666666666666666666666666666666666666666666666666666666666666666666666666666
6666666666666666666666666666666666666666666666666666666666666666666666666666666666
66666666666666666666666666666666   6666666666666   666      66666666666666666666666666666666
666666666666666666666666666666666666   6666666666   6666   66666666666666666666666666666666
666666666666666666666666666666666666   666666666   66666   66666666666666666666666666666666
66666666666666666666666666666666666666   6666666   666666   66666666666666666666666666666666
66666666666666666666666666666666666666   66666   6666666   66666666666666666666666666666666
6666666666666666666666666666666666666666   666   66666666   66666666666666666666666666666666
6666666666666666666666666666666666666666   6   666666666   66666666666666666666666666666666
66666666666666666666666666666666666666666666   6666666666   66666666666666666666666666666666
6666666666666666666666666666666666666666666666666666666666666666666666666666666666
6666666666666666666666666666666666666666666666666666666666666666666666666666666666
```

Portfolio Revision

Portfolio analysis is a "one-period" portfolio optimization technique which uses expected returns, variances, and covariances as statistical inputs for the analysis. In developing the optimum portfolio the security analyst must refine his estimates of the future into values for these statistics as of some future date. This future time period is then the horizon—it furnishes an upper limit on the period the resulting portfolio is designed to span. However, as history unfolds and the planning horizon draws nearer, new information becomes available and expectations are revised. As a result, the existing portfolio becomes suboptimal in terms of the newer expectations. Likewise, when the planning horizon is reached, the portfolio is based on a set of expectations that have most likely become obsolete.

Even if the security analyst's expectations do not change, owing to dividend income and changes in the assets' market prices, the participation levels (that is, w_i's) of the various assets will become suboptimal. Thus, portfolio revision is necessary to consider under almost any circumstances.[1]

---

[1] For a survey of policies for portfolio building that are not based on portfolio analysis, see H. A. Latane and W. E. Young, "Test of Portfolio Building Rules," *Journal of Finance*, September 1969, pp. 595–613.

The Objective of Portfolio Management

Different people do not desire the same portfolio: each person has a unique set of indifference curves. For example, a timid, risk-averting investor might prefer point A in Fig. 6.1. An aggressive investor might prefer the portfolio at point B on the Capital Market Line. Every investor selects the point where his highest-valued utility isoquant is just tangent to the CML in order to maximize his utility. Clearly, not all points on the CML yield the same utility to the investor.

A mutual fund should not be content to be just on the CML. If Fund X was originally at point A in Fig. 6.1 but it changed to point B, the holders of that fund might all sell shares in Fund X and buy shares in a fund that would place them closer to point A in order to maximize their utility.

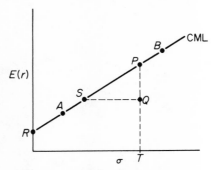

Fig. 6.1   Portfolios in Risk-Return Space

Shareholders do not desire a fund that changes position on the CML. A shareholder would maximize utility if he bought an efficient fund that stayed in some desired risk class. Thus, the objective of portfolio management becomes one of simply maximizing return in a risk class, or *preferred risk habitat*. In the initial formation of a portfolio, management should select and publicize the risk class in which they plan to maintain the portfolio, so that only investors whose preferences concur will be attracted to ownership. Of course, this is what is occurring (as a first approximation) when some mutual funds promote themselves as "growth funds" while other funds stress dividend payout.

With changing expectations, the securities that a fund has in its portfolio may cease to be optimal. In other words, a fund manager may have bought a particular portfolio with the expectations that this portfolio will lie at point P in Fig. 6.1. But, because of changing expectations, the fund finds that the portfolio is at point Q, below the CML and clearly non-optimal. The triangle QPS represents more desirable portfolios; that is, each point in the triangle QPS dominates point Q. However, the portfolio management should seek to remain in the preferred risk habitat (that is, along the line segment QP). Thus, the best revision would not be to move to any point in the triangle QPS, but only to those points that would increase return *in* the preferred risk habitat. This assumes that the objective of portfolio management is to maximize portfolio return within a preferred risk habitat.

Portfolio Revision Policies

Given the above objective (that is, maximize portfolio return within a selected risk class), portfolio management policies regarding revision of participation levels may be categorized into four groups. In descending order with respect to the degree of change and concurrent revision costs, the four policies are described as follows.

Complete Revision

A policy of complete revision entails recomputation of the efficient set each time the security analyst's latest expectations indicate the portfolio is "significantly" suboptimal. This will likely entail completely liquidating the portfolio and reinvesting the proceeds from time to time. Such a policy will result in large revision costs due to the computation expenses associated with revision, selling and buying commissions, and absorption of any capital losses incurred in liquidation.

The amount of revision costs incurred by a policy of complete revision will depend on how significant a departure from the efficient frontier will be tolerated, how often a determination is made to detect suboptimality, and how revision costs are weighed in the decision to revise.

Controlled Revision

A second possible policy is a heuristic policy which will tolerate suboptimal portfolios on a continuing basis. Unlike the complete-revision policy, the controlled-revision policy will result in continual minor portfolio revisions. This controlled revision process would proceed as follows. First, securities are forced into the solution by varying their participation levels (w_i's). The effects of the change in the weights on $E(r_p)$, σ_{r_p}, and the concurrent revision costs are noted. If the marginal return from bringing the asset or assets under consideration into the portfolio exceeds the revision costs, and the portfolio will not be removed from its preferred risk habitat by the change, the change is made. Then, the investigation reexamines all remaining nonparticipating assets to determine if other securities may be profitably brought into the portfolio.

Figure 6.2 shows three suboptimum portfolios—A, B, and C. Assuming σ_o is the desired risk-class, portfolio D is the optimum revision. The impact of inserting new securities into the suboptimum portfolios A, B, or C is determined by calculating the resulting portfolios' returns and

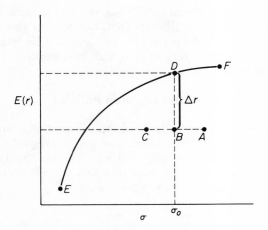

Fig. 6.2   Portfolio Revision Possibilities

risk as various new securities are introduced. Any portfolio revision that does not increase the portfolio's return within the desired risk class (σ_A) is discarded. Of those portfolio revisions which do increase the portfolio's return within the *desired* risk class, the revision which offers the largest expected marginal net increment in portfolio returns should be selected. Thus, equation (6.1) exists when no profitable portfolio revisions are possible.

$$(\Delta r) \text{ less \$ revision cost/total \$ assets} = \text{net marginal return gained.} \qquad (6.1)$$

The controlled-revision policy is based on iteratively performing marginal analysis. The objective of this revision policy is to capture the majority of the expected return that could be achieved with a complete revision but at a fraction of the revision cost.

If the portfolio's risk class is allowed to vary, such marginal-analysis techniques are of dubious value. By allowing the portfolio's risk class to change, the relevant search area becomes the area within the triangular figure bounded by QPS in Fig. 6.1. Searching within this area requires consideration be given to both risk and return.[2] If selection is to be made in $(E(r), \sigma)$ space, some weighting scheme must be devised to evaluate both risk and return simultaneously. Any such weighting scheme will not be satisfactory to all investors since risk-return preferences differ.

---

[2] See K. V. Smith, "Alternative Procedures for Revising Investment Portfolios," *Journal of Finance and Quantitative Analysis*, December 1968, pp. 383–384. Smith suggests how to consider risk by evaluating portfolios in terms of "risk-equivalent" returns.

Maintaining the Initial Proportions

A third policy with respect to portfolio revision is to maintain the initial proportions (w_i's). This policy implicitly assumes that the original set of optimal weights remains optimal. As a result, income from dividends and capital gains must be invested so as to maintain the initial participation levels of all securities unchanged. Or, if capital losses exceed dividend income, some holdings must be liquidated to purchase shares in the depreciating securities. If the forecasted statistics upon which the portfolio is based are accurate, this policy is reasonable. However, as a practical matter, transactions costs will likely render this policy unprofitable. And, maintaining the initial participation levels furnishes no guard against changes in the portfolio's risk class or expected return. If estimates of the securities' expected returns, variances, or covariances change, the portfolio's position changes in $[E(r), \sigma]$ space, although its initial participation levels have not changed.

Doing Nothing

A fourth possible policy is simply to do nothing. This policy enjoys the benefits of simplicity and minimum revision costs. Dividend income is allowed to accumulate or be reinvested. No effort is made to offset changes in participation levels due to changes in market values.

In its pure form, doing nothing as a matter of policy has little to speak for it. But, doing nothing with the original investment, combined with the policy of controlled revision as applied only to dividend income, may have its merits. This mixed policy offers a small chance to revise the portfolio using dividend income. And, it offers simplicity with minimum revision costs while providing for an opportunity to maintain the portfolio near full efficiency.

Smith's Empirical Tests of Portfolio Revision Policies

Very little work has been done to determine the efficacy of the various portfolio revision policies. It is difficult to say which policy is best.

Professor K. V. Smith has run some tests to determine the desirability of the various policies and to determine if an optimal period for revision exists. Smith's results did not clearly affirm or deny the desirability of any one revision policy or revision interval. However, Smith reached some tentative conclusions.

Concerning the efficacy of the various revision policies, Smith found the "controlled" and "complete" revision policies resulted in higher ex post yields than did the alternate policies. He also found that the controlled-revision policy could achieve near efficiency at a fraction of the revision cost of a complete revision. Concerning frequency of revision, Smith indicated that portfolio yields can be improved by revising the portfolio as often as quarterly. Using the controlled-revision policy quarterly can thus result in near-efficient portfolios without sacrificing conservative portfolio turnover ratios.

Maximizing the Utility of the Investors

To date, little progress has been made in delineating the indifference map for a group or organization.[3] However, if an indifference map could be devised to appropriately represent the preferences of all parties concerned with a portfolio, it might look as graphed in Fig. 6.3.

In Fig. 6.3, assume an initial portfolio at C was selected from the opportunity set bounded by BCD based on the hypothesized utility map for the group. Then, due to new information, the opportunity set shifted to EFG. Using the unchanged utility map, the portfolio manager could maximize the "joint utility" for the participants in the portfolio by revising portfolio C to become portfolio F. Such changes can be made if and only if the investors' utility map is explicitly known. This approach can be suggested as a practical policy only if all investors are informed before purchasing their shares in the portfolio exactly what utility map is to be used.

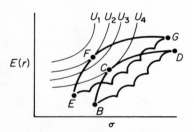

Fig. 6.3   A Group Utility Map in Risk-Return Space

Revision Costs Make True Efficient Frontier Unattainable

Portfolio revision is a costly process. When a portfolio is revised, previously purchased securities which didn't perform as expected may have to be liquidated at a capital loss. The security analysis expense of updating the risk and return statistics for many securities and the computer operation necessary to determine the new efficient frontier are not trivial. And the commissions on any securities bought or sold must be paid too.

---

[3] For a discussion of the problems associated with the construction of group preference orderings, many readings could be cited. The interested reader is directed to pp. 217–224 of Henderson and Quandt's *Microeconomic Theory* (New York: McGraw-Hill, Inc., 1958). Those authors present a concise summary of the problem and a representative list of references.

As a result of these portfolio revision costs, it is not possible for a revised portfolio to attain the true efficient frontier along the curve *EBCF* in Figure 6.4. Instead, the constrained semi-efficient frontier along the curve $E'C'F'$ represents the optimum attainable investments. The vertical difference between the unconstrained efficient frontier curve *EBCF* and the *semi-efficient frontier* curve $E'C'F'$ is the revision costs as a percentage of the portfolio's total assets.[4] As shown in Figure 6.4, the semi-efficient frontier is closer to the true efficient frontier for low-risk, low-return portfolios than for portfolios with higher returns. This is due to the fact that the low-risk, low-return portfolios presumably contain many bonds and the sales commissions for buying and selling bonds are much lower than for stock; therefore, revision costs are less.

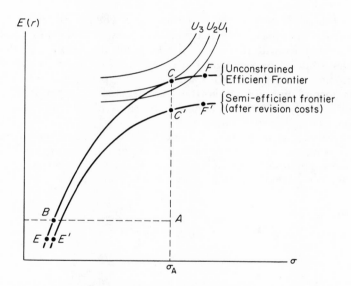

Fig. 6.4   Portfolio Revision Possibilities

In situations like the one depicted in Figure 6.4, portfolio A should be revised to attain point C'. Revisions of this nature should occur as often as they are possible according to the controlled revision policy—this may be a month, a quarter, or perhaps even longer after portfolio A was originally purchased. There is no single optimum time schedule for portfolio revision. Due to revision costs, it is impossible to attain the most efficient portfolio, C, in the desired risk-class, σ_A. But there is no reason that portfolio C' should

[4] A. H. Y. Chen, F. C. Jen, and S. Zionts, "The Optimal Portfolio Revision Policy," *Journal of Business*, January 1971, 44, No. 1, 51–61.

not be obtained directly and immediately. And, in order to maintain the portfolio in the risk-class its investors chose when they bought shares in it, portfolios which are in significantly different risk-classes should not be selected even though they may dominate the portfolio under revision.

Appendix 6A
Sensitivity Analysis and Portfolio Revision[1]

In the process of portfolio revision and when considering "what if" questions, the portfolio's management may wonder how changes in market activity will affect the portfolio. This appendix shows the mathematics to make the weights (that is, participation levels of the securities) a function of the forecasted market index's expected value and variance. This formulation allows portfolio management to perform sensitivity analysis that may throw light on decisions about competing revision policies or revised portfolios.

In the two-security example of portfolio analysis in Appendices 4B and 4C, it was shown that the optimum set of portfolio weights could be found by solving systems of linear equations. Using Cramer's rule, the solution to (4C.7) was shown as equations (4C.11) and (4C.12).

$$W_1 = \frac{\phi E(r_2) - \phi E(r_1) + 2\sigma_{12} - 2\sigma_{22}}{4\sigma_{12} - 2\sigma_{11} - 2\sigma_{22}}, \qquad (4C.11)$$

$$W_2 = \frac{\phi E(r_1) - \phi E(r_2) - 2\sigma_{11} + 2\sigma_{12}}{4\sigma_{12} - 2\sigma_{11} - 2\sigma_{22}}. \qquad (4C.12)$$

In Appendix 4E, the following relations were derived.

$$E(r_i) = a_i + b_i E(r_I) \qquad (4E.1)$$

$$\text{Var } (r_i) = (b_i \mid {}_I)^2 \, (\text{Var } (r_I)) + \sigma^2_{(r_i \mid r_I)} \qquad (4E.2)$$

$$\text{Cov } (r_i \mid r_j) = (b_{i \mid I}) \cdot (b_{j \mid I})(\text{Var } (r_I)) \qquad (4E.3)$$

---

[1] This appendix is of a mathematical nature. It assumes an understanding of Chapter 4 and its appendices in order for the reader to grasp the analysis.

Substituting equations (4E.1), (4E.2), and (4E.3) into equations (4C.11) and (4C.12) yields equations (6A.1) and (6A.2) below.

$$w_1 =$$

$$\frac{\phi[a_2 + b_2 E(r_I)] - \phi[a_1 + b_1 E(r_I)]}{4[(b_{1|I})(b_{2|I}) \text{ Var } (r_I)] - 2[(b_{1|I})^2 \text{ Var } (r_I))} , \quad (6A.1)$$

$$+ 2[(b_{1|I})(b_{2|I})(\text{Var } (r_I)] - 2[(b_{2|I})^2 (\text{Var } (r_I)) + \sigma^2_{(r_2|r_I)}]$$

$$+ \sigma^2_{(r_1|r_I)}] - 2[(b_{2|I})^2 (\text{Var } (r_I) + \sigma^2_{(r_2|r_I)}]$$

$$w_2 =$$

$$\frac{\phi[a_1 + b_1 E(r_I)] - \phi[a_2 + b_2 E(r_I)] - 2[(b_{1|I})^2 (\text{Var } (r_I))}{4[(b_{1|I})(b_{2|I})(\text{Var } (r_I))] - 2[(b_{1|I})^2 (\text{Var } (r_I))} . \quad (6A.2)$$

$$+ \sigma^2_{1|I}] + 2[(b_{2|I})(\text{Var } (r_I))(b_{1|I})]$$

$$+ \sigma^2_{(r_1|r_I)}] - 2[(b_{2|I})^2 (\text{Var } (r_I)) + \sigma^2_{(r_2|r_I)}]$$

Since ϕ, a_i, b_i, $b_{i|I}$, and $\sigma^2_{(r_i|r_I)}$ are all simply constants, these values may be substituted into equations (6A.1) and (6A.2) in place of their symbols. This substitution will convert equations (6A.1) and (6A.2) into two linear equations with w_1 and w_2 as functions of $E(r_I)$ and Var (r_I).

Expressing the weights in the optimum portfolio as functions of the expected return of the index [that is, $E(r_I)$], and the variance of returns of the index [that is, Var (r_I)] provides valuable opportunities for sensitivity analysis. This formulation allows the analyst to see how various expected returns on the index and the degree of uncertainty surrounding this forecast [as measured by Var (r_I)] will affect the weights in the optimum portfolio. The results of this sensitivity analysis may yield insights into profitable paths for portfolio revision.

The brief discussion above was limited to the trivial case of a two-security portfolio analysis using one particular solution method. The student who is reading these appendices should have no difficulty extending this technique of sensitivity analysis to the Markowitz full variance-covariance problem or to the simplified models with large numbers of securities.

```
7777777777777777777777777777777777777777777777777777777777777777777777777777777777777
7777777777777777777777777777777777777777777777777777777777777777777777777777777777777
777777777777777777777777    7777777777777    777    777    77777777777777777777777777
777777777777777777777777777    7777777777    7777    777    77777777777777777777777777
7777777777777777777777777    77777777    77777    777    77777777777777777777777777
7777777777777777777777777777    777777    777777    777    77777777777777777777777777
7777777777777777777777777777777    77777    777777    777    7777777777777777777777777
77777777777777777777777777777777    777    7777777    777    7777777777777777777777777
77777777777777777777777777777777777    7    77777777    777    777777777777777777777777
7777777777777777777777777777777777777    777777777    777    77777777777777777777777
77777777777777777777777777777777777777    7777777777    777    77777777777777777777777
7777777777777777777777777777777777777777777777777777777777777777777777777777777777777
7777777777777777777777777777777777777777777777777777777777777777777777777777777777777
```

The Limits of Diversification

Naive diversification was defined as "not putting all your eggs in one basket." Naive diversification suggests owning many different securities—presumably, the more the better. Naive diversification ignores the covariance between securities and leads to superfluous diversification. Portfolios containing many securities selected by chartists or fundamental analysts would be examples of naively diversified portfolios, since they typically ignore covariances.[1]

Markowitz diverisfication was defined as combining securities that are less than perfectly positively correlated in an effort to reduce risk in the portfolio without reducing the portfolio's expected return. To the extent that securities' returns are all positively correlated, the risk-reduction benefits to be gained from Markowitz diversification are limited.

---

[1] Some chartist and fundamental analysts suggest selecting securities from different industries in order to diversify. The data show that few industries are negatively correlated and most are highly positively correlated. Thus, naive diversification even across different industries may not lower risk very much. See B. F. King, "Market and Industry Factors in Stock Price Behavior," *Journal of Business*, vol. XXXIX, no. 1, pt. II (January 1966), suppl., pp. 139–190; K. V. Smith, "A Portfolio Analysis of Conglomerate Diversification," *Journal of Finance*, June 1969, p. 422; L. Fisher and J. Lorie, "Some Studies of Variability of Returns On Investments In Common Stocks," *Journal of Business*, April 1970, pages 99–134.

Partitioning the Variance

It is an unfortunate fact that nearly all securities' returns are positively correlated with each other and with the market.[2] The portion of a security's variability of return that is correlated with the rest of the market was designated systematic risk; it cannot be eliminated from a portfolio containing many assets with any kind of diversification.

Using a sample of 63 firms from the New York Stock Exchange, King estimated what portion of the "average security's risk" is systematic risk. He used monthly price changes from 1927 to 1960 for the 63 firms from six industries for his study. King concluded that "the typical stock has about half of its variance explained by an element of price change that affects the whole market."[3]

In a separate study Evans and Archer gathered semiannual rates of return on 470 securities over the decade from 1958 to 1967.[4] For all 470 securities they found the average standard deviation of returns was .2094. Of this, they estimated that slightly over half of the risk was systematic. The similarity of the results of these two independent studies reinforces confidence in the estimate that about half of the total risk in most securities is systematic risk.

How Many Securities Are Needed for Diversification?

Since nearly all securities have a high proportion of systematic risk, precious few securities covary negatively with the market or with each other. As a result, risk cannot be reduced to zero in portfolios of any size. However, studies have shown that portfolios of randomly selected securities (that is, naively diversified portfolios) have risk that asymptotically decreases to a minimum level equal to the systematic risk in the market as the portfolio's size is increased. Figure 7.1 depicts the exact nature of this relationship.

Figure 7.1 represents the main conclusions of the Evans-Archer work.[5] The data for the figure came from 470 firms from the New York Stock Exchange. First, a data bank of semiannual rates of return for the decade from 1958 to 1967 for the 470 firms was stored in the memory of a computer. Then, a random-number generator was used to select individual securities from the data bank and form them into portfolios. Sixty portfolios—each containing two randomly selected securities—were formed. The standard deviation of returns was calculated on the 60 portfolios containing two securities each. Then the averages of the 60 portfolios' standard deviations were calculated and found to be .161. This process of

---

[2] King, "Market and Industry Factors in Stock Price Behavior," pp. 149–150.
[3] *Ibid*, p. 151.
[4] John L. Evans and S. H. Archer, "Diversification and the Reduction of Dispersion: An Empirical Analysis," *Journal of Finance*, December 1968, pp. 761–769.
[5] *Ibid*.

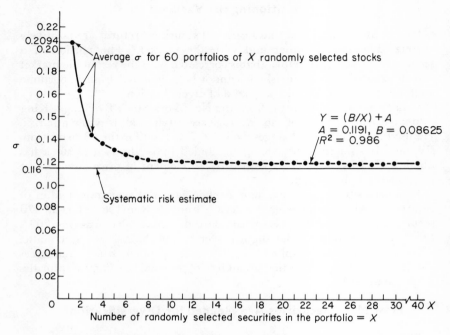

Fig. 7.1   Naive Diversification Reduces Risk to the Systematic Level

generating sixty portfolios was done for portfolios of size 3, 4, 5, . . . , 38, 39, and 40 securities, respectively. Thus, a total of 60 random portfolios were formed of each size from 1 to 40 securities inclusive. The average standard deviation of returns for the 60 portfolios at each of the 40 different sizes was calculated. Figure 7.1 is a graph with the average standard deviation of returns plotted for each of the 40 different sizes of naively diversified portfolios.

How Naive Diversification Works

Naive diversification reduces risk to the systematic level by allowing the independent random errors (that is, unsystematic variability of return) from the combined securities to average out to zero, leaving only the systematic risk. Lintner says:[6]

> Apart from negatively correlated stocks, all the gains from diversification come from "averaging over" the independent components of the returns and risks of individual stocks. Among positively correlated stocks, there would be no gains from diversification if independent variations (i.e., unsystematic risk) were absent.

---

[6] J. Lintner, "Security Prices, Risk, and Maximal Gains from Diversification," *Journal of Finance*, December 1965, p. 589 (words in parentheses added).

Since naive diversification ignores covariances, it does not generally reduce risk below the systematic level.

Minimum-Risk Portfolios Require Low-Covariance Securities

Fig. 7.2 is similar to Fig. 7.1. In Fig. 7.2 Markowitz diversification is considered rather than naive diversification. Beneath the systematic risk line in Fig. 7.2 is a dotted line asymptotically rising to the level of systematic risk. The dotted line is a very subjective estimate of the minimum variance portfolio attainable at each size if Markowitz portfolio analysis

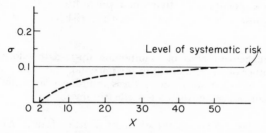

Fig. 7.2   Markowitz Diversification Can Reduce Risk Below the Systematic Level

has been used. Note that risk in the minimum-risk portfolios rises steadily as the portfolio's size increases from two.[7] The widely used definition of naive diversification implies that risk should fall instead of rise as securities are added to the portfolio. This cannot occur, owing to the scarcity of securities which covary inversely with each other. As more and more securities are forced into a Markowitz efficient portfolio, even the most desirable additions will contain increasingly large positive covariances which increase the portfolio's risk.

Superfluous Diversification

This analysis highlights the folly of the time-honored axioms about diversification currently used by most investment fund managers and legislators. The traditional investment fund manager naively defines diversification as "not putting all of your eggs in one basket." Such thinking seems to imply that a twenty-security portfolio is twice as well diversified as a ten-security portfolio. This type thinking was apparently the

---

[7] To attain zero risk in a two-security portfolio two securities that are perfectly negatively correlated must be combined in exactly the correct proportions—this was shown graphically in Fig. 2.10. Finding two securities whose returns are perfectly negatively correlated is quite unlikely, but not unimaginable. For example, a few securities are negatively correlated (in the range $0 > r_{iM} > -.4$) with the market index; one of these may move perfectly inversely with one of the numerous securities positively correlated with the market index.

basis for the Investment Company Act of 1940, Subchapter M of the Internal Revenue Code, and various state laws. In effect, these laws require that an open-end investment company (that is, mutual fund) hold no more than 5 percent of its total assets in any given security if it is to obtain favorable tax treatment.

Most large mutual fund managers and their staffs of fundamental analysts and chartists have carried the dubious logic of naive diversification too far by spreading their assets over dozens of different securities. In fact, it is quite common for large mutual funds to hold well over 100 different securities in their portfolios. Of course, such superfluous diversification will likely reduce risk to the systematic level. But, the average return of such superfluously diversified portfolios is doomed to remain below the highest return available in that risk class for the following reasons:

1. excessive management costs of maintaining up-to-date information on the excessive number of securities held in the portfolio, and
2. acceptance of securities with poor returns resulting from a policy of owning numerous securities rather than a few efficient ones.

Graphically, Fig. 7.3 shows the efficient frontier (curve EF) that could be achieved with portfolio analysis if the portfolios were not forced to hold an excessive number of securities. The curve OD shows the most efficient frontier that can be attained with an "overly" or superfluously diversified portfolio. Figure 7.3 shows that portfolio analysis will always result in a

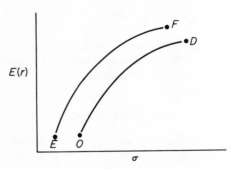

Fig. 7.3   Superfluous Diversification Reduces Efficiency

higher-expected return portfolio at every risk class. This conclusion can be demonstrated mathematically. However, such a proof is unnecessary, since it is already well known by econometricians, mathematicians, operations researchers, and other analytical researchers that constrained optima are never more optimal than unconstrained optima. Of course, accurate ex ante input statistics are required to achieve these (or any) benefits from portfolio analysis.

Appendix 7A

Diversification Can Increase the Geometric Mean Return

In Chapter 7 it was shown that Markowitz diversification, which considered the covariance (or correlation) between assets, was at least as effective at reducing risk as naive diversification. It was pointed out that the Markowitz diversification would not reduce an efficient portfolio's expected return. In fact, diversification of any kind can be expected to *increase* a portfolio's (geometric mean) rate of return over time.[1] A simple numerical example will be used to illustrate this point.

Table 7A.1   Hypothetical Data for Three Assets

Asset	$1 + r_1$	$1 + r_2$	$[(2 + r_1 + r_2)/2] = \overline{VR}$
A	1.4	1.0	1.2
B	1.4	1.0	1.2
C	1.0	1.4	1.2

All three assets in Table 7A.1 have an arithmetic average value relative (that is, $VR = 1 + r$) of 1.2 over the two periods. If assets A and B are combined half and half into a portfolio, call it N, variance of the portfolio's value relatives is calculated as follows:

$$\text{Var}(VR_N) = \sum_i^2 p_i(VR_i - \overline{VR})^2 = (\tfrac{1}{2})(1.4 - 1.2)^2 + (\tfrac{1}{2})(1.0 - 1.2)^2$$

$$= (\tfrac{1}{2})(.04) + (\tfrac{1}{2})(.04) = .04.$$

If assets B and C are combined half and half into a portfolio, the portfolio's average value relative is also 1.2. However, this portfolio of inversely correlated assets has a variance of zero. This Markowitz diversified portfolio, denote it M, has a variance of zero because the portfolio's value relative equals 1.2 in both periods.

The geometric mean of the value relatives for portfolios M and N are calculated as follows:

$$\text{gr}_N = \sqrt[2]{(1.4)(1.0)} = \sqrt{1.40} = 1.18,$$

$$\text{gr}_M = \sqrt[2]{(1.2)(1.2)} = \sqrt{1.44} = 1.2.$$

---

[1] The reader should master Appendix 1A before reading this appendix.

Portfolio M grew to 144 percent of its beginning value while portfolio N only grew to 140 percent of its beginning value. Portfolio M had a higher geometric mean value relative than portfolio N, although both had an arithmetic mean value relative of 1.2, because portfolio M had less variance. Better diversification reduced portfolio M's variance to zero. Thus, portfolio M grew at a constant factor of 1.2 and outperformed its poorly diversified counterpart, which grew erratically.

In general, the product of n value relatives with a given arithmetic average $\left[(1/n) \sum_{i}^{n} VR_i = \bar{V}R \right]$, will be larger the less the variance of those n value relatives. In terms of the geometric mean returns (gr) and arithmetic mean returns (ar) defined in Appendix 1A, this relationship may be restated as equation (7A.1).[2]

$$ \text{gr} \cong (\text{ar}^2 - \sigma^2)^{1/2}. \tag{7A.1} $$

Clearly, gr increases as the variance of the period-by-period rates of return decreases.

Period	Asset	M	Q	N
1	$VR_1 = 1 + r_1$	1.2	1.3	1.4
2	$VR_2 = 1 + r_2$	1.2	1.1	1.0
	Arithmetic average return	20%	20%	20%
	Geometric mean return	$\sqrt[2]{(1.2)(1.2)}$ $>$ $\text{gr}_M = \sqrt{1.44}$	$\sqrt[2]{(1.3)(1.1)}$ $>$ $\text{gr}_Q = \sqrt{1.43}$	$\sqrt[2]{(1.4)(1.0)}$ $>$ $\text{gr}_N = \sqrt{1.40}$

The data above summarize the teaching point of this appendix. Three portfolios—say, M, Q, and N—all having an arithmetic average rate of return of 20 percent per period, are shown. But all three portfolios have different geometric mean returns over the two periods they are in existence. The portfolio with the least variability of return (that is, M) has the highest geometric mean return over the two periods.

---

[2] W. E. Young, "Common Stock Ex Post Holding Period Returns and Portfolio Selection," Ph.D. thesis, University of North Carolina, 1968, Chapel Hill, N.C.; W. E. Young and R. H. Trent, "Geometric Mean Approximations of Individual Security and Portfolio Performance," *Journal of Financial and Quantitative Analysis*, vol. IV, June 1969; E. F. Renshaw, "Portfolio Balance Models in Perspective: Some Generalizations That Can Be Derived from the Two Asset Case," *Journal of Financial and Quantitative Analysis*, vol. II, June 1967, pp. 123–149; H. Markowitz, *Portfolio Selection*, New York: John Wiley & Sons, Inc., 1959, p. 122.

```
8888888888888888888888888888888888888888888888888888888888888888888888888888888888888888888888888
8888888888888888888888888888888888888888888888888888888888888888888888888888888888888888888888888
8888888888888888888888888   8888888888888   888      888      888   8888888888888888888888888888
8888888888888888888888888    88888888888    8888     888      888   8888888888888888888888888888
8888888888888888888888888     888888888     88888    888      888   8888888888888888888888888888
8888888888888888888888888888    8888888    888888    888      888   8888888888888888888888888888
88888888888888888888888888888    88888    8888888    888      888   8888888888888888888888888888
88888888888888888888888888888    888     88888888    888      888   8888888888888888888888888888
888888888888888888888888888888    8     888888888    888      888   8888888888888888888888888888
8888888888888888888888888888888         8888888888   888      888   8888888888888888888888888888
88888888888888888888888888888888       88888888888   888      888   8888888888888888888888888888
8888888888888888888888888888888888888888888888888888888888888888888888888888888888888888888888888
8888888888888888888888888888888888888888888888888888888888888888888888888888888888888888888888888
```

Investment Funds

ALTHOUGH mutual funds and other large public portfolios are widely advertised, touted in the financial press, and the subject of much conversation, few truly analytical studies or studies grounded in portfolio analysis have been made of their performance.[1] There is institutional and descriptive material out on various portfolios explaining their corporate charters, their management structure, the mechanics of their day-to-day activities, the value and composition of their holdings, and so on. But, not enough work has been done to discredit or support widely held beliefs within the industry concerning the use of charting, traditional views on diversification, the fundamental analyst's approach to searching out undervalued securities, the interrelation of security price movements, and other vital subjects. Hopefully, more research will be done in these areas

---

[1] Jack L. Treynor, "How to Rate Management of Investment Funds," *Harvard Business Review*, January–February 1965, pp. 63–75; William F. Sharpe, "Mutual Fund Performance," *Journal of Business*, January 1966, pp. 119–138; M. C. Jensen, "The Performance of Mutual Funds in the Period 1945–1964," *Journal of Finance*, May 1968, pp. 389–416; Don E. Farrar, *The Investment Decision Under Uncertainty* (Englewood Cliffs, N.J.: Prentice-Hall, Inc., 1962); M. C. Jensen, "Risk, The Pricing of Capital Assets, and the Evaluation of Investment Portfolios," *Journal of Business*, April 1969; Irwin Friend, Marshall Blume, and Jean Crockett, *Mutual Funds and Other Institutional Investors: A New Perspective* (New York: McGraw-Hill, Inc., 1970); J. L. Treynor and Kay K. Mazuy, "Can Mutual Funds Outguess The Market?" *Harvard Business Review*, July–August 1966, pp. 131–136.

in the future and will reach the hands of investment fund managers and the investing public.

An abundance of erroneous but widely accepted folklore is used in the investments industry. Only when erroneous beliefs are discredited and the folklore replaced with an awareness of ignorance will the foundation be laid for acceptance of analytical techniques like portfolio analysis. In the meantime, loanable funds will be misallocated, resources squandered to pay for the services of charlatans, and effort will be wasted tending to the insignificant.

Table 8.1   Performance of 34 Mutual Funds, 1954–1963

Mutual Fund	Average Annual Return (Percent)	Std. Dev. of Annual Return (Percent)	Risk Premium to Standard Deviation Ratio*
Affiliated Fund	14.6	15.3	.75896
American Business Shares	10.0	9.2	.75876
Axe-Houghton, Fund A	10.5	13.5	.55551
Axe-Houghton, Fund B	12.0	16.3	.55183
Axe-Houghton, Stock Fund	11.9	15.6	.56991
Boston Fund	12.4	12.1	.77842
Broad Street Investing	14.8	16.8	.70329
Bullock Fund	15.7	19.3	.65845
Commonwealth Investment Company	10.9	13.7	.57841
Delaware Fund	14.4	21.4	.53253
Dividend Shares	14.4	15.9	.71807
Eaton and Howard, Balanced Fund	11.0	11.9	.67399
Eaton and Howard, Stock Fund	15.2	19.2	.63486
Equity Fund	14.6	18.7	.61902
Fidelity Fund	16.4	23.5	.57020
Financial Industrial Fund	14.5	23.0	.49971
Fundamental Investors	16.0	21.7	.59894
Group Securities, Common Stock Fund	15.1	19.1	.63316
Group Securities, Fully Administered Fund	11.4	14.1	.59490
Incorporated Investors	14.0	25.5	.43116
Investment Company of America	17.4	21.8	.66169
Investors Mutual	11.3	12.5	.66451
Loomis-Sales Mutual Fund	10.0	10.4	.67358
Massachusetts Investors Trust	16.2	20.8	.63398
Massachusetts Investors—Growth Stock	18.6	22.7	.68687
National Investors Corporation	18.3	19.9	.76798
National Securities—Income Series	12.4	17.8	.52950
New England Fund	10.4	10.2	.72703
Putnam Fund of Boston	13.1	16.0	.63222
Scudder, Stevens & Clark Balanced Fund	10.7	13.3	.57893
Selected American Shares	14.4	19.4	.58788
United Funds—Income Fund	16.1	20.9	.62698
Wellington Fund	11.3	12.0	.69057
Wisconsin Fund	13.8	16.9	.64091

* Ratio = (average return − 3.0 percent)/variability. The ratios shown were computed from original data and thus differ slightly from the ratios obtained from the rounded data shown in the table. These ratios may be thought of as being a sort of index of desirability which considers risk and return simultaneously.

Testing the Capital Market Line

In Chapter 5, the rationale for the CML was developed. The theory hypothesized that the expected return of an efficient portfolio should be a positive linear function of the portfolio's risk as measured by its standard deviation of returns. Perhaps a good place to begin examining funds is to compare empirical evidence about their performance with what the theory predicts. Although the theory is cast in terms of expectations, it is not unreasonable to expect historical data to conform to the hypothesis in at least some rough sense.

To test the CML, data previously tabulated and reported by Professor William F. Sharpe will be used.[2] Table 8.1 shows the historical average annual rates of return ($\bar{r}$) in column one and standard deviation of these annual returns (σ) in column two over the decade from 1954 to 1963 for 34 mutual funds. These 34 funds were selected by Sharpe from the Weisenberger data because they had annual returns published for twenty consecutive years. This criteria may bias the sample because new, small funds were not included.

Using the standard least-squares technique, a simple linear regression line of the form $\bar{r}_i = a + b\sigma_i + e$ was fitted to the 34 pairs of observations, where a and b are the intercept and slope regression statistics. The regression line over the range that the data cover is shown in Fig. 8.1

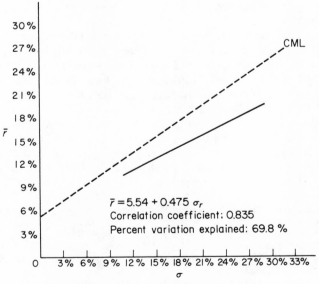

$$\bar{r} = 5.54 + 0.475\,\sigma_r$$
Correlation coefficient: 0.835
Percent variation explained: 69.8 %

Fig. 8.1   Estimates of the CML

[2] See "Risk Aversion in the Stock Market: Some Empirical Evidence," *Journal of Finance*, September 1965, pp. 416–422.

as the solid line. This regression line represents the average performance
that could be achieved using naive diversification. The regression slope
coefficient ($b = .475$) is significantly different than zero at the .01 level
of significance.[3] The correlation coefficient is .835. The percentage of
variation explained by the regression line (that is, the coefficient of
determination) is 69.8 percent. The historical data conform to the CML
hypothesis.[4]

Funds Not Efficient

In Fig. 8.1 a dashed line labeled the CML has been graphed to give an
extremely subjective estimate of where the true efficient frontier would lie
if all the portfolios were Markowitz efficient. Although the regression
line conforms to the relationship hypothesized in the capital market
theory, it is doubtlessly dominated by the true CML owing to several poor
management practices followed by mutual funds. These inefficiencies are
discussed next.

Superfluous Diversification

In the previous chapter it was shown that portfolio risk could typically
be reduced to near the minimum level imposed by systematic variation
with as few as eight *randomly* selected securities—see Fig. 7.1 for a graphical summary of the analysis leading to this conclusion. It was also pointed
out that by using portfolio analysis fewer securities could achieve even
more reduction in risk.

Various legal guidelines require open-end mutual funds to spread their
assets across a minimum of twenty different portfolios in order to obtain
certain income tax exemptions. This requirement does not seem to frustrate
the mutual funds, pension funds, and so forth. In fact, many funds
have well over 100 securities in their portfolios by choice. As a glance
at Fig. 7.1 reveals, such excessive diversification tends to reduce portfolio
risk to the minimum level imposed by systematic variation. But this
is no impressive accomplishment, since the number of securities owned
is excessive and leads to at least three types of portfolio inefficiency.

First, experience with the portfolio-analysis techniques discussed in
this book shows that unleveraged Markowitz efficient portfolios without

---

[3] The standard error of b is .055, so $t = (b - B)/\sigma_b = (.475 - 0)/.055 = 8.6$ for the null
hypothesis $b = 0$.

[4] W. F. Sharpe, "Risk Aversion in the Stock Market: Some Empirical Evidence,"
Journal of Finance, September 1965, pp. 416–422. For a critique of Sharpe's study see R. R.
West, "Mutual Fund Performance and the Theory of Capital Asset Pricing: Some Com-
ments," *Journal of Business*, April 1968, pp. 230–234.

Sharpe's regression slope parameter is likely biased. Both variables in the regression
model represent observations that are subject to various errors. It has been shown that
this "errors-in-variables" problem results in inconsistent, inefficient, and biased regression
slope coefficients. J. Johnston, *Econometric Methods* (New York: McGraw-Hill, Inc., 1963),
chap. 6.

any constraints on the number of securities held are frequently composed of less than 20 securities. Furthermore, the lowest-risk portfolios in the efficient set typically contain *less than the systematic level of risk*. These minimum-risk portfolios are composed of only a few uncorrelated securities.[5] As additional securities are forced into a Markowitz efficient portfolio, it becomes more risky, and its risk asymptotically approaches the level of risk in the market portfolio—that is, the level of systematic risk. Superfluous diversification can *increase* risk rather than reduce it. Thus, the larger portfolios are more prone to fluctuate with the market than the lowest-risk Markowitz efficient portfolios. Even if they used portfolio analysis, most investment funds are simply too large to be well diversified—they are forced by their size to pursue superfluous diversification.

Second, a portfolio that has 120 securities has at least 100 more securities than it needs to be efficient or to satisfy the law. The administrative cost of keeping current information on these 100 excess securities and the recurring management cost of reviewing them periodically runs up unduly high management fees for the mutual fund. This reduces the net return to owners. In fact, Sharpe's data indicate that mutual funds with a *low* ratio of management expense to net assets do *better* than funds that spend a larger proportion on management.[6] Such evidence speaks poorly for current mutual fund managements.

Third, mutual funds that purchase many different securities will be forced to accept securities offering lower and lower returns. In highly efficient markets such as the New York Stock Exchange, very few significantly undervalued investments (that is, disequilibrium returns) will exist at any moment. Thus, a portfolio containing over one hundred securities must surely contain a majority of lackluster performers.

The three effects of superfluous or naive diversification discussed above explain why the CML in Fig. 8.1 must surely dominate the regression-line fit to the actual data. In defense of the charge they diversify superfluously, investment fund managers frequently reply that their fund is too large to own only a few securities. That is, if a large fund invested all its assets in less than twenty securities, its activities would affect the price of these issues. Of course, these contentions are correct. Thus, the law would do better to limit the total dollar size of funds than to require superfluous diversification. Or, large funds could be broken down into smaller specialized funds, managed independently. These latter changes would tend to make the capital markets more competitive and lead to more efficient capital allocation.

---

[5] Homestake Mining, Pan-Am, General Portland Cement, and Pepsi-Cola were found to have negatively correlated returns with the market over a recent 10-year period. Such securities allow portfolio risk to be reduced below the systematic level if this counter-cyclical behavior can be expected to continue.

[6] Sharpe, "Mutual Fund Performance," p. 132.

Searching for Underpriced Securities

Most mutual funds devote resources to searching for underpriced securities in hopes of earning substantial capital gains. This search is typically performed either by fundamental security analysts or technical analysts (that is, chartists). It is unlikely that such activity will ever earn a return above a naive buy-and-hold strategy.[7]

Charting-reading is based on the assumption that the successive price changes of securities are not random. But impressive evidence has been gathered showing these price changes are actually random.[8] Meanwhile, the chartists have offered little in the way of economic rationale or proof that their activity has any merit.[9]

Fundamental analysis, on the other hand, is a more defensible process. It involves collecting facts and then reaching a rather subjective estimate of the intrinsic value of a security based on these facts.

In spite of its rationale, fundamental analysis offers a negligible opportunity to earn a return above what could be achieved with a naive buy-and-hold strategy. There are thousands of full-time professional fundamental analysts constantly poring over new information as it becomes available and constantly rechecking market values against their own estimates of intrinsic value. Thus, market prices in efficient markets such as the New York Stock Exchange at any moment are excellent, unbiased, up-to-the-moment estimates of the securities' true intrinsic value. The efforts of an "army" of fundamental analysts cause market prices to be so accurate that fundamental analysis offers virtually no possibility of consistently finding a significantly undervalued security—or an overvalued one for that matter. This should not be interpreted to mean that no fundamental analyst (or chartist or dart-thrower) will not "pick a winner" and know it from time to time. Rather, the point is, after deducting the losses from the "losers" and the costs of fundamental analysis (or charting), the net returns from fundamental analysis (or charting) will not exceed what could have been earned with random selection.

Lorie and Fisher found that about a 10 percent before-tax annual return compounded annually could be earned over recent decades by selecting

---

[7] The phrase "naive buy-and-hold strategy" refers to the process of randomly selecting securities (for example, with a dart or a roulette wheel), buying them, and holding them as long-run investments. See L. Fisher and J. Lorie, "Rates of Return on Investments in Common Stock," *Journal of Business*, July 1968.

[8] E. F. Fama, "Efficient Capital Markets: A Review of Theory and Empirical Work," *Journal of Finance*, May 1970, pp. 383–717.

[9] Levy has articulated a case for technical analysis better than most. R. A. Levy, "Random Walks: Reality or Myth," and M. C. Jensen, "Random Walks: Reality or Myth—Comment," both in November–December 1967, *Financial Analysts Journal*, pp. 69–85. "Random Walks: Reality or Myth—Reply," *Financial Analysts Journal*, January–February 1968, pp. 129–132.

many securities randomly (for example, with a *dart*) and holding them.[10] Over a period of years, the studies published seem to indicate that no large open-end mutual fund has been able to consistently outperform these naive buy-and-hold strategies.

Charting and fundamental analysis have not only failed to earn average returns exceeding those attainable by randomly selecting securities, but the costs of this fruitless search seem to have lowered mutual funds' *net returns to below* what could be attained by using a dart.[11]

Perhaps if the capital market theory of Chapter 5 were used to highlight securities whose prices were in disequilibrium[12] and then fundamental analysis performed on these, the search for undervalued securities could be made fruitful. At this time, however, the authors know of no investment fund that uses such analytical techniques. Instead, they more or less aimlessly conduct an expensive and evidently fruitless search for undervalued securities.

No Consistently Superior Funds

In an effort to determine if any open-end mutual funds were consistently superior, Fama ranked 39 common stock funds that were in existence throughout the decade from 1950 to 1960. Calculating annual rates of return with dividends reinvested and compounded, Fama ranked all 39 funds based on their annual returns in each of the ten years. These data are shown in Table 8.2.

As Fama points out, the most striking feature of Table 8.2 is the inconsistency of the rankings. Although some funds did significantly better than average in some years, no fund consistently ranked high. Of the 39 funds, no single fund consistently had returns high enough to place it among the top twenty funds in each of the ten years.

In column one of Table 8.2 the funds' compound rate of return over the decade is shown. The average return of all 39 funds is 14.1 percent for the decade. This is the return on the shareholder's actual investment after load charges (salesman's commissions). This return on net investment flatters the funds. Their return on gross investment (that is, on the actual investment, plus the salesman's commission) would be lower, of course. The Lorie and Fisher data showed the market average return over this same period was 14.7 percent. This means that the average investor who used a dart to select securities for the decade from 1950 to 1960 would have earned a higher return than the average mutual fund share owner.

---

[10] Lorie and Fisher, "Rates of Return on Investments in Common Stocks . . . , " *Journal of Business*, vol. XL, no. 3 (July 1968), pp. 1–26.

[11] See Fama's comments, "Behavior of Stock Prices," *Journal of Business*, January 1965, pp. 90–92.

[12] See the discussion accompanying Figs. 5.8 and 5.7.

Table 8.2 Year-By-Year Ranking of Individual Fund Returns[13]

Fund	Return on Net (1)	1951 (2)	52 (3)	53 (4)	54 (5)	55 (6)	56 (7)	57 (8)	58 (9)	59 (10)	1960 (11)
Keystone Lower Price	18.7	29	1	38	5	3	8	35	1	1	36
T. Rowe Price Growth	18.7	1	33	2	8	14	15	2	25	7	4
Dreyfuss	18.4	37	37	14	3	7	11	3	2	3	7
Television Electronic	18.4	21	4	9	2	33	20	16	2	4	20
National Investors Corp.	18.0	3	35	4	19	27	4	5	5	8	1
De Vegh Mutual Fund	17.7	32	4	1	8	14	4	8	15	23	36
Growth Industries	17.0	7	34	14	17	9	9	20	5	6	11
Massachusetts Investors Growth	16.9	5	36	31	11	9	1	23	4	9	4
Franklin Custodian	16.5	26	2	4	13	33	20	16	5	9	4
Investment Co. of America	16.0	21	15	14	11	17	15	23	15	15	15
Chemical Fund, Inc.	15.6	1	39	14	27	3	33	1	27	4	23
Founders Mutual	15.6	21	13	25	8	2	20	16	11	13	28
Investment Trust of Boston	15.6	6	3	25	3	14	26	31	20	29	20
American Mutual	15.5	14	13	4	22	14	13	16	25	25	4
Keystone Growth	15.3	29	15	25	1	1	1	39	11	13	38
Keystone High	15.2	10	7	3	27	23	36	5	27	25	11
Aberdeen Fund	15.1	32	23	9	25	9	7	10	27	7	30
Massachusetts Investors Trust	14.8	8	9	14	16	9	15	20	18	32	28
Texas Fund Inc.	14.6	3	15	9	32	23	26	5	27	37	7
Eaton & Howard Stock	14.4	14	9	4	17	20	15	13	37	29	17
Guardian Mutual	14.4	21	26	25	34	31	29	13	20	15	2
Scudder, Stevens, Clark	14.3	14	23	14	19	27	15	29	9	15	30
Investors Stock Fund	14.2	8	28	21	22	27	20	23	5	29	23
Fidelity Fund, Inc.	14.1	21	26	25	34	31	29	13	20	15	23
Fundamental Inv.	13.8	14	15	31	15	9	11	31	18	25	30
Century Shares	13.5	14	28	35	25	3	20	23	31	34	2
Bullock Fund Ltd.	13.5	29	9	21	19	14	9	20	34	34	20
Financial Industries	13.0	26	15	31	13	19	29	34	20	9	35
Group Common Stock	13.0	38	8	25	27	27	33	8	20	34	17
Incorporated Investors	12.9	14	13	37	6	3	13	37	11	18	39
Equity Fund	12.9	14	27	21	32	31	33	13	31	18	23
Selected American Shares	12.8	21	15	21	31	23	20	23	15	32	30
Dividend Shares	12.7	32	7	14	34	20	32	4	37	37	11
General Capital Corp.	12.4	10	28	9	38	35	39	23	34	13	23
Wisconsin Fund	12.3	32	26	4	37	35	38	10	34	18	7
International Resources	12.3	10	37	39	22	35	1	37	39	1	11
Delaware Fund	12.1	36	23	25	27	39	26	29	9	23	30
Hamilton Fund	11.9	38	28	9	34	35	36	10	31	18	17
Colonial Energy	10.9	10	15	35	39	20	4	36	20	39	10

[13] E. Fama, "The Behavior of Stock Prices," Table 18, p. 93.

Near Efficiency

Probably the most complimentary remarks about mutual fund performance in an analytical study were made by Farrar.[14] Using monthly observations from 1946 to 1956 on 23 mutual funds, the risk-return of each
portfolio and the efficient frontier were determined. These results are
shown in Fig. 8.2.[15]

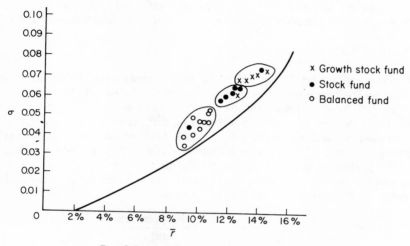

Fig. 8.2   Data on 23 Mutual Funds

The figure shows the funds are near the Markowitz efficient frontier.
Farrar says:[16]

> The plots do seem to follow closely along the frontier of optimal portfolios.
> Even more encouraging, however, is the tendency of the funds to cluster
> along the boundary in almost perfect groups of balanced funds, stock
> funds, and growth funds, respectively.

One-Parameter Portfolio Performance Measures

In an effort to measure the performance of investment portfolios,
various devices have been proposed.[17] The more sophisticated of these

[14] Donald E. Farrar, *The Investment Decision Under Uncertainty* (Englewood Cliffs, N.J.:
Prentice-Hall, Inc., 1962).

[15] *Ibid.*, p. 73.

[16] *Ibid.*, p. 74.

[17] J. Treynor, "How to Rate the Management of Mutual Funds," *Harvard Business
Review*, vol. 43 (January-February 1965), pp. 63–75. William Sharpe, "Mutual Fund
Performance," *Journal of Business*, vol. 39 (January 1966), pp. 119-138. M. Jensen, "The
Performance of Mutual Funds in the Period 1945–1964," *Journal of Finance*, vol. 23 (May
1968), pp. 389–416. M. Jensen, "Risk, Capital Assets, and the Evaluation of Investment
Portfolios," *Journal of Business*, vol. 42 (April 1969), pp. 167–247.

techniques sought to take both the risk and return of a portfolio into consideration. Treynor and Sharpe have developed models for portfolio performance measurement that consider both risk and return and allow the portfolios to be ranked. These models develop one ordinal number to measure the performance of each portfolio. This number is a function of the portfolio's risk and return.

All the portfolio performance measures discussed in the remainder of this chapter are outgrowths of capital market theory. As such, they are based upon the simplifying assumptions listed and discussed in Chapter 5.

Sharpe's Ranking Technique

Sharpe analyzed 34 mutual funds' performance over the decade from 1954 to 1963 inclusive. His data are shown in Table 8.1. He subtracted from each fund's gross average return ($\bar{r}$) his estimate of the riskless return over the decade—that is, 3 percent. The difference is a *risk premium* for investing in assets with more than zero risk. He then divided each security's risk premium by its standard deviation of annual returns (σ), a measure of the portfolio's total risk. The resulting number is the ratio of risk premium per unit of risk borne. Let this ratio of risk premium per unit of risk borne be denoted S_i for the ith mutual fund.

$$S_i = \frac{\bar{r}_i - .03}{\sigma_i} = \frac{\text{risk premium}}{\text{total risk}}. \qquad (8.1)$$

S is Sharpe's index of desirability. S is developed for comparing assets in different risk classes. Consider Fig. 8.3, which graphically represents S_i for assets 1, 2, and 3. Asset 1 is the most desirable, since $S_1 > S_2 > S_3$. These S_i's or reward-to-variability ratios for the 34 mutual funds are

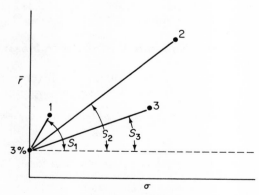

Fig. 8.3   Sharpe's Ranking Technique

shown in column 3 of Table 8.1. Sharpe then calculated the same ratio for the Dow-Jones Industrial Averages (DJIA) and prepared Fig. 8.4.[18]

The average ratio for the 34 funds was .633, which is considerably below the .667 for the DJIA. Of the 34 funds only 11 did better than the DJIA in Sharpe's ranking. Had Sharpe netted out sales commissions (which are

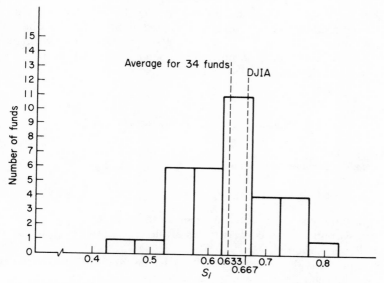

Fig. 8.4   Frequency Distribution of Risk Premium-to-
Variability Ratios

typically 8 percent of the original investment), the mutual funds would have done even worse in comparison with the DJIA.

Conclusions about Empirical Data

If a superior open-end mutual fund exists, it has yet to be detected. In general, most funds seem to earn a gross return a little below that which would be achieved using a naive buy-and-hold strategy. The net return they pay to shareholders is significantly below what the investor could have averaged with a naive buy-and-hold strategy. Most funds own too many securities and spend too much searching for underpriced securities. None

---

[18] Sharpe, "Mutual Fund Performance," Fig. 9, p. 136.

of the mutual funds discussed here were Markowitz efficient.[19] A discussion of models for evaluating investment funds is provided in the remainder of this chapter.

Treynor's Ranking Device

In Chapter 3 [equations (3.4) and (3.5)] and Chapter 5 [equations (5.1) and (5.2)] individual securities' returns were regressed on the market index to determine Sharpe's beta coefficient [equation (5.4)]. Sharpe's beta coefficient is an index of a security's systematic or undiversifiable risk. Similarly, the returns on portfolio p, denoted r_p, may be regressed on the returns of an index—denoted r_I.

$$r_p = A + B_p(r_I) + e_p, \qquad (8.2)$$

where the e_p's are random errors and it is assumed that

(1) $E(e_p) = 0$,
(2) $\text{Var}(e_p) = $ some finite constant,
(3) $\text{cov}(e_p, r_I) = 0$, and
(4) $\text{cov}(e_{p,t}, e_{p,t+k}) = 0$.

These assumptions assure that the regression parameters A and B are minimum-variance, unbiased estimates of the true values of A and B for the whole population.[20]

The expected value of equation (8.2) is the conditional expectation (that is, regression line) shown in equation (8.3) below.

$$r_p = E(r_p \mid r_I) = A + B(r_I). \qquad (8.3)$$

This regression line will be called the characteristic line of the portfolio. Two possible forms the characteristic line might assume are graphed in Figure 8.5.

The regression slope coefficient (B) in equations (8.2) and (8.3) will be referred to as the *portfolio's beta*—it is a measure of the systematic risk of the portfolio. A portfolio's beta coefficient is a measure of the volatility or responsiveness of the portfolio to changes in the market index.[21] Portfolios classified as "balanced funds" would have lower B_p's than "growth

---

[19] These conclusions agree with those of Ira Horowitz, "The Varying Quality of Investment Trust Management," *Journal of the American Statistical Association*, December 1963, pp. 1011–1032; M. C. Jensen, "The Performance of Mutual Funds in the Period 1945–1964," *Journal of Finance*, May 1968, pp. 289–415—especially 406; and M. C. Jensen, "Risk, The Pricing of Capital Assets, and the Evaluation of Investment Portfolios," *Journal of Business*, April 1969, pp. 167–247.

[20] By the Gauss-Markov theorem.

[21] J. L. Treynor, "How to Rate Management of Investment Funds," *Harvard Business Review*, January–February 1965, pp. 64–65. Treynor calls equation (8.3) the *characteristic line* of a portfolio and the slope coefficient (B) a measure of its *volatility*.

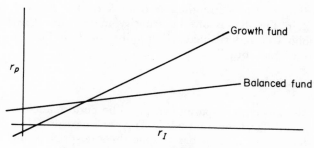

Fig. 8.5   Characteristic Lines

funds." The portfolio beta is the weighted average of the Sharpe's beta coefficients of the securities in the portfolio. Symbolically,

$$B_p = \frac{\text{cov}\,(r_p, r_m)}{\sigma_m{}^2} \qquad \text{by definition}$$

$$= \frac{\text{cov}\left(\sum_i^{i\in p} w_i r_i, r_m\right)}{\sigma_m{}^2} \qquad \text{substituting } \sum_i^{i\in p} w_i r_i = r_p$$

$$= \sum_i^{i\in p} w_i \frac{\text{cov}\,(r_i, r_m)}{\sigma_m{}^2} \qquad \begin{array}{l}\text{by expectation theorem E8}\\ \text{in Math Appendix C}\end{array}$$

$$= \sum_i^{i\in p} w_i b_i \qquad \text{since } b_i = \text{cov}\,(r_i, r_m)/\sigma_m{}^2 \qquad (8.4)$$

Treynor's portfolio-ranking device utilizes the portfolio beta to measure risk. Treynor's index of portfolio desirability, denoted T_i for the ith portfolio, is defined in equation (8.5) below.

$$T_i = \frac{E(r_i) - R}{B_i} = \frac{\text{risk premium}}{\text{systematic risk index}}. \qquad (8.5)$$

Graphically, Treynor's ranking device is represented in Fig. 8.6. Portfolio 1 is more desirable than portfolio 2 because $T_1 > T_2$. The T_i

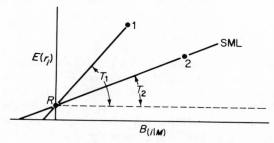

Fig. 8.6   Treynor's Ranking Device

measures the slope of a straight line from R to the ith asset. Assuming portfolio 2 in Fig. 8.6 is on the security market line (SML) implies that portfolio 1 is undervalued. High values of T_i indicate that the ith portfolio is a "good buy."

Jensen's Measure

Jensen developed a one-parameter portfolio performance measure that resembles, yet differs from Sharpe's or Treynor's measures. Like Treynor's measure, Jensen's measure is based upon the asset-pricing implications of the SML. In Chapter 5 [see equations (5.4) and (5.5) or the proof of Proposition 4 in Appendix 5A] the formula for the SML was shown to be equation (8.6).

$$E(r_i) = R + b_i[E(r_M) - R]. \tag{8.6}$$

The SML is shown graphically in Fig. 8.7. Two hypothetical portfolios are represented by points 1 and 2 in Fig. 8.7. Portfolio 1 is underpriced and offers a high expected return relative to the equilibrium prices and returns represented by the SML.

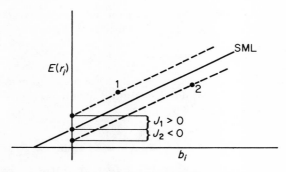

Fig. 8.7   Jensen's Measure

Jensen measures the desirability of portfolios with the coefficient J_i in equation (8.7).

$$E(r_i) = R + J_i + b_i[E(r_M) - R]. \tag{8.7}$$

J_i measures the vertical distance which a portfolio's return lies above or below the SML shown in Fig. 8.7. High values of J_i represent underpriced portfolios with unusually high returns, such as J_1 in Fig. 8.7. $J_2 < 0$ implies portfolio 2 is overpriced and offers a poor return for the amount of systematic risk associated with that portfolio. Since J_i only measures vertical deviations from the SML (but ignores the risk dimension) it cannot be used for one-parameter portfolio rankings (as S and T can).

Jensen suggests measuring J_i by fitting regression equation (8.8) for $t = 1, 2, \ldots, T$.

$$r_{it} - R_t = J_i + b_i[r_{Mt} - R_t] + e_{it}. \tag{8.8}$$

Over T periods the e_{it}'s will average zero and J_i will be the regression intercept coefficient. Equation (8.7) is the expected value of equation (8.8). Jensen suggests using a different value for the risk-free rate (R_t) in each period to hold the variation in the level of interest rates constant while J_i is estimated.

Conclusions about One-Parameter Portfolio Performance Measures

Sharpe's technique measures risk premium per unit of total risk and is satisfactory for portfolio selection but not for individual assets. Sharpe's S_i is an index of efficiency of the portfolio. Treynor's measure considers systematic risk and is suitable for individual assets or portfolios.

All three of the portfolio performance measures discussed above have one serious flaw that exerts a bias against selection of high-risk portfolios.[22] As discussed in Chapter 5, the borrowing and lending rates differ. This causes the CML and SML to become nonlinear (for example, Figs. 5.10 and 5.9). The nature of these nonlinearities implies lower equilibrium expected returns for the high-risk portfolios than indicated by the CML and SML. Since none of the three portfolio evaluation models discussed above makes adjustments for these nonlinearities, they are all biased against selection of high-risk portfolios.

An appendix at the end of this chapter shows the mathematical relationship between the three portfolio performance measures.

A Model for Evaluating Various Aspects of Portfolios

It is possible that a rational Markowitz efficient investor may desire to own shares in several Markowitz *inefficient* portfolios. If the shares in these inefficient portfolios are assembled into an overall portfolio that is Markowitz efficient, the investor has ultimately made an efficient investment. Thus, it is not clear that a portfolio manager's objective should necessarily be to maintain a Markowitz efficient portfolio. In fact, at least two portfolio objectives suggest themselves: (1) selection of undervalued securities in an effort to earn returns above those appropriate for the securities' risk class, or (2) maintaining a Markowitz efficient portfolio.

Since either or both of these two portfolio objectives may be appropriate, it seems that multiple criteria may be required for evaluating the performance of portfolios. Some new theoretical apparatus will be required to carry out this evaluation.

---

[22] I. Friend and M. Blume, "Measurement of Portfolio Performance Under Uncertainty," *American Economic Review*, September 1970.

The Naive Market Portfolio—The Index

Consider the Dow-Jones Average, or some other index (I) that is used as a surrogate for the market portfolio (M). These real-life analogues to M are like a naively formed market portfolio. They differ from M in two respects: (1) the indices are not Markowitz efficient portfolios. The indices did not have their risk minimized. (2) The indices are not perfectly positively correlated with M. Since the indices only enjoyed the benefits of naive diversification (see Fig. 7.1), their risk is equal to or above the systematic level—the indices most likely contain unsystematic risk.

The Naive CML Based on the Indices

As was mentioned above, the stock market indices used in the financial world are surrogates for M. The indices are not Markowitz efficient portfolios. If the average return and standard deviation of returns for some index are plotted in ($E(r)$, σ) space, a point like I in Fig. 8.8 would result. Then, if the riskless rate (R) is estimated and plotted, a

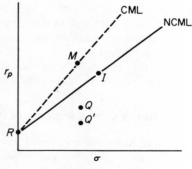

Fig. 8.8   The Naive CML

naive capital market line (*NCML*) may be drawn. The NCML is the line passing through R and I. The NCML should correspond to a regression line for naively diversified portfolios' expected returns and standard deviations (such as the solid line in Fig. 8.1). Of course, the NCML will be dominated by the CML because M is Markowitz efficient and I is not. The CML (developed in Chapter 5) is drawn in Fig. 8.8 as a dotted line. The solid line in Fig. 8.1 is analogous to the NCML.

Both the NCML or CML may be used to evaluate the performance of portfolios such as mutual funds, trust funds, and pension funds. Portfolios on the CML are Markowitz efficient and perfectly positively correlated. Portfolios between the NCML and the CML in Fig. 8.8 are more efficient than the average portfolio—but they are not Markowitz efficient. Portfolios lying below the NCML in Fig. 8.8 are not only inefficient, they are more inefficient than a naively selected portfolio.

A portfolio may not be Markowitz efficient because: (1) its securities have poor returns, or (2) the portfolio's risk is not being properly reduced, or (3) some combination of both. In the remainder of this chapter a portfolio evaluation model is outlined that will enable analysts to determine which of these weaknesses is the cause of any given inefficient portfolio. This model may also be used to determine if a portfolio is efficient owing to its ability to find securities that earn abnormally high returns although it is poorly diversified. That is, portfolios that are able to "pick winners" may be detected.

Portfolio Betas and the SML

Earlier in this chapter, it was shown that the returns on portfolio p, denoted r_p, may be regressed on the returns of an index—denoted r_I.

$$r_p = A + B(r_I) + e_p, \qquad (8.2)$$

where the e_p's are random errors and conform to the assumptions of regression analysis. This was called the portfolio's characteristic line.

Since portfolios' expected returns and beta coefficients are merely linear combinations of the expected returns and betas of the securities in the portfolio, portfolios' returns and beta coefficients should also be on the SML in equilibrium.[23] The SML is graphed in Fig. 8.9. The SML represents the linear relationship between a portfolio's or individual security's systematic risk and its expected return in equilibrium.

If a portfolio is doing an average job of finding undervalued securities, its $E(r)$ and B_p should plot on the SML. But, if a portfolio's $E(r)$ and B_p

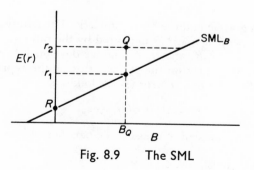

Fig. 8.9   The SML

---

[23] Friend and Blume show that the linearity of the SML is an oversimplification. Friend and Blume, "Measurement of Portfolio Performance under Uncertainty."

plot between the SML and the $E(r)$ axis, the portfolio is better than average at "picking winners." Conversely, a portfolio located below the SML is picking overvalued securities (that is, "losers").

If a portfolio like Q in Fig. 8.9 is investigated further, it may turn out to be inefficient. As shown in Fig. 8.8, portfolio Q is less efficient than average. In fact, portfolio Q would be at a point like Q' in Fig. 8.8 if it weren't so adept at picking winners that it raised its average return to point Q. It can be concluded that portfolio Q is good at picking winners but poor at diversification. All in all, Q is less efficient than average and far from being Markowitz efficient.

The Index of Total Portfolio Risk and B_p

The relationship between a portfolio's systematic risk (as measured by B_p) and its total risk (as measured by σ_p) may be more clearly seen in terms of Fig. 8.10. Figure 8.10 is like Fig. 8.9 except that an additional

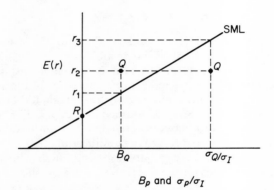

$$B_p \text{ and } \sigma_p/\sigma_I$$

Fig. 8.10   Tools for Evaluating Portfolio Performance

variable has been graphed on the horizontal axis. The additional variable is the *index of total portfolio risk*,[24] as measured by the ratio σ_p/σ_I.

Relationships between B_p and σ_p/σ_I may be developed from equations (8.2) and (8.3). The returns on the pth security can be represented as a linear function of the index's returns (r_I) as follows:

$$r_p = A + B(r_I) + e_p. \tag{8.2}$$

The pth security's variance of returns can be partitioned into two sources:

---

[24] The index of total portfolio risk is

$$\frac{\sigma_p}{\sigma_I} = \frac{\text{standard deviation of returns on the portfolio}}{\text{standard deviation of returns on the index}}.$$

$$\text{Var } (r_p) = \text{Var } (A + B_p r_I + e_p)$$
$$= \text{Var } (B_p r_I) + \text{Var } (e_p) = B_p{}^2 \, \text{Var } (r_I) + \text{Var } (e_p) \qquad (8.9)$$
$$= \text{systematic variance} + \text{unsystematic variance} = \text{total risk}.$$

If the pth security is efficient, its unsystematic variance must be zero by the definition of efficiency—namely, Var $(e_p) = 0$. Thus, equation (8.9) can be written as follows for an efficient asset.

$$\text{Var } (r_p) = B_p{}^2 \, \text{Var } (r_I) + 0.$$

The relation between B_p and the index of total portfolio risk for efficient portfolios is derived below from equation (8.9).

$$\text{Var } (r_p) = B_p{}^2 \, \text{Var } (r_I) + 0 \qquad \text{since Var } (e_p) = 0,$$

$$\frac{\text{Var } (r_p)}{\text{Var } (r_I)} = \frac{\sigma_p{}^2}{\sigma_I{}^2} = B_p{}^2, \text{ by dividing by Var } (r_I)$$

$$\frac{\sigma_p}{\sigma_I} = B_p.$$

The same relationship can be derived by examining the definition of the beta coefficient.

$$B_p = \frac{\text{Cov } (r_p, r_M)}{\sigma_M{}^2} = \frac{(r_{pM})(\sigma_p)(\sigma_M)}{\sigma_M{}^2} = \frac{\sigma_p}{\sigma_M},$$

since $r_{pM} = 1$ for all efficient portfolios. Thus, B_p is identical to the index of total portfolio risk for an efficient portfolio; they are in the same units. For an *inefficient* portfolio

$$\sqrt{\frac{\text{Var } (r_p)}{\text{Var } (r_I)}} = \sqrt{\frac{\text{Var } (B r_I) + \text{Var } (e_p)}{\text{Var } (r_I)}} > B_p \qquad \text{since Var } (e_p) > 0.$$

It was shown in Fig. 7.1 that naive diversification can reduce portfolio risk to the systematic level. At that point $\sigma_p = \sigma_I$ and the index of total portfolio risk equals unity. And, $B_p = 1$ when $\sigma_p = \sigma_I$. When risk is above the systematic level, $B_p > 1$ and $\sigma_p > \sigma_I$. Likewise, when $B_p < 1$, then $\sigma_p < \sigma_I$ for an efficient portfolio. The ratio σ_p/σ_I is in the same units as B_p, and σ_p/σ_I will equal B_p when the portfolio is efficient.

Referring to portfolio Q again, Fig. 8.10 shows that portfolio Q earned a higher return (r_2) than normal (r_1) for its level of systematic risk (B_q). This is just what Fig. 8.9 showed. But Fig. 8.10 also shows that for its level of total portfolio risk (σ_q/σ_I) portfolio Q had a return (r_2) below normal (r_3)—this is what Fig. 8.8 showed. These new devices allow a more discriminating evaluation of a portfolio's performance. What appeared to be an outstanding portfolio in Fig. 8.9 showed up very poorly in Fig. 8.8. Figure 8.10 resolved the seeming paradox by showing that portfolio Q "picked winners" but that it did not diversify well.

It was pointed out at the beginning of this section that a portfolio manager's objective need not necessarily be to operate an efficient portfolio. Thus, Markowitz efficient investors may want to buy shares in portfolio Q in an effort to reap the abnormally high return. But they must combine shares of Q with shares of other assets if they are going to minimize risk. To the extent that such multiple criteria are applicable, the more discriminating tools shown here are necessary for portfolio evaluation.

Appendix 8A

Mathematical Relations of Portfolio Performance Measures

Equation (8A.1) below represents the SML in terms of Sharpe's beta coefficient.

$$E(r_i) - R = b_i[E(r_M) - R]. \qquad (8A.1)$$

If all assets are correctly priced, all $(b_i, E(r_i))$ pairs fit equation (8A.1). To recognize explicitly that not all assets are in equilibrium, equation (8A.2) may be written:

$$E(r_i) - R = N_i + b_i[E(r_M) - R], \qquad (8A.2)$$

where N_i is a measure of disequilibrium for asset i. If $N_i = 0$, then asset i is correctly priced.

Treynor's one-parameter portfolio performance measure (T_i) is obtained by dividing both sides of (8A.2) by the beta coefficient.

$$\frac{E(r_i) - R}{b_i} = \frac{N_i}{b_i} + [E(r_M) - R] = T_i. \qquad (8A.3)$$

Equation (8A.3) may be written as (8A.4). Equation (8A.4) shows that Treynor's measure is a linear transformation of Jensen's measure (J_i), since $[E(r_M) - R]$ is a constant.

$$\frac{N_i}{b_i} = \frac{E(r_i) - R}{b_i} - [E(r_M) - R] = \frac{J_i}{b_i}. \qquad (8A.4)$$

Sharpe's portfolio performance index (S_i) may be derived from (8A.2) by noting that $b_i = [(r_{iM})(\sigma_i)(\sigma_M)]/\sigma_M^2$.

$$E(r_i) - R = N_i + \left[\frac{(r_{iM})(\sigma_i)(\sigma_M)}{\sigma_M{}^2}\right] \cdot [E(r_M) - R]. \qquad (8A.2')$$

For efficient portfolios $(r_{iM}) = 1.0$. Substituting for the correlation coefficient and dividing (8A.2') by σ_i yields Sharpe's portfolio measure (S_i).

$$\frac{E(r_i) - R}{\sigma_i} = \frac{N_i}{\sigma_i} + \frac{E(r_M) - R}{\sigma_M} = S_i. \qquad (8A.5)$$

Since $[E(r_M) - R]/\sigma_M$ is a constant, S_i is seen to be a transformation of Jensen's N_i. That is to say, $S_i = (N_i/\sigma_i) + \text{constant}$.

The models above are formulated in terms of ex ante quantities. Equation (8A.6) may be used in place of (8A.2) if these quantities are to be estimated with ex post data.

$$r_{it} - R_t = N_i + b_i[r_{Mt} - R_t] + e_{it}. \qquad (8A.6)$$

Assuming: $E(e_{it}) = 0$, cov $(e_{it}, r_{Mt}) = 0$, and homoscedasticity, regression analysis will generate minimum-variance, unbiased estimates of the equations above.[1]

---

[1] The authors are indebted to Marshall Blume and Irwin Friend, of the Wharton School, for the use of the material in this appendix.

"Beating the Market"

FROM time to time various authors have published books with such provocative titles as *How to Beat the Stock Market, Get Rich Quick, How to Make a Million in the Stock Market,* ad nauseum. The purpose of this chapter is to define what it means to "beat the market," to point out a few of the naiveties of such titles, to suggest how it may be possible to achieve an expected return that is above the market average using portfolio analysis, and to make it clear that portfolio analysis is not a procedure to "beat the market."

The discussion will begin by defining what it means to "beat the market." Second, some brief comments will be made about stock price movements. Technical analysis, fundamental security analysis, and the so-called random-walk theory[1] will be discussed. Third, the possibility of earning speculative profits by using Sharpe's beta coefficient will be discussed. Fourth, a method of finding "underpriced" assets will be examined. Fifth, it will be shown how an investor might be able to earn a rate of return above the average if the investment is held over a period long enough to be "representative." Finally, it will be concluded that none of these devices actually "beat the market." The securities markets tend to operate like an omniscient "invisible hand," setting the prices

---

[1] Technically, stock price movements are not a rigorously defined random walk. Rather, stock prices are a submartingale sequence.

and returns on each security at levels suppliers and demanders of capital deem appropriate for the risk associated with that security. Thus, only if the hopeful investor naively ignores the risk burden associated with each security or has a piece of "good luck" can he say he is "beating the market."

"Beating the Market" Defined

Naive investors sometimes believe they have beaten the market merely by leaving the market with more wealth than they had when they entered the market. This is like concluding that someone is a fast runner if he can run faster than a stationary object. Some advertisements by mutual funds and other investment funds capitalize on this naive conception of "beating the market." These advertisements show graphs or figures depicting the fund's growth in value over time. It never occurs to some naive investors that a positive return is a poor return if it could have easily been exceeded in numerous other investments without assuming more risk.

All things are relative. Before concluding that "X is a winner" or "X is big" or "X excels" in any way a standard of comparison is required. Professors Lawrence Fisher and James Lorie have compiled excellent data that are appropriate to use for comparing stock market performances.[2] Working at the University of Chicago's Center for Research in Security Prices, these men expended many man-years, many hours of computer running time, and many thousands of dollars to determine a standard for comparison of investments in the New York Stock Exchange. The study assumes an equal amount of money is invested in every NYSE stock on January 1 of each year from 1926 to 1965. Then, on December 31 of each year, this investment is liquidated and that year's rate of return is calculated. These calculations are performed for every year and every series of years in the interval. Different calculations are performed for different tax brackets, different assumptions about reinvesting the dividend income, and so on. The study thus indicates what different investors could expect to earn from various naive buy-and-hold strategies. For example, an investor who picked stocks on the NYSE randomly with, say, a dart, could expect to earn what the Lorie-Fisher study showed if he had neither better-than-average nor poorer-than-average luck in his random pickings.

The study shows, for instance, that the naive buy-and-hold strategy would have earned 28.3 percent before taxes and sales commissions if the dividends were reinvested over the year of 1965.[3] Thus, an investor who earned only 25 percent in 1965 could expect to have done better picking stocks on the NYSE with a dart. On the other hand, if the same strategy

---

[2] L. Fisher and J. Lorie, "Rates of Return on Investments in Common Stock: The Year-by-Year Record, 1926–1965," *Journal of Business*, vol. XXXIX, no. 1, pt. II (January 1966), pp. 291–316, © 1966 by the University of Chicago. All rights reserved.

[3] *Ibid.*, Table 1, pt. A, pp. 296–297.

lost only 25 percent from December 31, 1928, to December 31, 1932, the investor *beat* the NYSE average. The Lorie-Fisher data show a *negative* 30.5 percent return (compounded annually) before sales commissions and taxes for these four years.

In evaluating the merits of various investments, the Lorie-Fisher data may be used as a standard for comparison. But risk must also be considered. To truly *beat the market* an investor must either earn a higher rate of return than the market without assuming more risk than the market average or, conversely, find an investment that is less risky than the market average but earns as much rate of return.

The Behavior of Stock Prices

Very few professors, economists, or financiers would fit neatly into one of the three categories to be delineated below. Nevertheless, only the views from the three polar extremes of thinking on the behavior of stock prices will be presented in order to simplify the discussion.[4] The three main groups that have emerged in the literature about the behavior of stock prices are:

1. the chartists or technical analysts,
2. the fundamentalists, and
3. the random-walk theorists.

Technical Analysis

Technical analysts contend that all information about a stock is subsumed into the patterns traced out by its price and/or volume movements. These technicians believe that by studying charts of the movement of market indices and the securities prices they can see a handy summary of the firm's earning power, the "market psychology," and *all* other factors influencing that price.[5] Some chartists prefer to ignore the firms' annual reports, its prospectuses, and other financial data. A few are even opposed to reading the business news because it may bias their interpretation of the price patterns.[6]

The Dow theory is probably the most widely discussed technical approach. However, there are many other tools in the technician's box.

---

[4] Brealey has a readable discussion on stock price movements, which goes into more depth: R. A. Brealey, *An Introduction to Risk and Return from Common Stocks* (Cambridge, Mass.: The M.I.T. Press, 1969), chaps. 1–6.

[5] R. A. Levy, "Conceptual Foundations of Technical Analysis," *Financial Analysts Journal*, July-August 1966, pp. 83–89.

[6] A favorite book of many chartists is R. Edwards and Magee, *Technical Analysis of Stock Trends*, 1948. The interested reader may read this book to obtain more details.

The bar charts, point and figure charts, Elliot's wave principle, the confidence index, odd-lot statistics, short interest, breadth indexes, relative-strength measures, statistics on brokerage balances, and other theories are espoused by technicians.

The bar-chart technicians, for example, graph time (usually trading days) on the horizontal axis and price level and probably volume on the vertical axis. The next-to-the-last page of the *Wall Street Journal* carries current examples of bar charts of market averages, and the adjacent column entitled "Abreast of the Market" provides a smattering of chartist patter. Bar chartists are particularly fond of stocks that are at their alltime highs. To justify this preference the chartists reason that when a stock is selling below its previous high, investors who lost on the stock as it fell will sell out as it regains its previous peak. Supposedly, they do this in order to recover some or all of their previous losses. This supply of sales tends to offset price rises and a "resistance area" is said to exist. But, when the stock finally attains its previous high, no such resistance to further price rises remain. Then chartists say the stock has "clear sailing" ahead. Other chartist prognostications appear to lack even the dubious logic present in the resistance-area hypothesis. Patterns such as "heads and shoulders," "triangles," "flags," "pennants," and others appear to be virtually void of analytical content or logic.

Point and figure charts are even more mysterious and confusing to the nontechnician than bar charts. Point and figure purists believe that the formation of patterns can be obscured by using equal time intervals as one axis for their charts. Thus, point and figure chartists begin a new column only when a "significant" price reversal occurs. A significant reversal is usually defined as a price reversal larger than one dollar. Point and figure charts based on one-dollar reversals are called one-point reversal charts. Three- and five-point reversal charts are also used for the higher-priced securities. For each significant successive advance, the chartist makes the column one more x high. For reversals a new column is started at the existing price and extended in the opposite direction. If no significant change occurs for 15 trading days, the chart is not changed for three weeks. If, say, five significant declines occur, after previously advancing prices, then the column extends downward five x's below the price where the last reversal occurred.

Point and figure chartists search for patterns such as "inverse fulcrums," "delayed endings," "inverted V's," "inverse saucers," and even "heads and shoulders" (evidently, changing the nature of the graph doesn't distort the formation of "heads and shoulders"). They also measure the width of "congestion areas"—a series of short columns caused by a series of reversals. Then they predict how high or low the price should proceed during its next rise or fall by measuring the width of the congestion area and projecting this distance upward or downward to determine the new "price target." When questioned about the reasoning behind this procedure (or others too, for that matter) most chartists are not able to convey answers that satisfy analytical minds.[7] John W. Schulz, the writer of a chartist newsletter, has written the following about establishing "price targets."[8]

> On the question of where, in actual practice, measurements of lateral action should be taken, we are far from doctrinaire . . . we advocate the utmost flexibility because this tends to obviate the dangerous rigidity of preconceived notions.

Such "flexible" procedures also defy testing. Space does not permit a discussion of all the technical theories. The interested reader may find the other technical tools mentioned above explained elsewhere.[9]

In general, much of the technical analysis literature is characterized by such maddening words as "usually," "probably," and "perhaps"— and little rationale for the procedures is suggested. The phrase "well-recorded folklore" has been suggested as a description of this literature. The evidence published to date seems to indicate that technical analysis is not capable of beating the market. Furthermore, most technical analysis tools are not appropriate for portfolio management even if they performed as claimed. Most technical analysis tools are supposed to detect short-run price rises in advance. They ignore the long-run considerations essential to rational management.

Fundamental Security Analysis

Fundamental analysis is the antithesis of charting. Fundamental analysis is the activity typically carried on by traditional security analysts.[10] As the name implies, fundamentalists are engaged in investigating and interpreting pieces of fundamental financial, economic, and managerial data about the firms in whose securities they are interested. In their efforts to discern the true value of a firm, fundamental analysts typically calculate financial ratios.

Liquidity ratios are calculated to measure the firm's ability to pay its short-term creditors. Profitability ratios are used to tell if the firm is earning an acceptable level of profit. Leverage ratios measure the firm's

---

[7] R. A. Levy is one of the few technical analysts who has articulated the conceptual and theoretical foundations of his technique. The interested reader is directed to the following articles by Levy, which all appeared in *Financial Analysts Journal:* (1) "Conceptual Foundations of Technical Analysis," July–August 1966, pp. 83–89. (2) "Random Walks: Reality or Myth," November–December 1967, pp. 69–76. An article commenting on Levy's article follows directly in the same issue. (3) "Random Walks: Reality or Myth—Comment," by M. C. Jensen, *The Financial Analysts Journal*, November–December 1967, pp. 77–85. (4) "Random Walks: Reality or Myth—Reply," *The Financial Analysts Journal*, January–February 1968, pp. 129-132.

[8] Quote from Dan Seligman, "The Mystique of Point and Figure," *Fortune*, March 1962.

[9] J. B. Cohen and E. D. Zinbarg, *Investment Analysis and Portfolio Management* (Homewood, Ill.: Richard D. Irwin, Inc., 1967); Chapter 14 has a nice discussion of the main technical theories, and other references are given.

[10] *Ibid.*, especially Chapter 5.

involvement in debt financing. And activity ratios are used to measure the turnover of the various inventories of the firm and gauge how efficiently capital is being utilized.

Fundamental analysts also consider economic forecasts. Beginning with certain assumptions about the course of world events, a national economic forecast is made of GNP. Then activity in the various sectors of the economy is projected, as well as inflation, unemployment, and credit. This national forecast is then used to predict sales for the industry of the firm being analyzed. Finally, the firm's competitive position is analyzed, and sales, price, and cost prospects for the firm are determined.

Fundamental analysts may also interview the management of the firm being analyzed. Information about the firm's research and development activities, new products, possible mergers, and the like are gathered. A general management appraisal is made.

Weighing the information from the ratio analysis, the prospects for the company relative to its competitors, the future of its products, new developments, management ability, and so forth, the fundamental analyst then makes an estimate of the profit outlook for the firm. Based on the profit outlook, the fundamental analyst estimates the true value of the firm and its shares. Called the *intrinsic value*, this estimate is subjective.[11] But it is grounded in objective fundamental facts about the firm.

There are thousands of professional fundamental security analysts at work in the United States. They all perform more or less the sort of analysis described above. As a result of the efforts of this army of professional fundamental analysts, the price of any publicly listed and traded security represents the best estimate available at that moment of the intrinsic value of that security. In fact, the fundamental analysts do such a good job, there is no reason for anyone who is not a full-time professional to bother with fundamental analysis—it will not enable the investor to beat the market. This high degree of market efficiency is the basis for the random-walk hypothesis. That is,[12]

> . . . in a random-walk market the security analysis problem of the average investor is greatly simplified. If actual prices at any point in time are good estimates of intrinsic values, he need not be concerned with whether individual securities are over- or underpriced.

---

[11] Typically, fundamental analysts multiply the firm's earnings per share times the "appropriate" price-earnings ratio to obtain the estimated price per share. However, earnings per share is subject to the vagaries of the accounting procedure. And, the price-earnings ratio is determined very subjectively. Thus, the intrinsic value estimates are also quite subjective.

[12] E. Fama, "The Behavior of Stock Market Prices," p. 40. The conclusion that fundamental analysis is not necessary for some investors is applicable only in an efficient, intrinsic-value, random-walk market such as Fama describes on pp. 36–40. Fundamental analysis is practically the only tool in several common situations. For example, fundamental analysis is essential in pricing securities in the following situations: (1) a first public issue of securities by a firm; (2) buying into a small privately owned firm where the destiny of the company depends on one or a few personalities, products, or patents; and (3) in poorly regulated over-the-counter markets when trading in the securities of closely held firms.

Random-walk Theorists

Random-walk theorists believe that short-term price *changes* and the *changes* in the rates of return are basically like a series of random numbers that follow no predictable pattern. Like the pure fundamental analysts, random-walk theorists deny the validity of charting techniques. However, random-walk theorists do not deny the validity of fundamental analysis. Random-walk theorists believe the price of a security printed in the newspaper each day is an unbiased estimate of the true intrinsic value of the security. They don't believe the stock price is a random number; it represents the best estimate of the intrinsic value. Rather, the short-run *price changes* are random about the true intrinsic value. Thus, it is only the price changes that are random, rather than the general level of a security's price. Note that this position does not deny the existence of long-run trends in the market or in the prices of individual securities.

A number of hypotheses about the source of the random short-run price fluctuations exist—random errors in fundamental analyst's estimates, random information arrival, trading by chartists, and others. However, none of these hypotheses suggest that the stock prices themselves are random numbers. Only the price *changes* and concurrent *changes* in rates of return are hypothesized to be random.

Random-walk theorists have conducted statistical tests to determine if price changes are random. To date some impressive evidence has been compiled. As a result, the burden of proof has been shifted to the advocates of nonrandom price changes to demonstrate some predictable pattern in security prices.

Random-walk theorists do not believe stock price movements are perfectly statistically independent—only independent enough to deny stock-price chartists an opportunity to beat the market. "Patterns" emerge from time to time appearing to discredit the random-walk hypothesis. The student of stock price movements should be wary about concluding such findings discredit the random-walk hypothesis. The random-walk hypothesis is a *very negative* hypothesis which denies the existence of *any* patterns in successive stock price changes. Naive persons finding some pattern—although it is not predictable, never repeats itself, does not last long, and is not very different from random behavior—may too quickly claim to have discredited the random-walk hypothesis. Patterns will appear. Even in series of truly random numbers one may delineate what appears to be patterns. But these "patterns" are useless for prediction purposes. Rigorous analysis rather than subjective, intuitive interpretations should be used to disprove the random-walk hypothesis.

Rather than review the statistical tests that have been conducted to verify the hypothesis that price changes are random, the reader is referred to a few of the sources.[13] Here, the discussion is limited to some implications of the random-walk hypothesis.

Symbolically, a strong form of the random walk (RW) hypothesis is expressed by the following probability statement.

$$f(\Delta P_t \mid \Delta P_{t-k}, V_{t-k}, \Delta V_{t-k} \quad \text{for } k = 1, 2, \ldots, \infty) = f(\Delta P_t), \quad (9.1)$$

where ΔP_t is the price change in a given security at time t, ΔP_{t-k} is the price change in the given security k periods in the past, V_{t-k} is the market volume of the security k periods in the past, ΔV_{t-k} is the change in trading volume in the given security k periods in the past, and $k = 1, 2, 3, \ldots, \infty$. In probability language, this statement says that the conditional probability distribution equals the unconditional probability distribution. Intuitively, this means that if a random-walk (RW) theorist were about to purchase a stock and all historical prices and trading volume data for that stock were on the next page of a book in front of the RW theorist, he wouldn't bother to turn the page to see the historical prices before purchasing the stock.

The RW theory does not deny the presence of the upward trend in the prices and dividends of securities that Fisher and Lorie found.[14] Nor does the theory deny long-run trends in individual securities. The theory only asserts that the short-run price movements are not predictable. The RW hypothesis does not say that no chartist or speculator ever did or ever will make a speculative profit in the stock market. The theory does not deny that some investors will use "insider" information to their advantage or that some speculators will have runs of naive luck. The RW hypothesis merely asserts that in the long run, over thousands of transactions, speculators will not beat the market.

Sometimes the random-walk theory is asserted in the form shown in equation (9.2):

$$f(\Delta P_t \mid \Delta P_{t-1}, \Delta P_{t-2}, \ldots) = f(\Delta P_t). \quad (9.2)$$

Equation (9.2) says that the entire probability distribution of price changes for an asset is independent of the preceding sequence of price changes. More commonly, the random-walk theory is assumed only to

[13] Paul H. Cootner, ed., *The Random Character of Stock Market Prices*, (Cambridge, Mass.: M.I.T. Press, 1964); Benoit Mandelbrot, "The Variation in Certain Speculative Prices," *Journal of Business*, October 1963, pp. 394–419; E. F. Fama, "Efficient Capital Markets: a Review of Theory and Empirical work." *Journal of Finance*, May 1970, pp. 383–417.

[14] L. Fisher and Lorie, "Rates of Return on Investments in Common Stocks," *Journal of Business*, July 1968.

imply the martingale model[15] of equation (9.3), possibly with a few additional conditions relating to lack of serial correlation.

$$E(\Delta P_t \mid \Delta P_{t-1}, \Delta P_{t-2}, \ldots) = E(\Delta P_t).\tag{9.3}$$

Equation (9.3) only asserts that the expected price changes are not predictable. A model represented by equation (9.3) is less restrictive than a random-walk model. Technically, short-term stock price changes are a martingale, rather than a pure random walk.[16] The martingale model (9.3) does not require the complete independence of the pure random-walk model (9.1). And the distribution of price changes may depend on the distribution of the preceding price changes in a martingale. The main assertion of the martingale is that historical price data cannot be used to forecast future price changes. The stock prices themselves do not conform to a martingale. Prices are a submartingale, as shown in (9.4).

$$E(P_{t+1} \mid I_t) > P_t,\tag{9.4}$$

where I_t represents that information existing at time t which led to the formation of $E(P_{t+1})$. Various writers have defined I_t differently.[17]

The generation of random security price changes can occur through what Fama has called an *intrinsic-value-random-walk market*.[18] In this market professional security analysts constantly retest prices. No single investor is large enough (or cannot legally use this power if it exists) to manipulate the prices of securities. Information arrival is a random process. New information is analyzed and security prices adjust almost immediately (that is, no learning lags exist to cause trends). Each investor's expectations are independent enough of the others so that a wide variation of opinion may exist (for example, chartists and fundamentalists disagree). As a result of this type market, it is argued that security price changes are random, independent, and conform to a stable distribution; charting techniques will not net more than a naive buy-and-hold strategy using a dart for selection. The average investor need not bother with fundamental analysis because this task is adequately performed by an army of professionals who remove the profit potential for all but the most expert of their ranks. Market prices are excellent estimates of a stock's true intrinsic value and it is impossible to outguess short-run movements in security prices.

---

[15] William Feller, *An Introduction to Probability Theory and Its Applications*, vol. II (New York: John Wiley & Sons, Inc., 1966), pp. 189–193, 210–215, and others.

[16] P. A. Samuelson, "Proof that Properly Anticipated Prices Fluctuate Randomly," *Industrial Management Review*, vol. VI (Spring 1965), pp. 41–49.

[17] Benoit Mandelbrot, "Forecasts of Future Prices, Unbiased Markets, and Martingale Models," *Journal of Business*, vol. XXXIX, no. 1, pt. II (January 1966), pp. 242–255.

[18] Fama, "The Behavior of Stock Market Prices," p. 36.

In general, the random-walk devotees conclude that some security markets are near-perfect markets and investors should merely determine their preferences in $(E(r), \sigma)$ space and select a Markowitz efficient portfolio which fits those preferences.[19]

Speculative Profits

The random-walk hypothesis denies that speculative profits can be made using charts. However, if a speculator can accurately forecast the market indices, a speculative profit on short-run trading exceeding that available from a naive buy-and-hold strategy could be earned Of course, accurately forecasting the index is the difficult trick.[20] Assuming rates of return on the index (r_I) can be forecast accurately, equation (5.2), fit using historical data or intuition, provides a basic model to use for speculation.[21]

$$r_i = a_i + b_i(r_I) = E(r_i \,|\, r_I). \qquad (5.2)$$

Given a value for r_I, equation (5.2) yields a forecasted rate of return (r_i) on the ith security. Since it is not difficult to fit numerous regression lines like (5.2), numerous securities' returns may be forecasted with this model from a single forecast of r_I.

For successful speculation those securities which possess the following characteristics are best:

1. A high positive value for the regression coefficient (b_i) in equation (5.2) will indicate that the returns of the firm tend to be sensitive to changes in the index (r_I). These volatile securities will experience large capital gains and losses as r_I varies.
2. A high correlation coefficient between r_i and r_I will tend to indicate a dependable ability to predict. Of course, if the nature of the firm or any of the processes underlying the model have changed, then equation (5.2) fit with historical data must be adjusted.

Recalling equation (1.1), it is clear that if the ith firm's rate of return is predicted to make a large drop quickly, this change is usually due to capital losses (since the dividends do not typically vary).

$$r = \frac{\text{(capital gain or loss)} + \text{(dividend income)}}{\text{beginning price}} \qquad (1.1)$$

---

[19] *Ibid.*, p. 40.
[20] Jensen found that *none* of the 115 mutual funds he investigated showed any ability to forecast security prices sufficiently well to cover just their brokerage commissions associated with their buying and selling. M. C. Jensen, "The Performance of Mutual Funds in the Period 1945–1964," *Journal of Business*, May 1968, pp. 389–416.
[21] See Figs. 5.4 and 5.5 for a graph of equation (5.2).

Thus, when equation (5.2) above predicts a falling r, the speculator should sell short in the short run. Likewise, when the model predicts a sharp rise in r, capital gains are predicted, and the speculator should buy long in the short run. Research discussed in Chapter 3 has shown that the b_i's tend to be stationary over time—this increases the usefulness of this model. Of course, predicting r_I and the timing of its movements is the real problem. If r_I cannot be predicted accurately, investing in assets with high b_i's will be quite risky.

Using equation (5.2) to make speculative profit is not "beating the market." First of all, the investor's ability to predict r_I with sufficient accuracy to earn a significant profit is dubious. Second, securities with high b_i's have high expected returns to induce investors to buy such risky securities. Thus, if a speculative profit is made, it was earned. The speculator didn't get something for nothing: the high expected return is the result of rational supply and demand forces and is necessary to induce aggressive investors to bear the systematic risk associated with the high b_i's.[22]

Finding Underpriced Securities

Figure 5.8 is reproduced from Chapter 5 to supplement the following discussion. The previous discussion of the figure won't be repeated here. Capital market theory supplies an apparatus with which to reveal under- or overpriced securities. In Fig. 5.8, point L represents underpriced securities and point H represents a security whose price is too high. The prices and equilibrium returns of these securities should be revised until new points on the SML are attained.

Of course, Fig. 5.8 is based on simplifying assumptions. In reality, the SML is a fuzzy band, and only significant departure from the band

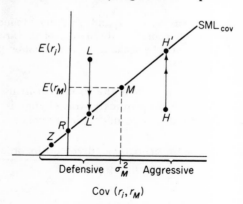

Fig. 5.8   The SML in [Cov, $E(r)$] Space

---

[22] A variation of this thesis is known as the "free-lunch theorem." The free-lunch theorem asserts the widely quoted cynicism that "there is no such thing as a free lunch." That is, you can't expect to get something for nothing.

may be expected to cause movement in the direction the theory indicates. Even when points far off the SML are discovered, the analyst should not invest without first investigating. Points off the SML may merely represent poor $E(r)$ and risk estimates. Fundamental analysis should be performed to determine why the apparent disequilibrium exists. Thus used, the capital market theory is a heuristic device which can be used to decrease the wasted expense of aimless fundamental analysis. Any profits earned will tend to correct the disequilibrium.

Using capital market theory as suggested above is not truly "beating the market." In large, efficient markets, such as the NYSE, the investor may expect that other competent fundamental analysts are also aware of any security he investigates. If a security's price remains in what appears a disequilibrium, the capital market analyst should first question his $E(r)$ and risk estimates. New information may not have been included in his estimates of $E(r)$ and risk. Even if a true disequilibrium security is found and a capital gain is obtained, the market hasn't been "beaten." The equilibrating mechanism of the market is what allowed the capital gain. And, taking these gains removes the profitable disequilibrium. Furthermore, most points far off of the SML may not be there owing to a true disequilibrium but rather owing to poor information. This method too is not without its costs of investigation and risks of error. A disequilibrium is easier to detect ex post than it is ex ante.

Above-Average Long-Run $E(r)$

The rationale for the CML and SML was reviewed earlier. Suffice it to say, expected return is a function of risk. Thus, if an investor buys a risky security or portfolio, high on the CML or SML, and holds it over a "representative period," he may expect to earn a higher-than-average rate of return.

Here again, the investor has not "beaten the market." Rather, the individual merely selected an investment to which the market mechanism assigned a high return in order to induce investors to buy it. To earn this high return the investor was exposed to more than average variability of return and the concurrent possibilities of loss of principle; that is, he did not get "something for nothing."

Conclusions About "Beating the Market"

Hopefully, by now the reader has developed some doubts as to whether the market can be easily "beaten." Apparently no simple rules, tricks, charts, or devices will earn a return above the average that could be earned merely by using a dart to select securities to be held. The market is quite a rational, efficient, responsive mechanism that usually cannot be outguessed, manipulated, waylaid, or "beaten" by any single individual.

Using econometric analysis, the equilibrium tendencies of the market may be discerned. With a knowledge of the market's equilibrium tendencies and the resulting opportunities, an investor may select an investment that concurs with his personal preferences for risk and return. Selecting such securities or portfolios in this manner will maximize the investor's expected utility. But, the market wasn't "beaten" by such action.

SECTION FOUR

OTHER ISSUES

```
101010101010101010101010101010101010101010101010101010101010101010101010101010101010
101010101010101010101010101010101010101010101010101010101010101010101010101010101010
1010101010101010101010101010101010101    10101    101010101010101010101010101010101010
1010101010101010101010101010101010101010    010    0101010101010101010101010101010101010
10101010101010101010101010101010101010101    1    10101010101010101010101010101010101010
1010101010101010101010101010101010101010    0101010101010101010101010101010101010101010
1010101010101010101010101010101010101010101    1010101010101010101010101010101010101010
1010101010101010101010101010101010101010    0101010101010101010101010101010101010101010
10101010101010101010101010101010101010101    1    10101010101010101010101010101010101010
1010101010101010101010101010101010101010    010    0101010101010101010101010101010101010
1010101010101010101010101010101010101    10101    101010101010101010101010101010101010
101010101010101010101010101010101010101010101010101010101010101010101010101010101010
101010101010101010101010101010101010101010101010101010101010101010101010101010101010
```

Some Elements of Utility Analysis

UTILITY analysis is an analysis of human decisions. The objective of the analysis is to rationalize decisions.

Utility measures the magnitude of desire or nonhedonistic satisfaction someone derives from something. Utility is an index of psychic gain or loss. If a person is faced with a decision, the alternative with the highest utility (that is, the most utiles) is the preferred choice. Thus, if the utility of a spanking is less than the utility of ice cream, the ice cream is preferred to the spanking. Symbolically, $U(\text{ice cream}) > U(\text{spanking})$.

Utility is derived from numerous things. For example, people derive utility from portfolios. Thus, choice among portfolios may be rationalized with utility analysis; that is the task of this chapter.

Basic Assumptions of Utility Analysis

Utility analysis is based on the following assumptions:[1]

1. People have consistent preferences. Thus, given a choice between A and B, a person can tell whether he prefers A to B, $U(A) > U(B)$; is indifferent between A and B, $U(A) = U(B)$; or prefers B to A, $U(B) > U(A)$.

---

[1] For the classic discussion of the basic assumptions see John von Neumann and Oskar Morgenstern, *Theory of Games and Economic Behavior* (Princeton, N.J.: Princeton University Press, 1953), 3rd ed., chap. 3. For a less rigorous discussion see W. J. Baumol's *Economic Theory and Operations Analysis*, 2nd ed. (Englewood Cliffs, N.J.: Prentice-Hall, Inc., 1965), chap. 22.

2. A person's choices are transitive. Thus, if a man preferred A to B and preferred B to C, then it follows directly that A is preferred to C.
3. Objects with equal utility are equally desirable. Symbolically, if $U(A) = U(D)$ and $U(A) > U(B)$, then $U(D) > U(B)$ follows directly, since A and D are desired equally.
4. If $U(A) > U(B)$ and $U(B) > U(C)$, then there is some risky lottery involving A and C that is as satisfying as B. Symbolically,

$$P(A) \cdot U(A) + P(C) \cdot U(C) = U(B)$$

for some values of $P(A)$ and $P(C)$, where $P(A)$ and $P(C)$ are the probabilities of A and C.
5. If someone has ranked objects of choice, then adding some irrelevant additional object to each of the already ranked alternative objects of choice should not change their ranking. Symbolically, if $U(A) > U(B)$, then $U(A) + U(E) > U(B) + U(E)$, where E does not affect A or B.
6. *The expected-utility maxim:* The utility of a risky object is equal to the expected utility of the possible outcomes. Symbolically, if an object has n possible outcomes, its expected utility is

$$E(U) = \sum_{i=1}^{n} P(O_i) \cdot U(O_i),$$

where O_i is the ith outcome and $P(O_i)$ is the probability of O_i.

The expected-utility maxim given in assumption 6 is the heart of utility analysis. The expected-utility maxim implies that people act so as to maximize their *expected utility* rather than so as to maximize the *utility of the expected outcome.*

Before the analysis of risky alternatives can be performed, the analyst must be supplied with a probability distribution of outcomes and utility function to give the utility of the outcomes. For example, in selecting among alternative portfolios a probability distribution of returns is needed for each portfolio. A utility function assigning utiles to each possible rate of return that the portfolios might earn is also required. Only after the utility function and the probability distributions are known may utility analysis proceed.

Numerical Example of Utility Analysis of Risky Assets

Consider three objects of choice—portfolios named, say, A, B, and C. Table 10.1 defines the probability distribution of returns for portfolios

Table 10.1

Portfolio	Portfolios' Outcomes and Their Probabilities					Portfolio Characteristics	
	Outcomes: -3%	0	3%	6%	9%	$E(r)$	σ_p
A	Probabilities:		.5	$+$		.5 $= 1.0$	$E(r_A) = 3\%$ $\sigma_A = 6.0\%$
B		.5	$+$	.5	$= 1.0$		$E(r_B) = 3\%$ $\sigma_B = 3.0\%$
C			1.0				$E(r_C) = 3\%$ $\sigma_C = 0$

A, B, and C. The three portfolios' characteristics are calculated using equations (2A.1′) and (2A.3′) as shown below.

$$E(r_A) = \sum_{i=1}^{2} w_i E(r_i) = (\tfrac{1}{2})(-.03) + (\tfrac{1}{2})(.09) = .03 = 3 \text{ percent,}$$

$$E(r_B) = (\tfrac{1}{2})(0) + (\tfrac{1}{2})(.06) = 3 \text{ percent,}$$

$$E(r_C) = (1.0)(.03) = 3 \text{ percent,}$$

$$\sigma_A = \sqrt{\sum p_i (r_i - E(r))^2} = \sqrt{(\tfrac{1}{2})(-.03 - .03)^2 + (\tfrac{1}{2})(.09 - .03)^2}$$
$$= \sqrt{.0036} = 6 \text{ percent,}$$

$$\sigma_B = \sqrt{(\tfrac{1}{2})(0 - .03)^2 + (\tfrac{1}{2})(.06 - .03)^2} = \sqrt{(\tfrac{1}{2})(.0009) + (\tfrac{1}{2})(.0009)}$$
$$= 3 \text{ percent,}$$

$$\sigma_C = \sqrt{(1)(.03 - .03)^2} = 0.$$

Figures 10.1, 10.2, and 10.3 below represent the utility functions for a risk-averting, risk-indifferent, and risk-seeking investor, respectively.[2] Since all three portfolios offer the same expected return of 3 percent, investors can rank the portfolios purely on the basis of risk.

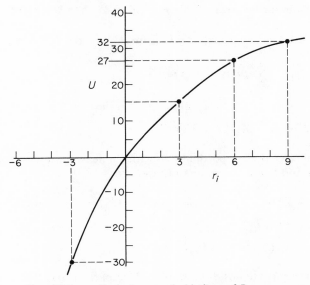

Fig. 10.1   Risk-Averter's Utility of Returns

[2] The utility functions in Figs. 10.1, 10.2, and 10.3 all pass through the origin merely for intuitive appeal. The preference rankings from a utility function are invariant under a positive monotone transformation of the function. Thus, the functions could have been drawn quite differently without changing the preference ranking.

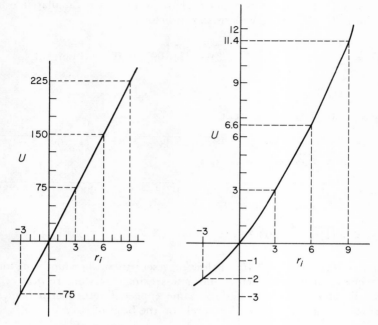

Fig. 10.2   Fig. 10.3
Risk-Indifferent Investor's Utility   Risk-Lover's Utility of Returns

The risk-averter's expected utility from A, B, and C is calculated below.

$$E[U(A)] = \sum_{i=1}^{2} P(O_i) \cdot U(O_i) = (\tfrac{1}{2})(32) + (\tfrac{1}{2})(-30) = 1 \text{ utile,}$$

$$E[U(B)] = (\tfrac{1}{2})(0) + (\tfrac{1}{2})(27) = 13.5 \text{ utiles,}$$

$$E[U(C)] = (1.0)(15) = 15 \text{ utiles.}$$

The risk-averter prefers portfolio C—with the least variance.
    The risk-indifferent investor's utilities are

$$E[U(A)] = (\tfrac{1}{2})(225) + (\tfrac{1}{2})(-75) = 75 \text{ utiles,}$$

$$E[U(B)] = (\tfrac{1}{2})(150) + (\tfrac{1}{2})(0) = 75 \text{ utiles,}$$

$$E[U(C)] = (1.0)(75) = 75 \text{ utiles.}$$

Since the three portfolios differ only with respect to risk, the risk-indifferent investor ranks all three portfolios equally. Symbolically,

$$E[U(A)] = E[U(B)] = E[U(C)].$$

The risk-lover's utility calculations follow.

$$E[U(A)] = (\tfrac{1}{2})(11.4) + (\tfrac{1}{2})(-2) = 4.7 \text{ utiles,}$$
$$E[U(B)] = (\tfrac{1}{2})(6.6) + (\tfrac{1}{2})(0) = 3.3 \text{ utiles,}$$
$$E[U(C)] = (1.0)(3) = 3 \text{ utiles.}$$

The risk-lover prefers the large variability of return exhibited by portfolio A.

The preceding numerical examples of the preference orderings of a risk-averting, risk-indifferent, and risk-loving investor show how choices can be rationalized in terms of expected utility. These examples also show how expected utility is a function of both expected return and risk in an uncertain world; that is, $E(U) = f[E(r), \sigma]$.

The Statistical Moments of a Probability Distribution

Before proceeding further, it is necessary to introduce some statistical language about probability distributions that will be needed later.

The *moments* of a probability distribution are statistical measures that define the distribution.[3] For a probability distribution of returns the *first moment about the origin* is defined as follows;

$$E(r) = \sum_{i=1}^{n} p_i r_i. \tag{2A.1'}$$

The first moment about the origin of a distribution is the same thing as its expected value or mean. The first moment about the origin is a measure of location or central tendency for the distribution.

Moments about the mean are different than *moments about the origin*. The first moment about the mean is defined as:

$$M_1 = \sum p_i (r_i - E(r)) = 0. \tag{10.1}$$

Of course, the first moment about the mean is always zero. It has no use in the analysis. However, higher-order moments about the mean are called statistical moments and are useful.

The second moment about the mean of a distribution of returns is defined below:

$$\sigma_i{}^2 = E(r_i - E(r))^2 = \sum p_i (r_i - E(r))^2. \tag{2A.2'}$$

---

[3] For a discussion of moments see J. E. Freund, *Mathematical Statistics* (Englewood Cliffs, N.J.: Prentice-Hall, Inc., 1962), chap. 4. For a more elementary discussion of moments and various approximations for moments, see S. B. Richmond, *Statistical Analysis*, 2nd ed. (New York: The Ronald Press Company, 1964), chap. 4. Of course, those probability distributions for which moments do not exist cannot be described by their moments (for example, Cauchy distribution).

Second statistical moment is a synonym for variance. The second statistical moment measures the distribution's dispersion or wideness.

Technically speaking, portfolio analysis assumes investor utility is derived from the first moment about the origin and the second moment about the mean—namely, $E(r)$ and σ^2. But usually this assumption is stated by merely saying "utility is a function of the first two moments," with the technical distinction concerning what type moments being understood.

The *third moment* of a distribution of returns is

$$M_3 = E(r - E(r))^3 = \sum p_i (r_i - E(r))^3. \qquad (10.2)$$

The third statistical moment measures the skewness or lopsidedness of the distribution—see Figs. 10.4, 10.5, and 10.6.[4] A distribution that is

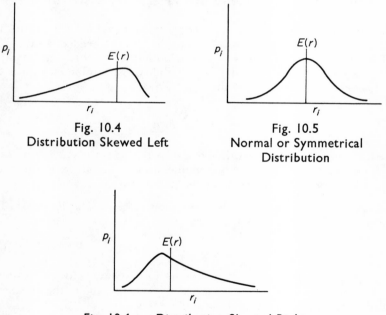

Fig. 10.4
Distribution Skewed Left

Fig. 10.5
Normal or Symmetrical
Distribution

Fig. 10.6   Distribution Skewed Right

skewed left will have a long left tail and a negative third moment. A normal or any symmetrical distribution will have a third moment of zero. Distributions that are skewed right will have positive third moments and a longer right tail.

---

[4] The third moment is sometimes normalized by dividing it by the standard deviation cubed. Skewness refers to this normalized third moment. However, in this book the authors will refer to the raw third moment as a measure of skewness.

The *fourth moment* (M_4) measures kurtosis or peakedness in a probability distribution.[5] For a probability distribution of returns the fourth moment is defined as

$$M_4 = E(r - E(r))^4 = \sum p_i(r_i - E(r))^4. \qquad (10.3)$$

Figure 10.7 shows a probability distribution of returns that is more peaked than normal. This is called a leptokurtic distribution. Figures 10.8 and 10.9 represent other forms of distributions. Although all three of these

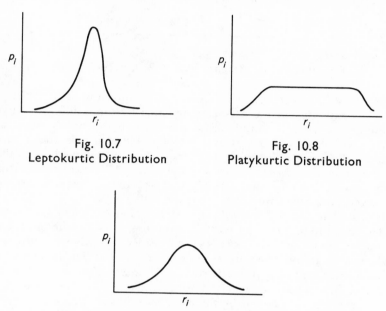

Fig. 10.7
Leptokurtic Distribution

Fig. 10.8
Platykurtic Distribution

Fig. 10.9   Normal or Mesokurtic Distribution

distributions may have first, second, and third moments that are identical, they would all have different fourth moments.

Portfolio Analysis is Based on Only the First Two Moments

One of the basic assumptions underlying portfolio analysis is that investors can base their decisions on only the first two statistical moments of the probability distribution of returns. Symbolically, $U = f(E(r), \sigma)$. Figure 10.10 is a graph of a utility map for a risk-averter's utility function

---

[5] Kurtosis refers to the normalized fourth moment rather than the raw fourth moment itself—technically speaking. However, the authors won't take space to develop and maintain this distinction in the text. See I. Kaplansky, "A Common Error Concerning Kurtosis," *American Statistical Association Journal*, vol. 40, for a discussion about whether the fourth moment actually measures peakedness.

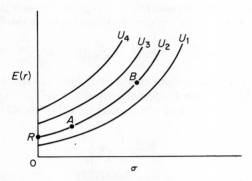

Fig. 10.10   Indifference Map in Risk-Return Space

of the form $U = f(E(r), \sigma_r)$. Every point on any given indifference curve is equally satisfying to the person represented by the indifference map. Indifference curves are utility isoquants. Where the utility isoquants intersect the $E(r)$ axis $\sigma = 0$ and the expected return is known with certainty. Thus, on indifference curve U_2 in Fig. 10.10 it can be seen that R is the *certainty equivalent* of risky assets A and B.[6] The assumption that utility is a function of only variability of return and expected return begs several important questions.

First, students of the *expected-utility maxim* often wonder how it can satisfactorily rationalize risky portfolio decisions based on the mean and variance of returns when it does not even consider the variance of utility— only expected utility. The numerical example given earlier should suffice to explain this confusing point. Portfolios A, B, and C all had 3 percent $E(r)$, and only their variances of returns differed. The lower expected utilities assigned to A and B by the risk-averse investor are due to their larger variability of returns. And, the larger expected utility the risk-lover associated with portfolio A reflects this investor's preference for risk. Thus, the two parameters—mean and variance of returns—are both reflected in expected utility. Thus, risk is incorporated into utility analysis without resort to the variance of utility. Of course, if the utility function in Fig. 10.1 had been drawn convex to the r_i axis (for a risk-lover), the preference ordering for the three portfolios would have been reversed. In either case, expected utility measures the effects of both $E(r)$ and σ.

A second question typically raised by students of the utility implications of portfolio analysis concerns the third and fourth moments of the probability distribution of returns. For example, imagine two portfolios with identical expected returns and variances but which have different third and fourth moments. In this situation the distribution most skewed to the left will have a larger probability of a large downward variation —perhaps even enough to bankrupt the portfolio. Or, if one of the

---

[6] Don E. Farrar, *The Investment Decision Under Uncertainty* (Englewood Cliffs, N.J.: Prentice-Hall, Inc., 1962), see sect. 1.4.

distributions is platykurtic, the range of possible returns is wider than a normal distribution. In this situation the student may ask if portfolio analysis will find both securities equally desirable. The answer is yes.

Portfolio-analysis techniques presented here ignore third and fourth moments. However, these are not flaws in the model for two reasons: (1) Statistical evidence shows that, historically, distributions of returns are symmetrical.[7] Thus, consideration of skewness is not necessary. (2) Unless investors' utility functions are of degree four, or higher, the fourth moment does not affect utility. Furthermore, there is some question about what the fourth moment actually measures.[8]

The assumption that utility is only a function of the first two moments begs a third question. How does the investor's level of wealth affect his utility of returns? That is, what consideration is given to the investor's wealth if utility is only a function of risk and return? The answer is that the investor's initial wealth affects the curvature of his utility of returns function.[9] Later in this chapter it is shown that the utility function for returns does imply certain things about the investor's utility of wealth.

Quadratic Utility Functions

A quadratic utility function implies certain things about the investor's utility. Consider the following quadratic utility function:

$$U = a + br - cr^2, \tag{10.5}$$

where a, b, and c are constants.

Finding the expectation of the quadratic utility function yields an insight.

$$
\begin{aligned}
E(U) &= E(a + br - cr^2) \\
&= a + bE(r) - cE(r^2) \\
&= a + bE(r) - c[E(r)]^2 - c(\sigma_r^2),
\end{aligned} \tag{10.5'}
$$

since $E(r^2) = [E(r)]^2 + \sigma_r^2$.[10] Equation (10.5') shows that the expected utility of a quadratic utility function is determined by the first two

[7] The following research has found distributions of returns to be symmetrical: E. Fama, "The Behavior of Stock Prices," *Journal of Business,* January 1965; M. G. Kendall, "The Analysis of Economic Time Series, I: Prices," *Journal of the Royal Statistical Society,* sec. A, 1953, pp. 11–25; M. F. M. Osborne, "Brownian Motion in the Stock Market," *Operations Research,* vol. VII, 1959, pp. 145–177; M. Blume, "Portfolio Theory: A Step Toward its Practical Application," *Journal of Business,* April 1970, pp. 163–164.

[8] I. Kaplansky, "A Common Error Concerning Kurtosis," op. cit.

[9] Jan Mossin, "Optimal Multiperiod Portfolio Policies," *Econometrica,* October 1966, pp. 215–218.

[10] See Theorem E2 in Appendix C for proof.

moments. Symbolically. $E[U(r)] = f[E(r), \sigma]$. Solving $(10.5')$ for σ^2 yields (10.6).

$$\sigma^2 = \left(\frac{a - E(U)}{c}\right) + \left(\frac{b}{c}\right)E(r) - E(r)^2$$

$$= \text{constant} + \left(\frac{b}{c}\right)E(r) - E(r)^2. \tag{10.6}$$

Equation (10.6) is quadratic in $[E(r), \sigma]$ space. Varying the constant generates an indifference map in $[E(r), \sigma]$ space. For an investor with diminishing utility (that is, a risk-averter), this indifference map must be composed of quadratic functions that are concave to the $E(r)$ axis as shown in Figs. 2.6, 2.7, and 2.8.[11] These figures show graphically that investors with diminishing quadratic utility functions will maximize their expected utility by selecting portfolios with the minimum risk for any given rate of return (that is, efficient portfolios). Thus, portfolio analysis can maximize expected utility for investors with quadratic utility functions. In fact, an investor with a utility of wealth (or returns) function of any form may maximize expected utility using portfolio analysis if the probability distribution of wealth (or returns) is a two-parameter distribution (for example, a normal distribution),[12] and marginal utility is diminishing.

Marginal Utility

The preceding graphical, arithmetic, and algebraic illustrations of utility analysis may be extended by using calculus. Consider the utility function

$$U = \sqrt{r} = r^{1/2}, \tag{10.7}$$

where U is the number of utiles and r is the rate of return. Figure 10.11 represents equation (10.7) graphically. Since the utility function is concave downward, the function is for a risk-averse investor.

Unless wealth becomes undesirable at some point, marginal utility should be a positive function of returns. That is, if $r_2 > r_1$, then $U(r_2) > U(r_1)$ for all r_i if more wealth is always desirable. Mathematically, this means the first derivative of the utility function, which measures marginal utility, should be positive. Specifically,

$$\frac{dU}{dr} = \frac{1}{2}(r)^{-1/2} > 0 \qquad \text{for all } r > 0.$$

---

[11] J. Tobin, "Liquidity Preference as Behavior Towards Risk," *Review of Economic Studies*, February 1968, pp. 65–86, especially sec. 3.

[12] M. K. Richter, "Cardinal Utility, Portfolio Selection, and Taxation," *Review of Economic Studies*, June 1960, pp. 152–166, esp. 153–154. Briefly, the proof goes as follows:

$$E[u(r)] = \int f(r|m_1, m_2) u(r) dr$$
$$= E[u(r)|m_1, m_2]$$

where $f(r|m_1, m_2)$ is a 2 parameter probability distribution of rates of return. Clearly, expected utility is a function of m_1 and m_2 as long as the distribution is completely described by two parameters.

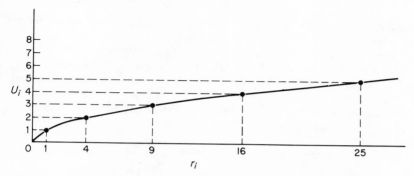

Fig. 10.11   Risk-Averter's Utility of Returns

Risk-aversion requires diminishing marginal utility. Mathematically, whether marginal utility is increasing or decreasing is measured by the second derivative, and should be negative for risk-aversion (that is, dim. marg. ut.):

$$\frac{d^2U}{dr^2} = \frac{-1}{4(\sqrt{r})^3} = \left(\frac{-1}{4}\right)r^{-3/2} < 0 \qquad \text{for all } r > 0.$$

Clearly, utility function (10.7) is for an investor who prefers more wealth to less wealth but is nevertheless a risk-averter since he experiences diminishing marginal utility.

A Problem with Quadratic Utility Functions

The marginal utility of returns of equation (10.5) is the change in utility with respect to a change in return as shown below.

$$\frac{du}{dr} = b - 2cr. \tag{10.8}$$

The marginal utility of additional returns is positive for $r < b/2c$. At $r = b/2c$ marginal utility is zero—this is where the utility curve in Fig.

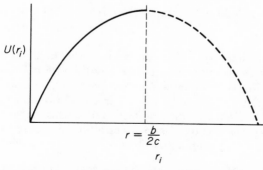

Fig. 10.12   Quadratic Utility of Returns Function

10.12 reaches a peak. And for returns above $b/2c$ the investor receives negative marginal utility—that is, returns above $b/2c$ are distasteful! In order to avoid that unlikely portion of the indifference map where returns have negative marginal utility (that is, the dotted portion of Fig. 10.12), the analysis must be restricted to returns below $b/2c$. To assume that a quadratic utility of returns function has an upper bound is not so unrealistic. After all, people are not observed paying large prices for a small chance at an infinitely large return.

Linear Transformations of Utility Functions

Utility functions may be multiplied by a positive constant and/or have a constant added or subtracted without changing their ranking of objects of choice[13]. This means, for example, that if every value on the vertical axis of Figs. 10.1, 10.2, and 10.3 underwent some positive linear transformation, the preference rankings of portfolios A, B, and C would be unchanged. Only the number of utiles assigned would be changed. However, since utility only has ordinal (not cardinal) significance, the preference ordering would not be changed by such transformations.

Among the important characteristics of utility functions that are invariant under a linear transformation of the function are:

1. the power or degree of the function,
2. the concavity, convexity, linearity, or other general shape of the graph of the function, and
3. the preference ranking resulting from the function.

Invariance under linear transformation is a property of utility functions that allows some interesting insights about the utility of wealth function.

Quadratic Utility of Wealth

It is possible to define the rate of return in terms of investor wealth (W) as follows:

$$r = \frac{W_T - W_0}{W_0} = \frac{\text{terminal price less purchase price}}{\text{purchase price}}, \quad (10.9)$$

where W_T = terminal wealth at the end of the holding period, and W_0 = beginning wealth, a constant. Defining the rate of return in terms of the random variable terminal wealth and the purchase price (which is a positive constant) results in a simple linear transformation from returns to additions to terminal wealth. The fact that returns are a linear transformation of terminal wealth (or vice versa) implies that the utility of wealth and utility of return functions have common characteristics.

---

[13] von Neumann and Morgenstern, *Theory of Games and Economic Behavior*, pp. 22–23.

Since the quadratic utility function for returns is simply a linear transformation of the investor's utility of wealth function, it follows that portfolio analysis makes implicit assumptions about investor's utility of wealth. Specifically, portfolio analysis implies that an investor's attitude toward risk can be well approximated by a utility function that is quadratic in the range of market values of wealth that exist at the terminal date for the portfolio.[14] Portfolio analysis enables investors to maximize the expected utility of terminal wealth for a quadratic utility of wealth function.

Of course, not all investors have quadratic utility of wealth functions. Various utility functions have been suggested which pose problems for portfolio analysis.[15] Some of these problems will be discussed in the last chapter of this book. For a more complete discussion of utility theory and portfolio analysis see Part IV of Markowitz's book.[16]

"One-Period" Expected Utility Maximization

As discussed earlier, portfolio analysis is a "one-period" model. The investor makes estimates of $E(r)$, σ and the covariances to correspond to the desired planning horizon, or holding period. The investor's utility is assumed to be solely a function of the portfolio's expected return and risk over the holding period for which these estimates were prepared. Thus, the investor's utility function corresponds only to the holding period or planning horizon for which the estimates were prepared.

In more comprehensive economic models, individuals are assumed to act so as to maximize their lifetime utility. Typically, the lifetime utility function is of the form

$$U = f(C_1, C_2, C_3, \ldots, C_T, W_T), \qquad (10.10)$$

where C_t is consumption in the tth period, T is the last period of the individual's life, and W_T is a bequest to heirs.

Fama has shown that under general conditions an investor maximizing a lifetime utility function like equation (10.10) will tend to behave *as if* he were maximizing a single period utility function of the form

---

[14] H. Markowitz, *Portfolio Selection* (New York: John Wiley & Sons, Inc., 1969), pp. 282–287.

[15] See F. D. Arditti, "Risk and the Required Rate of Return," *Journal of Finance*, March 1967, pp. 19–21, for development of an investor's utility function based on the first three moments of the distribution of returns the investor's wealth. Or, a Friedman-Savage utility curve is not amenable to portfolio analysis because it is not a quadratic function. See M. Friedman and L. Savage, "The Utility Analysis of Choices Involving Risk," *The Journal of Political Economy*, August 1948, pp. 279–304.

[16] Markowitz, *Portfolio Selection*, Part IV.

assumed in portfolio analysis—namely, $U = f(E(r), \sigma)$.[17] Thus, the "one-period" nature of the utility of returns function underlying portfolio analysis is consistent with rational, long-term behavior.

[17] E. Fama, "Multi-Period Consumption-Investment Decisions," Reports No. 6830 and 6831, University of Chicago: Center for Mathematical Studies in Business and Economics, June 1968. Also see Jan Mossin, "Optimal Multiperiod Portfolio Policies," *Journal of Business*, April 1968, pp. 215–229.

Technically, Fama showed an investor characterized by (10.10) will act as though he was maximizing (10.11).

$$U = f(C_t, W_{t+1}). \qquad (10.11)$$

If transactions costs are absent, Fama showed maximizing (10.11) will lead to selection of single-period efficient portfolios.

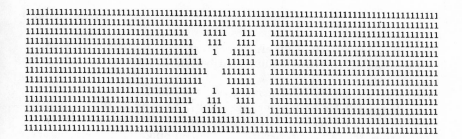

Some Unanswered Questions and Some Conclusions About Portfolio Analysis

THUS far the foundations underlying portfolio analysis have been explained, the portfolio-analysis model has been presented, and implications of portfolio analysis for capital market behavior, portfolio evaluation, and other areas have been pointed out. Where it was particularly convenient or appropriate, some implications of portfolio analysis were examined critically (for example, the simplifying assumptions of capital market theory). But some serious questions about the entire analysis have been passed over.

Some Unanswered Questions

The purpose of this chapter is to consider some criticisms and shortcomings of the preceding analysis. Some brief concluding remarks will also be made.

Are the First Two Moments Enough?

Portfolio analysis assumes investor utility is determined solely by the first two statistical moments of the probability distribution of returns.[1]

---

[1] See Chapter 10 for a discussion of statistical moments; specifically see equations (10.2), (10.3), and the accompanying discussion.

The third and fourth moments are ignored in the analysis—this is a simplification. Consider the probability distribution of returns for securities i and j shown in Fig. 11.1.

The expected return is 10 percent and the standard deviation of returns is 9 percent for both securities i and j. Security i's distribution is symmetrical and has a third statistical moment of zero. However, security j's returns are skewed right. Security j offers an opportunity for a higher return than is possible with security i. Security j's distribution is also more peaked than security i's, as indicated by the larger fourth statistical moment.

To an investor following a maximin policy (that is, maximize the minimum possible return), security j is more desirable than i. Likewise, a maximax policy (that is, maximize the maximum possible return) will result in a preference for j over i. In fact, many selection criteria would result in some preference for i over j or vice versa. Obviously, investors may well consider more than the first two moments when selecting securities. But, since portfolio analysis is based on only the first two moments of the distribution, securities i and j would be equally desirable candidates for inclusion in the portfolio (assuming their covariances were identical).

By ignoring higher-order moments, the portfolio-analysis model wastes information that might be used to increase investor satisfaction. Thus viewed, portfolio analysis is a heuristic technique. To what extent this oversimplification results in suboptimal (that is, less than the maximum possible investor utility) portfolios is not known. However most securities distributions of return seem to be symmetrical and will therefore possess third moments of zero. As a result, little if any information is lost by ignoring third moments. And, it is not entirely clear what fourth moments measure or how they affect investor utility.[2] Thus, most investors would probably ignore fourth moments even if they were known.

What Is the Best Portfolio Risk Surrogate?

Portfolio analysis is based on the assumption that the standard deviation (or variance) of returns is the proper surrogate for portfolio risk. No conclusive evidence supporting this hypothesis has been published.[3] Furthermore, numerous other intuitively pleasing measures of risk have been suggested.

---

[2] I. Kaplansky, "A Common Error Concerning Kurtosis," *American Statistical Association Journal*, vol. 40.

[3] Sharpe's data were very suggestive. See W. F. Sharpe, "Risk-Aversion in the Stock Market: Some Empirical Evidence," *Journal of Finance*, September 1965, pp. 416–422. The high correlation coefficient Sharpe found tends to support σ as a measure of risk. But much more work needs to be done with other risk surrogates.

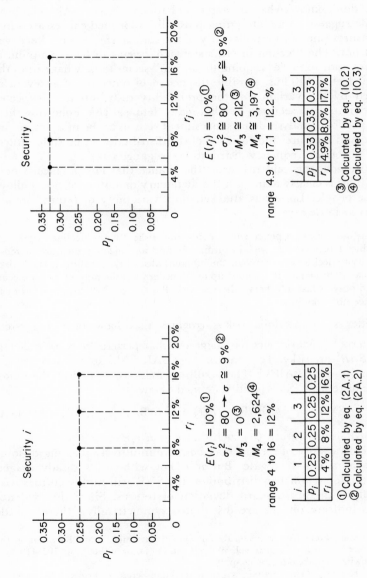

Fig. 11.1 Two Different Probability Distributions of Returns with Identical $E(r)$ and σ

Security i

$E(r_i) = 10\%$ [1]
$\sigma_i^2 = 80 \rightarrow \sigma \cong 9\%$ [2]
$M_3 = 0$ [3]
$M_4 = 2,624$ [4]

range 4 to 16 = 12%

i	1	2	3	4
p_i	0.25	0.25	0.25	0.25
r_i	4%	8%	12%	16%

[1] Calculated by eq. (2A.1)
[2] Calculated by eq. (2A.2)

Security j

$E(r_j) = 10\%$ [1]
$\sigma_j^2 \cong 80 \rightarrow \sigma \cong 9\%$ [2]
$M_3 \cong 212$ [3]
$M_4 \cong 3,197$ [4]

range 4.9 to 17.1 = 12.2%

j	1	2	3
p_j	0.33	0.33	0.33
r_j	4.9%	8.0%	17.1%

[3] Calculated by eq. (10.2)
[4] Calculated by eq. (10.3)

213

In an effort to determine how the public at large views *risk*, one of the authors has casually asked numerous unsophisticated people to define the term. A few respondents said, "The nervous feeling in my stomach when I don't know what is going to happen" is risk. Although this definition suggests some interesting possibilities for medical research into risk measures (measuring the acidity of the stomach?), it is not very well thought out. The "feeling in one's stomach" seems to be a symptom of risk. "Not knowing what is going to happen" seems to be what causes the "nervous feeling." Thus, possible dispersion of outcome of an event as measured by the variance of the probability distribution of expected outcomes implicitly seems to be what many define as risk. Following these people, portfolio analysis defines investment returns as the most important outcome and measures the variance of the distribution of possible returns (or of a historical frequency distribution) to gauge risk.

Some respondents said risk was "the chance that loss or harm would occur." This is clearly akin with the dictionary definition of risk. Following these people, Lorie has attacked the "variability of return" definition of risk. Lorie says:[4]

> It is not variation per se which constitutes risk; it is the decline in price or value. I believe that we will ultimately find an objective measure of sensitivity to decline which avoids the inherent absurdity of calling a stock risky because in the past it has gone up much faster than the market in some years and only as fast in others, whereas we call a security which never varies in price not risky at all.

Consider some portfolio risk surrogates that have been suggested.

Semi variance   Markowitz has suggested that perhaps only *below average returns (BAR)* are risky. To measure these BAR's Markowitz adopted the variance for only BAR's.[5] The resulting measure is called the semi-variance of returns (SVR) and is defined below.

$$\text{SVR} = \sum p_i(\text{BAR} - E(r))^2 = E(\text{BAR} - E(r))^2, \qquad (11.1)$$

where BAR is any return (r_i) such that $r_i < E(r_i)$.

The semivariance of returns may be more intuitively pleasing to some investors as a risk surrogate. But it is not without its disadvantages. First of all, for symmetric distributions the SVR will rank securities' risk identically with the standard deviation of returns. Since the evidence seems to indicate returns are distributed symmetrically,[6] there is little

---

[4] J. H. Lorie, "Some Comments on Recent Quantitative and Formal Research on the Stock Market," *Journal of Business*, vol. 39. no. 1, pt. II (January 1966), pp. 107–110.

[5] Markowitz, *Portfolio Selection*, chap. 9.

[6] M. G. Kendall, "The Analysis of Economic Time Series, I: Prices," *Journal of the Royal Statistical Society*, ser. A, 1953, pp. 11–25; M. F. M. Osborne, "Brownian Motion in the Stock Market," *Operations Research*, vol. VII, 1959, pp. 145–173; M. E. Blume, "Portfolio Theory: A Step Toward Its Practical Application," *Journal of Business*, April 1970, p. 163.

point in using the SVR. Second, the SVR is mathematically difficult to manipulate and computationally cumbersome.

Coefficient of variation   The coefficient of variation is the standard deviation divided by the mean or expected value. The coefficient of variation of returns (CVR) is defined as

$$\mathrm{CVR} = \frac{\sigma}{E(r)}. \tag{11.2}$$

The CVR is a "normalized" standard deviation of returns. It measures *relative* variability of returns. The CVR is intuitively appealing and has been used as a measure of financial risk.[7] However, it suffers from certain shortcomings.

One problem with the coefficient of variation occurs when the mean or expected value approaches zero. As the denominator of equation (11.2) approaches zero, the coefficient of variation approaches infinity. A second problem with the CVR arises because the standard deviation of returns is already a risk measure that allows portfolios and securities of different absolute value to be directly compared. Thus, the linear transformation to *relative* variability of returns (that is, the CVR) is not necessary. Third, the CVR has one property that reduces its intuitive appeal. Consider Fig. 11.2 where $E(r)$ and σ are graphed for securities i and j.

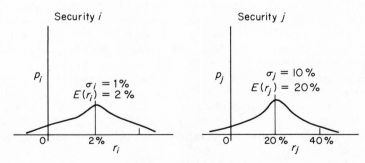

Fig. 11.2   Two Different Probability Distributions

Securities i and j have equal CVR's, namely, $\mathrm{CVR}_i = 2\%/1\% = 2 = 20\%/10\% = \mathrm{CVR}_j$. In fact, as shown in Fig. 11.3, any securities lying on the same ray from the origin in $(E(r), \sigma)$ space will have identical CVR's. Since Var (r) is already a risk measure void of distortions due to security price or portfolio size differences, it is disturbing that i and j have the same CVR when their σ's differ so much.

---

[7] Archer and D'Ambrosio, *Business Finance: Theory and Management* (New York: The Macmillan Co., 1966), chap. 5.

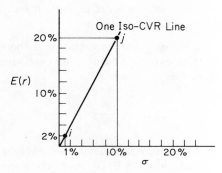

Fig. 11.3   Iso-CVR Graph

On the other hand, the coefficient of variation of dollar amounts rather than returns is more reasonable. Lawrence Fisher used the coefficient of variation of accounting profit as a measure of risk to predict risk premiums on bonds.[8] The coefficient of variation was found to have a significant positive relationship with risk premiums as used by Fisher.

Mean Absolute Deviation (MAD)   The mean absolute deviation of returns (MADR) is defined as

$$\text{MADR} = \sum p_i \, |r_i - E(r)|, \qquad (11.3)$$

where $|r_i - E(r)|$ is the absolute value of the ith returns deviation from $E(r)$. The MADR is in the same units as the basic random variable. The MADR enjoys many of the benefits of the standard deviation of returns plus some additional benefits. Since the standard deviation and the variance both square deviations from the mean, they give heavier weight to large deviations than to small ones. As a result, the standard deviation for samples erratically jumps around the true parameter for the underlying population whenever large deviations occur.

On the other hand, the MADR is always less than or equal to the standard deviation and is less erratic—that is, has less sampling error. As shown in Fig. 11.4, as the sample size (n) is increased from zero to 1200 and the statistics σ and MADR are recalculated for each n, they smooth down toward their true values for the underlying population.[9] But note that the MADR is less erratic and gives a more efficient estimate of its underlying parameter than σ. This quality of the MADR is especially desirable for random variables having much dispersion—as stock price movements and rates of return have.

---

[8] L. Fisher, "Determinants of Risk Premiums on Corporate Bonds," *Journal of Political Economy*, June 1959, pp. 217–237. Reprinted in Wu and Zakon, *Elements of Investments* (New York: Holt, Rinehart and Winston Inc., 1965), pp. 268–299.

[9] E. Fama, "The Behavior of Stock Prices," *Journal of Business*, January 1965, graph from p. 96.

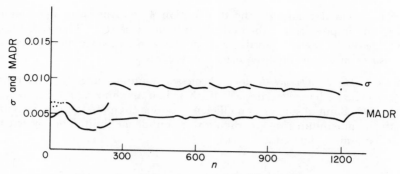

Fig. 11.4   Sequential σ's and MADR's for ATT as the Sample Increases

However, the MADR is not without its difficulties. The MADR is mathematically intractable in some applications (for example, calculus is difficult for variables within absolute-value signs). Furthermore, the MADR is computationally cumbersome.

Semi-interquartile deviation (SID)   The semi-interquartile deviation of returns (SIDR) is a possible risk measure. It is defined as

$$\text{SIDR} = \frac{Q_3 - Q_1}{2}, \tag{11.4}$$

where Q_3 is the third quartile and Q_1 is the first quartile. In words, the SIDR is equal to half the range encompassed by the central 50 percent of the distribution. The SID is a measure of dispersion useful with open-ended distributions, since it is not affected by extreme values.

The distribution drawn with the dotted line in Fig. 11.5 is an open-ended distribution. An open-ended distribution has an infinite variance. Of course, any finite sample will always possess a finite variance. But sample variances from open-ended distribution will be erratic estimates of the variance of the underlying population.

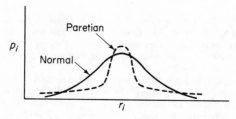

Fig. 11.5   Two Probability Distributions

Some evidence suggests the distribution of returns is an open-ended distribution possessing a theoretically infinite variance.[10] Thus, the SIDR may be one of the few possible risk measures to use, since most other risk measures suggested here require a finite variance.

Baumol's lower confidence limit   Professor Baumol suggested amending Markowitz's efficiency criteria.[11] Rather than maximizing returns at each risk level, Baumol suggests an efficient frontier composed of the portfolios with the maximum $E(r_p)$ at each lower confidence limit. The lower confidence limit is defined as L.

$$L = E(r_p) - k\sigma, \tag{11.5}$$

where k is the number of standard deviations below $E(r_p)$ required to yield the desired probability that the portfolio's returns will not fall beneath $E(r_p)$. L varies inversely with k. If returns are normally distributed, for $k = 2$ the probability of a portfolio return outside the range $E(r_p) \pm 2\sigma$ is .05. For example, consider two Markowitz efficient portfolios i and j, where $(E(r_i), \sigma_i) = (6\%, 2\%)$ and $(E(r_j), \sigma_j) = (20\%, 4\%)$. For $k = 2$, there is only a .025 probability that portfolio i's return will rise above 10 percent. And, there is also only a .025 probability that j's return will drop below 12 percent. Portfolio j offers higher expected returns. And, portfolio j has a lower limit on returns that is above i's top limit at the .025 confidence level. Thus, although $\sigma_j < \sigma_i$, Baumol says i is more risky since the chance of low returns is greater with i than with j. Baumol's criterion results in an efficient frontier which is a subset of the Markowitz efficient frontier. Baumol's L is merely an amendment to Markowitz's risk surrogate.

Sharpe's beta coefficient   It has been shown that individual assets and portfolio's returns are linearly related to some index of economic activity.[12] Sharpe's beta coefficient, the regression slope coefficient in equation (11.6), is a measure of this relation.

$$r_p = a + b(r_I) + e, \tag{11.6}$$

where r_p is the return on asset p, r_I is the rate of change in (or rate of return on) some market index (for example, $S \& P$ Composite), and a and b are regression coefficients.

---

[10] Fama, "The Behavior of Stock Prices," *Journal of Business*, January 1965, p. 49.

[11] See Appendix 4A, or see W. J. Baumol, "An Expected Gain-Confidence Limit Criterion for Portfolio Selection," *Management Science*, October 1963, pp. 174–182. Reprinted in E. G. Fredrickson's *Frontiers of Investment Analysis* (Scranton, Pa.: International Textbook Co., 1966), pp. 382–391.

[12] J. L. Treynor, "How to Rate Management of Investment Funds," *Harvard Business Review*, January–February 1965, pp. 63–75. W. Sharpe, "A Simplified Model for Portfolio Analysis," *Management Science*, January 1963, pp. 277–293 and "Capital Asset Prices: A Theory of Market Equilibrium Under Conditions of Risk," *Journal of Finance* September 1964, pp. 425–442.

The b is a measure of the volatility of the portfolio or other asset. The beta is an index of the systematic risk—that portion of risk which cannot be reduced via naive diversification.

The beta is defined as

$$b_p = \text{Cov } (r_p, r_I)/\sigma_I{}^2,$$

where cov (r_p, r_I) is the covariance of returns for the pth asset and the market index; and $\sigma_I{}^2$ is the variance of returns on the index. Since the denominator $\sigma_I{}^2$ is a constant for all assets' betas, this means cov (r_p, r_I) is an index of systematic risk which is equivalent to the beta.

The portfolio beta is the weighted average of the Sharpe's beta coefficients for all securities in the portfolio. The SML shows that assets' returns are proportional to their b_i's, as shown in Fig. 11.6. The beta

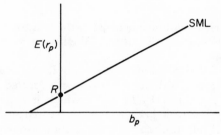

Fig. 11.6   The SML

coefficient is an intuitively pleasing surrogate for portfolio risk, as well as other assets' risk.

Adjusted variance   Professors Alberts and Segall have suggested a risk measure based on dollar amounts which are normalized to remove the scale factor.[13] Alberts called the measure the *adjusted variance*. In portfolio applications, the first step in calculating the adjusted variance for a security is to make terminal wealth (W_T) estimates. For a common stock, terminal wealth is defined as the sum of dividend income over some holding period (D) plus the market price at the end of the holding period (P_T). Figure 11.7 is a probability distribution for terminal wealth (W_T) and $E(W_T)$ is the mean of the distribution. Superficially, it seems that the variance of W_T might be a good risk measure. However, it is not. For two securities that are identical except their values differ by the scale factor a, the variance of the higher-priced security's variance will be a^2 times the

---

[13] W. Alberts and J. Segall, *The Corporate Merger* (University of Chicago Press, 1966), p. 263. Also see G. D. Quirin, *The Capital Expenditure Decision* (Homewood, Ill.: Richard D. Irwin, Inc., 1967), p. 217. As applied to a distribution of returns, Modigliani and Miller also suggest this risk measure. "The Cost of Capital, Corporation Finance, and the Theory of Investment," *American Economic Review*, June 1958, p. 266.

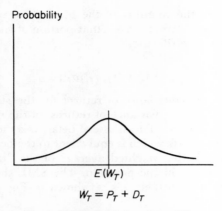

Fig. 11.7   Probability Distribution of Terminal Wealth

smaller-priced security's variance because of the relationship Var $(aW) = a^2 \text{Var} (W)$. Or, the standard deviation of the higher-priced asset will be a times the smaller one.

To remove this scale factor due to differences in securities' dollar values, the random variable W_T is divided by its own expected value to obtain the basic random variable $[W_T/E(W_T)]$, which is called "relative terminal wealth" here. The ratio $[W_T/E(W_T)]$ is treated as the basic random variable. The resulting probability distribution, shown in Fig. 11.8, shows that by dividing each of the W_T's in Fig. 11.7 by their expected value a normalized distribution with mean of one and a variance of Var $[W_T/E(W_T)]$ is obtained. This variance of the relative terminal values,

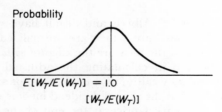

Fig. 11.8   Probability Distribution of Relative Terminal
Wealth

Var $[W_T/E(W_T)]$, is Alberts' adjusted variance. This risk measure is also quite useful in dynamic capital market theory applications—which will be discussed later. As defined here, the adjusted variance is another possible measure of portfolio risk. Its primary advantages are: (1) that it is independent of the initial price of a security—this has interesting implications for a dynamic theory since the risk-class does not change every time the beginning price of a security changes, and, (2) since the measure deals in cashflows it is amenable for capital budgeting.

Numerous surrogates for portfolio risk   Although the preceding list of possible surrogates for portfolio risk is certainly not exhaustive, it is suggestive.[14] Portfolio analysis and capital market theory are cast in terms of expectations about the future. It is impossible to measure expectations. Thus, it is impossible to accept or reject any given risk surrogate by empirical testing. Each different risk surrogate has its particular advantages and disadvantages. And each risk surrogate conceivably would be amenable to the general approach of Markowitz; each would generate a different efficient set; and each would imply a different set of capital asset prices. The particular analysis presented in the preceding chapters is just one particular form that would result from the general two-parameter model of Markowitz.

Infinite Variance

Mandelbrot, Fama, and others have suggested that stock price movements and rates of return are not distributed normally, as had long been thought.[15] Instead, evidence has been compiled showing successive changes in a stock's rates of return over time are independently and identically distributed random variables conforming to a stable Paretian distribution.

The particular form of the Paretian distribution that describes these random variables has parameters such that the tails of the distribution never touch the horizontal axis of the probability distribution. This implies that stock price movements (ΔP's) and rates of return are from a population with an infinite variance. Figure 11.5 compares the particular form of the Paretian distribution that the data suggest with a normal distribution having the same expected value. The normal distribution's tails asymptotically approach the horizontal axis, and the normal distribution has a finite variance.

If price changes form a Paretian distribution, problems are presented. The infinite variance of the distribution has serious implications for the analysis presented in the preceding chapters. Of course, a finite sample of price changes or rates of return will have a finite variance. But if these random variables are drawn from an underlying population with an infinite variance, certain statistics upon which portfolio analysis is based are not stationary from sample to sample.

Students of classical statistics study desirable properties that various statistics such as the mean and variance may or may not possess.[16]

---

[14] Markowitz, *Portfolio Selection*, pp. 286–297.

[15] See, for example: Benoit Mandelbrot, "The Variation of Certain Speculative Prices," *Journal of Business*, October 1963, pp. 394–419. E. Fama, "The Behavior of Stock Market Prices," *Journal of Business*, January 1965, pp. 34–105. W. Breen and J. Savage, "Portfolio Distributions and Tests of Security Selection Models," *Journal of Finance*, December 1968, pp. 805–819.

[16] See T. Yamane, *Statistics: An Introductory Analysis*, 2nd ed. (New York: Harper & Row, Publishers, 1967), chap. 10, for a nonrigorous discussion of desirable properties of estimates of parameters (that is, statistics).

Efficiency is one desirable property for a statistic. The most efficient statistic is the one that is the least erratic estimate of the population parameter being estimated. An inefficient statistic used to estimate the unknown parameter will be less dependable and from sample to sample it will jump around the true value more than an efficient statistic.

If the changes in prices and returns conform to a Paretian distribution with characteristic exponent less than two, as the Mandelbrot-Fama data suggest, the Markowitz full-covariance model and Sharpe's simplified model for portfolio analysis will not produce efficient results.[17] The Markowitz model uses securities' expected returns, variances and covariances of returns as inputs. These statistics will not be stationary in a Paretian market. Likewise, the simplified models of Sharpe and others are based on least-squares regression techniques. One requirement for regression parameters to be efficient is that the random variables possess finite variances.[18] If this assumption is violated, the least-squares regression parameters are erratic too. Thus, both the full-covariance model and the simplified models will tend to produce erratic, undependable solutions in a Paretian market.

If stock markets do generate price changes and returns distributed according to a Paretian distribution as the Mandelbrot-Fama data indicate, all is not lost. Fama has made an impressive first step toward restating the simplified model in such a manner that it is not so sensitive to random variables from a stable Paretian distribution.[19] And, with the model he develops, Fama shows that Markowitz diversification is still possible in a stable Paretian market where the distribution has a characteristic exponent within the range he estimates (Fama's estimates average from 1.7 to 1.95).[20]

Additional changes in the analysis may be made that will alleviate problems caused by the infinite variance. For example, defining risk in terms of the mean absolute deviation or semi-interquartile deviation of returns will stabilize the risk estimates. And, least absolute value of errors regression techniques may be used to develop the inputs for Fama's or Sharpe's simplified model. In any event, the model still has much value for normative economics even if its value in positive applications is diminished by the existence of Paretian markets.[21] A sampling theory for Paretian distributions is developing so that the degree of sampling error

[17] E. Fama, "The Behavior of Stock Market Prices," *Journal of Business*, January 1965, pp. 94–98.

[18] The Gauss-Markov theorem.

[19] E. Fama, "Portfolio Analysis in a Stable Paretian Market," *Management Science*, January 1965, pp. 404–419.

[20] Fama, "The Behavior of Stock-Market Prices," p. 67.

[21] For example, Tobin's conclusions about liquidity preference would still be accurate even if changes in prices and rates of return depart from normality. J. Tobin, "Liquidity Preference as Behavior Towards Risk," *Review of Economic Studies*, February 1958, pp. 65–86.

may be estimated accurately.[22] However, it is not universally accepted that stock price changes conform to a Paretian distribution.[23]

Capital Market Theory Static

Capital market theory is a static theory. The capital market line (CML) assumes risk is proportional to "variability of portfolio returns." Since

$$r_t = \left[\frac{(P_{t+1} - P_t) + D_{t+1}}{P_t} \right],$$

risk can be defined as follows:

$$\text{Var}(r) = \text{Var}\left[\frac{(P_{t+1} - P_t) + D_{t+1}}{P_t} \right] = \left(\frac{1}{P_t} \right)^2 \text{Var}(P_{t+1} + D_{t+1}), \quad (11.7)$$

where P_{t+1} is the beginning of the period market price for period $t + 1$, P_t is the tth period's beginning price—a constant for period t—and D_{t+1} are dividends earned during period t and received at the beginning of period $t + 1$.

The security market line assumes the risk of an individual security is "covariability of return" as measured by the covariance.

$$\text{Cov}(r_i, r_j) = E\{[r_i - E(r)][r_j - E(r)]\}$$

$$= \left(\frac{1}{P_{ti}} \right) \cdot \left(\frac{1}{P_{tj}} \right) \cdot E([(P_{t+1} + D_{t+1}) - E(P_{t+1} + D_{t+1})]_i$$

$$\cdot [(P_{t+1} + D_{t+1}) - E(P_{t+1} + D_{t+1})]_j). \quad (11.8)$$

Note that P_t, beginning price, is in both these risk surrogates. This is what constrains capital market theory to be a static model. Consider Figs. 11.9 and 11.10.

Assume an underpriced security such as U in Figs. 11.9 and 11.10 is observed over sequential time increments. Capital market theory says U is undervalued and will be in equilibrium at point E after a temporary disequilibrium during which its price will rise. But when it is actually observed, each time period it will have a different beginning of period

[22] E. Fama and R. Roll, "Some Properties of Symmetric Stable Distributions," *Journal of the American Statistical Association*, September 1968.

[23] ". . . there is no evidence of the long tails which Mandelbrot's hypothesis would predict . . . . No evidence was found in any of [the] series that the process by which they were generated behaved as if it possessed an infinite variance." M. D. Godfrey, C. W. J. Granger, and O. Morgenstern, "The Random Walk Hypothesis of Stock Market Behavior," *Kyklos*, vol. 17 (1964).

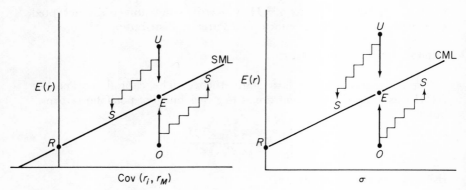

Fig. 11.9
The SML in a Dynamic Context

Fig. 11.10
The CML in a Dynamic Context

price (P_t). Since P_t will change each period as the security moves toward equilibrium, *the risk class of the security will also change each period*, although the distribution of P_{t+1} and D_{t+1} may not have changed. Thus, the time path for the security will follow the path like the ones ending at point S if this static theory is used for dynamic analysis. A symmetrical but opposite argument will show why an overvalued security such as O in Figs. 11.9 and 11.10 will increase its risk class as it moves toward equilibrium.

What is needed is a dynamic theory so that the market can be observed as it equilibrates. In a dynamic theory the securities would follow the time path to points like E rather than to points like S in Figs. 11.9 and 11.10. That is, the risk class of the security would be independent of the initial condition P_t.[24]

Until the model is adapted to dynamic analysis, capital market theory will not be able to deal with questions about the time paths of the variables. For example, consider the time derivative

$$\frac{dP}{dt} = f(D - S), \qquad (11.9)$$

where dP/dt is the change in price per time increment for some security, f is some positive function that could be estimated with difference equations; D is demand for a security and S is supply, so $(D - S)$ represents excess demand for the security. Estimates of such time derivatives might be useful in estimating security prices if the security's risk class determined f and would not change arbitrarily as the security moved toward equilibrium.[25]

---

[24] Sharpe refers to this problem in his footnote 17. William Sharpe, "Capital Asset Price: A Theory of Market Equilibrium Under Conditions of Risk," *Journal of Finance*, September 1964, pp. 425–442.

[25] P. A. Samuelson, *Foundations of Economic Analysis* (New York: Atheneum Publishers, 1965), chaps. X and XI.

Of course, many economic models are models that can only be used for comparative statics. Much rich analysis has come from some of these static models. However, the model would be more interesting if it were amenable to dynamics.

Problems with Utility

It can be shown that portfolio analysis is appropriate if the utility functions for rates of return and wealth are quadratic. Sometimes it is suggested that the utility of returns function for a risk-averter assumes the quadratic form $U = A + br - cr^2$. Such a quadratic utility-of-returns function is graphed in Fig. 11.12. Since the utility-of-wealth function is a linear transformation of the utility-of-returns function, it too is quadratic.

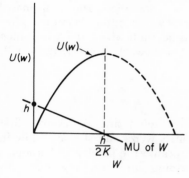

Fig. 11.11
Quadratic Utility of Wealth
Function

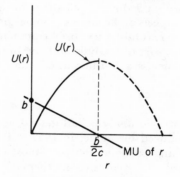

Fig. 11.12
Quadratic Utility of Returns
Function

As graphed in Fig. 11.11, the utility-of-wealth function for a risk-averter has the form $U = g + hW - kW^2$.

The marginal-utility (MU) functions are $dU/dr = b - 2cr$ for returns and $dU/dW = h - 2kW$ for wealth. These marginal utility functions imply marginal utility is negative for $r > b/2C$ and for $W > h/2K$. This means investors would dislike a rate of return larger than $b/2C$ or would dislike more wealth than $h/2K$. To avoid this absurdity, utility theoreticians require that the analysis be restricted to the range where $dU/dr > 0$ and $dU/dW > 0$. This assumption means that only the portion of the utility function with nonnegative marginal utility is relevant for the analysis.

These problems involving negative marginal utility and restrictions on the utility function are the result of unnecessarily assuming a quadratic utility function. Portfolio analysis can maximize expected utility for any form of utility function that has positive but diminishing marginal utility if the distribution of returns is a two-parameter distribution. This could occur, for example, if the probability distributions of the assets' returns are any form that possesses a finite variance—then the central limit theorem assures that the portfolio returns are a two-parameter normal distribution. Or, if the investor's utility function is well approximated by a quadratic function (over the range where its marginal utility is a nonnegative), portfolio analysis can "approximately maximize" the investor's expected utility. In any event, portfolio analysis itself does not presuppose restricted utility functions, negative marginal utility over some ranges, or any other perverse types of utility functions.

Some Conclusions

Not enough work has been done with portfolio analysis, capital market theory, and their implications to draw firm conclusions about all phases and aspects of the analysis. Some conclusions were mentioned in the earlier chapters. Only a few brief comments will be made about the acceptance of this sort of analysis and the future for such work. Some readers will, of course, reach different conclusions.

Acceptance

Portfolio analysis had gained acceptance slowly since Markowitz first introduced his model in 1952.[26] Universities were, and still are, slow in teaching portfolio analysis—most likely because the faculty and students lacked the requisite mathematical training and teaching materials (such as computer facilities). Financial managers were—and still are—slow in pressing the analysis into use, probably because they too lacked the necessary training.[27] And, apparently because managers were unaware how unsatisfactorily their traditional portfolio-management techniques were performing, they were satisfied with traditional techniques.

Now acceptance of the model seems to be accelerating—albeit slowly. Many business schools are requiring more tool courses and analytical courses of their students—this facilitates understanding of the model. The first generation of professors trained in the model are entering business classrooms as some finance departments reorient themselves toward econometrics. Portfolio managers are becoming dissatisfied with their performance as they and their investors read the recent reports evaluating the

---

[26] H. Markowitz, "Portfolio Selection," *Journal of Finance,* March 1952 pp. 77-91.

[27] Financial managers' lack of interest in portfolio analysis is most assuredly not due to lack of funds to spend or lack of curiosity. The authors have seen managers of large, well-known portfolios spend tens of thousands of dollars to investigate the possibility of a correlation between the stock market and physical phenomena, such as barometer readings, the ability of charting to predict asset prices, ad nauseam.

performance of various investment funds.[28] As a result, some college recruiters are beginning to ask for econometrically oriented finance graduates. Acceptance of the analysis should increase in the future—both in the classroom and in practical applications.

Future Research

For financial researchers, portfolio analysis is probably the most promising model since present-value theory. As the capital budgeting models are expanded to consider risk and the interdependence of assets is recognized, the variance-covariance matrix may furnish the engine of analysis to consider these interrelationships. Many researchers foresee a merging of capital budgeting and portfolio analysis into a more general model for capital allocation.[29] Admittedly, it does seem paradoxical to use one model (capital budgeting) to allocate capital to physical assets while using another model (portfolio analysis) to allocate capital among financial assets. Certainly the underlying principles of optimal capital allocation must not differ depending on the type of asset considered.

Portfolio analysis has fostered a new approach to valuation theory and the cost of capital—capital market theory.[30] Capital market theory provides a macro-model that rationalizes the determination of security prices. And the cost-of-capital dilemma will be solved only when a satisfactory security-valuation model is developed. Furthermore, it seems more logical to approach cost-of-capital determination externally to the firm through valuation theory before stepping inside the firm to see how the financial decision variables such as leverage affect the cost of capital.

Capital market theory is also having an impact upon thinking about the term structure of interest rates. Meiselman's error learning model may be rationalized in terms of Sharpe's beta coefficient.[31] There appear to be many valuable discoveries awaiting the analytical researcher.

---

[28] See Chapter 8.

[29] J. Mossin, "Security Pricing and Investment Criteria in Competitive Markets," *American Economic Review*, vol. LIX, no. 5 (December 1969), pp. 749–756.

[30] R. S. Hamada, "Portfolio Analysis, Market Equilibrium and Corporation Finance," *Journal of Finance*, March 1969, pp. 13–33.

[31] Richard Roll, *The Efficient Market Model Applied to U.S. Treasury Bill Rates*, University of Chicago doctoral dissertation, 1968, in monograph form from Basic Books, Inc., 1970. David Meiselman, *The Term Structure of Interest Rates* (Englewood Cliffs, N.J.: Prentice-Hall, Inc., 1962).

SIX MATHEMATICAL APPENDICES

A. The Summation Sign ($\sum$)

B. Probability

C. Some Proofs with the Expectation Operator

D. Simultaneous Solution of Linear Equations

E. Quadratic Equations

F. Computer Programs for Graphical
    Analysis of a Three-Asset Portfolio

Appendix A

The Summation Sign (Σ)

When discussing the sum of several unspecified quantities, say, five rates of return denoted r_1, r_2, r_3, r_4, and r_5, it is less cumbersome to write $\sum_{i=1}^{5} r_i$ than to write out $r_1 + r_2 + r_3 + r_4 + r_5$, although both expressions are equivalent. The symbol Σ is the upper-case Greek letter sigma. Σ is a mathematical *operator* denoting addition. The subscript $i = 1$ below the Σ is called the index of summation. The superscript 5 above the Σ is called the upper limit of summation.

The Σ can be used with any variable. Consider two variables, x and r, which are to be summed.

i	x_i value	r_i value
1	$x_1 = 5$	$r_1 = 2$
2	$x_2 = 9$	$r_2 = 7$
3	$x_3 = 2$	$r_3 = 4$
4	$x_4 = 7$	
5	$x_5 = 3$	

$$\sum_{i=1}^{3} r_i = r_1 + r_2 + r_3 = 2 + 7 + 4 = 13,$$

$$\sum_{i=2}^{3} r_i = r_2 + r_3 = 7 + 4 = 11,$$

$$\sum_{i=1}^{3} x_i = x_1 + x_2 + x_3 = 5 + 9 + 2 = 16.$$

In discussing half the sum of the first three r_i's, one could write

$$\frac{1}{2} \sum_{i=1}^{3} r_i = \sum_{i=1}^{3} \frac{r_i}{2} = \sum_{i=1}^{3} \left(\frac{1}{2}\right)(r_i) = \frac{2 + 7 + 4}{2} = \frac{13}{2} = 6.5.$$

All of these expressions are equivalent. For practice, the reader should verify the following:

$$\sum_{i=1}^{5} x_i = 26, \qquad \sum_{i=2}^{5} x_i = 21, \qquad \sum_{i=2}^{4} x_i = 18,$$

$$\frac{\sum_{i=1}^{5} x_i}{2} = 13, \qquad \sum_{i=3}^{4} 4x_i = 36, \qquad \sum_{i=1}^{5} (x_i + x_{6-i}) = 52.$$

Sometimes the limits of summation are left off the $\sum$ because they aren't known or don't matter. Several theorems about summations follow. The reader is invited to substitute numbers into the formulas to verify their validity.

SUMMATION THEOREM 1: *The summation of sums equals the sum of the summations. Thus,*

$$\sum_{i=m}^{n} (r_i + x_i) = \sum_{i=m}^{n} r_i + \sum_{i=m}^{n} x_i.$$

SUMMATION THEOREM 2: *A constant factor (k) times the summed variable equals the constant times the summation.*

$$\sum_{i=m}^{n} kx_i = k \sum_{i=m}^{n} x_i.$$

SUMMATION THEOREM 3: *The summation of a constant (for example, $k = 2$ or -10 or 11,002 or any unchanging number) is equal to the product of that constant times the number of times the summation is to be repeated.*

$$\sum_{i=1}^{n} k = nk.$$

SUMMATION THEOREM 4: *The product of the summations is not equal to the summation of the products in general, although a few cases can be found where this is true.*

$$\sum_i x_i \sum_i r_i \neq \sum_i x_i r_i.$$

For example

$$\left(\sum_{i=1}^{2} r_i\right)\left(\sum_{i=1}^{2} x_i\right) = (9)(14) \neq \sum_{i=1}^{2} x_i r_i = 10 + 63 = 73.$$

Multiple summation definition: Summation over two or more subscripts begins at the lower limits of both summations. The summation of one variable is completed before incrementing the other summation. The process is repeated until both summations reach their upper limits.

Multiple summation is encountered in tables and matrices. Letting i denote the row number and j denote the column number, the sum of the nine x_i's in the accompanying table can be written:

col. 1	col. 2	col. 3	
x_{11}	x_{12}	x_{13}	row 1
x_{21}	x_{22}	x_{23}	row 2
x_{31}	x_{32}	x_{33}	row 3

$$\sum_{i=1}^{3} \sum_{j=1}^{3} x_{ij} = \sum_{j=1}^{3} x_{1j} + \sum_{j=1}^{3} x_{2j} + \sum_{j=1}^{3} x_{3j}$$

$$= (x_{11} + x_{12} + x_{13}) + (x_{21} + x_{22} + x_{23}) + (x_{31} + x_{32} + x_{33}).$$

Appendix B
Probability

For the word *probability* we could substitute the phrase "relative frequency over an infinite number of repeated trials." In that case a probability is similar to an objectively measured percentage of past outcomes of an experiment that was repeated many times. On the other hand, when looking into the future a probability is an "*estimate* of the relative frequency of an event over an infinite number of trials." In this book, the probability of a future event will represent a measure of the "degree of confidence" that the event will occur. Sometimes these probabilities must be derived more or less subjectively.

Some statisticians make a distinction between subjective and objective probabilities. They refer to subjective probabilities as mere judgments about the future, as compared with objective probabilities which are measured from known outcomes or are inferred from the nature of the experiment. For portfolio analysis, the relative frequencies (that is, percentages or objective probabilities) of past data may be used for subjective probability estimates of the future if the process generating the given frequency is supposed to remain stationary in the future.

Probabilities can vary from zero to one. Thus, the limits on the probability of rainy weather or any other probability can be written: $0 \leq P(\text{rain}) \leq 1$. This is the notation commonly used when writing probabilities.

Like percentages, the probabilities always refer to outcomes of a given set of events. Thus, like percentages, the probabilities assigned to all the outcomes under discussion must add up to exactly one ($= 100\%$). So if the outcomes under discussion are rain and shine, their probabilities must be assigned so that $P(\text{rain}) + P(\text{shine}) = 1$ if rain and shine are mutually exclusive. Negative probabilities are not possible.

There are three basic kinds of probabilities. They may be defined in terms of the following situation. Imagine a file drawer containing a universe (Ω) of 1,000 personnel files. The numerical breakdown of the files is shown in Table B1.

Table B I

		Sex		
Age		Men (*M*)	Women (*W*)	Marginal Total
(A)	20–30	150	100	250
(B)	30–40	250	150	400
(C)	Over 40	200	150	350
Marginal total		600	400	1,000 $= \Omega$

The relative frequencies of the various categories of personnel are shown as Table B2. If individual personnel files are drawn randomly one at a time and then replaced, the probability of obtaining the file of someone in any particular category is the same as the relative frequency of that category.

Table B2

| | Sex | | |
Age	Men (M)	Women (W)	Marginal Probability
(A) 20–30	$P(A \text{ and } M) = .15$	$P(A \text{ and } W) = .1$	$P(A) = .25$
(B) 30–40	$P(B \text{ and } M) = .25$	$P(B \text{ and } W) = .15$	$P(B) = .4$
(C) Over 40	$P(C \text{ and } M) = .2$	$P(C \text{ and } W) = .15$	$P(C) = .35$
Marginal probability	$P(M) = .6$	$P(W) = .4$	$P(\Omega) = 1.0$

The three types of probabilities are:

1. Joint probabilities, such as the probability of selecting the file of someone who is a male *and* over 40. Symbolically, $P(M \text{ and } C) = .2 = P(C \text{ and } M)$.
2. Marginal probabilities, such as the probability of selecting the file of a male. Symbolically, $P(M) = .6 = P(A \text{ and } M) + P(B \text{ and } M) + P(C \text{ and } M)$. Note that marginal probabilities are the sum of joint probabilities.
3. Conditional probabilities—for example, *given* the file of a woman, what is the probability she is 20 to 30? Symbolically,

$$P(A \text{ given } W) = P(A \mid W) = P(A \text{ and } W)/P(W) = .1/.4 = .25.$$

The vertical bar represents the word "given." Note that conditional probabilities are the ratio of a joint probability over a marginal probability.

Some useful probability definitions are:

1. Definition of independence: If the probability of some event (such as A) does not vary or depend on the outcome of another event (such as M or W), the events are independent. For example, the probability of selecting someone aged 20 to 30 does not depend on which sex is given, so these events are independent. Symbolically, $P(A) = P(A \mid M) = P(A \mid W) = .25$. Note that if A and M are independent, this implies $P(A)$ times $P(M) = P(A \text{ and } M)$.
2. Definition of dependence: If the probability of some event (such as B) depends or varies with some other condition (such as M or W), the events are dependent. For example, the probability of selecting someone's file of age 30 to 40 depends on whether men's or women's files are used. Symbolically, $P(B \mid M) = .4166 \neq P(B \mid W) = .375$. Note that this implies $P(B)$ times $P(M) \neq P(B \text{ and } M)$ and $P(B)$ times $P(W) \neq P(B \text{ and } W)$.
3. Definition of mutually exclusive: If one event (say M) precludes the occurrence of another event (say W), the events are mutually exclusive. For example, if a male's file is picked, this precludes that file from being a female's file. Symbolically, $P(M \mid W) = 0$.

For a more enlightening elementary discussion, read Mosteller, Roarke, and Thomas, *Probability with Statistical Applications* (Reading, Mass.: Addison-Wesley Publishing Co., 1961), chaps. 1, 3, and 4. For a more rigorous treatment of finite probabilities, see Gangolli and Ylvisaker, *Discrete Probability* (New York: Harcourt, Brace & World, Inc., 1967).

Appendix C
Some Proofs with the Expectation Operator

The purpose of this appendix is to furnish proofs that may be studied to develop an understanding of the expected-value operator, and to explain certain mathematical statistics relationships that will aid in understanding the subject matter of this book.

Given two random variables X and Y having a joint probability distribution $p(X_i, Y_j)$ for $i, j = 1, 2, \ldots$, the following theorems may be derived using the expectation operator.

THEOREM E1: $\text{Var}(x) = E(x^2) - [E(x)]^2$

Proof:

$$\text{Var}(x) = E(x - E(x))^2 \qquad \text{by definition}$$
$$= E(x^2 - 2xE(x) + [E(x)]^2)$$
$$= E(x^2) - 2E(x) \cdot E(x) + [E(x)]^2$$
$$= E(x^2) - [E(x)]^2 \qquad \text{QED.}$$

THEOREM E2: $E(x^2) = \text{Var}(x) + [E(x)]^2$.

Proof:

$$\text{Var}(x) = E(x^2) - [E(x)]^2 \qquad \text{by Theorem E1}$$
$$\text{Var}(x) + [E(x)]^2 = E(x^2) \qquad \text{QED.}$$

THEOREM E3: $\text{Var}(ax + b) = a^2 \text{Var}(x)$ for any constants a and b.

Proof:

$$\text{Var}(ax + b) = E[ax + b - E(ax + b)]^2$$
$$= E[ax + b - aE(x) - b]^2$$
$$= Ea^2[x - E(x)]^2$$
$$= a^2E[x - E(x)]^2 = a^2 \text{Var}(x) \qquad \text{QED.}$$

Theorem E3 implies that the standard deviation of $(ax + b)$ equals $a\sigma_x$—the square root of $a^2 \operatorname{Var}(x)$.

THEOREM E4: $E(xy) = E(x) \cdot E(y)$ *if and only if x and y are independent.*

Proof:

$$E(xy) = \sum_i \sum_j [p(x_i \text{ and } y_j)(x_i)(y_j)]$$

but $p(x \text{ and } y) = (p_x)(p_y)$ if x and y are independent, so

$$E(xy) = \sum_i \sum_j [(p_{x_i})(p_{y_j})(x_i)(y_j)]$$

$$= \sum_i \sum_j [(p_{x_i}) \cdot (x_i) \cdot (p_{y_j}) \cdot (y_j)]$$

$$= \sum_i [(p_{x_i})(x_i)] \cdot \sum_j [(p_{y_j})(y_j)]$$

$$= E(x) \cdot E(y) \qquad \text{QED.}$$

THEOREM E5: $\operatorname{Cov}(x, y) = E(xy) - E(x) \cdot E(y)$.

Proof:

$$\operatorname{Cov}(x, y) = E[(x - E(x)) \cdot (y - E(y))] \qquad \text{by definition}$$

$$= E[xy - xE(y) - yE(x) + E(x) \cdot E(y)]$$

$$= E(xy) - E(x) \cdot E(y) - E(y) \cdot E(x) + E(x) \cdot E(y)$$

$$= E(xy) - E(x) \cdot E(y) \qquad \text{QED.}$$

THEOREM E6: $\operatorname{Cov}(x, c) = 0$, *where c is a constant.*

Proof:

$$\operatorname{Cov}(x, c) = E(xc) - E(x) \cdot E(c) \qquad \text{by Theorem E5}$$

$$= cE(x) - cE(x) = 0 \qquad \text{QED.}$$

THEOREM E7: $\operatorname{Cov}(ax + b, cy + d) = ac \operatorname{Cov}(x, y)$.

Proof:

$$\operatorname{Cov}(ax + b, cy + d) = E\{[ax + b - E(ax + b)] \cdot [cy + d - E(cy + d)]\}$$
$$\text{by definition}$$

$$= E\{[ax + b - aEx - b] \cdot [cy + d - cEy - d]\}$$

$$= E[a(x - Ex) \cdot c(y - Ey)]$$

$$= acE[(x - Ex) \cdot (y - Ey)]$$

$$= ac \operatorname{Cov}(x, y) \qquad \text{QED.}$$

THEOREM E8: $\mathrm{Cov}\,(x, y + z) = \mathrm{Cov}\,(x, y) + \mathrm{Cov}\,(x, z)$.

Proof:

$$
\begin{aligned}
\mathrm{Cov}\,(x, y + z) &= E[x(y + z)] - E(x) \cdot E(y + z) \qquad \text{by Theorem E5} \\
&= E(xy + xz) - [E(x) \cdot E(y) + E(x) \cdot E(z)] \\
&= E(xy) + E(xz) - [E(x) \cdot E(y) + E(x) \cdot E(z)] \\
&= [E(xy) - E(x) \cdot E(y)] + [E(xz) - E(x) \cdot E(z)] \\
&= \mathrm{Cov}\,(x, y) + \mathrm{Cov}\,(x, z) \qquad \text{QED.}
\end{aligned}
$$

THEOREM E9: *If the random variables x and y both undergo a linear transformation (for example, ax + b and cy + d, where a, b, c, and d are constants), their correlation coefficient (r_{xy}) is invariant. Symbolically,*

$$
r_{xy} = r(ax + b, cy + d).
$$

Proof:

$$
\begin{aligned}
r(ax + b, cy + d) &= \frac{\mathrm{Cov}\,(ax + b, cy + d)}{\sigma_{(ax+b)} \cdot \sigma_{(cy+d)}} \qquad \text{by definition of } r_{xy} \\
&= \frac{ac\,\mathrm{Cov}\,(xy)}{(a)(\sigma_x)(c)(\sigma_y)} \qquad \text{by Theorems E3 and E7} \\
&= \frac{\mathrm{Cov}\,(x, y)}{\sigma_x \sigma_y} \\
&= r(x, y) \qquad \text{by definition} \qquad \text{QED.}
\end{aligned}
$$

THEOREM E10: $\mathrm{Var}\,(\sum x_i) = \sum \sigma_i^2 + \sum_i \sum_j \sigma_{ij}$ *for* $i \neq j$.

Proof:

$$
\begin{aligned}
\mathrm{Var}\,(\sum x_i) &= E\left(\sum_i x_i - \sum_i u_i\right)^2 \qquad \text{where } u_i = E(x) \\
&= E\left(\sum_i (x_i - u_i)^2\right) \\
&= E\left(\sum_i \sum_j (x_i - u_i)(x_j - u_j)\right) \\
&= \sum_i \sum_j E[(x_i - u_i)(x_j - u_j)] \\
&= \sum_i \sum_j \sigma_{ij} \\
&= \sum_i \sigma_i^2 + \sum_i \sum_j \sigma_{ij} \qquad \text{for } i \neq j \qquad \text{QED.}
\end{aligned}
$$

Appendix D

Simultaneous Solution of Linear Equations

Consider the two linear equations:

(1) $$x + y = 5$$

and

(2) $$2x - y = 4.$$

There are many pairs of values of x and y that will satisfy either (1) or (2). The problem is to find whether there are pairs that will simultaneously satisfy both equations and, if so, how can they be found. If such pairs exist, the equations (1) and (2) are called simultaneous equations. Five methods of finding the simultaneous solutions to the two equations will be demonstrated.

Graphing

The first method consists of *graphing* the equations and observing where the graphs intersect. For each equation any point on its graph is a solution to that equation. The intersections are then simultaneous solutions of the equations. The tables used to determine the graph are shown here.

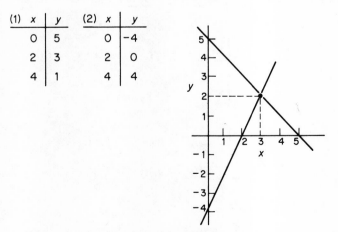

(1) x	y	(2) x	y
0	5	0	-4
2	3	2	0
4	1	4	4

Fig. D.1   Two Linear Equations

The intersection occurs at the point $x = 3, y = 2$ or $(3, 2)$ in (x, y) space. Notice that the graphs of the equations are straight lines and thus intersect at one point only. Such equations are called linear simultaneous equations, or a system of equations.

Elimination

The second method consists of multiplying one or both of the equations by appropriate constants and then adding or subtracting the equations. When this has been done, one of the unknowns will have been eliminated. This process is called the *elimination* method. If, for example, (1) is multiplied by -2 and added to (2), the result is

$$\text{negative two times } (1) = \quad -2x - 2y = -10$$

$$\begin{array}{rl}
\text{plus (2)} & +(2x - y = 4) \\
\hline
\text{equals} & -3y = -6
\end{array}$$

$$\text{so} \qquad y = 2$$

This value of y can be substituted into (1) or (2) to find x. Thus, from (1),

$$x + 2 = 5 \quad \text{or} \quad x = 5 - 2 = 3.$$

Again, the simultaneous solution is $(3, 2) = (x, y)$.

Substitution

The third method is called the *substitution* method. Using one of the equations, one unknown is solved for in terms of another. This solution is then substituted into the remaining equation, giving the value for the remaining unknown.

(1)
$$x + y = 5,$$

$$y = 5 - x,$$

(2)
$$2x - y = 4.$$

Substituting for y,

$$2x - (5 - x) = 4$$

or

$$3x = 9,$$

so

$$x = 3.$$

This value of x can be substituted into (1) or (2) to determine y. Using (2),

$$2x - y = 4,$$

$$6 - y = 4,$$

$$y = 2.$$

Once again, the solution is $(3, 2)$.

Cramer's Rule

Cramer's rule is the fourth method to be examined. *Cramer's rule* is based on matrix algebra.[1] The two equations in general form can be written:

(1) $a_1 x + b_1 y = c_1,$

(2) $a_2 x + b_2 y = c_2,$

where $a_1 = 1$, $b_1 = 1$, $c_1 = 5$, $a_2 = 2$, $b_2 = -1$, and $c_2 = 4$. The coefficients (that is: a_1, b_1, a_2, b_2) in matrix form and their determinant are

$$[A] = \begin{vmatrix} a_1 & b_1 \\ a_2 & b_2 \end{vmatrix} = \begin{vmatrix} 1 & 1 \\ 2 & -1 \end{vmatrix} = a_1 b_2 - a_2 b_1 = -1 - 2 = -3.$$

The determinant obtained by replacing the coefficients of x by the constants on the right side of the equations (that is, c_1 and c_2) is

$$[B] = \begin{vmatrix} c_1 & b_1 \\ c_2 & b_2 \end{vmatrix} = \begin{vmatrix} 5 & 1 \\ 4 & -1 \end{vmatrix} = c_1 b_2 - c_2 b_1 = -5 - 4 = -9.$$

The determinant obtained by replacing the coefficients of y by the numbers on the right side of the equations is

$$[C] = \begin{vmatrix} 1 & 5 \\ 2 & 4 \end{vmatrix} = 4 - 10 = -6.$$

Cramer's rule states that the value of the unknown is found by dividing the determinant of the matrix obtained by replacing the coefficients of

---

[1] See T. Yamane, *Mathematics for Economists* (Englewood Cliffs, N.J.: Prentice-Hall, Inc., 1962), p. 362.

that unknown by the constant values on the right of the equations, by the determinant of the original coefficients. Using Cramer's rule,

$$X = \frac{[B]}{[A]} = \frac{\begin{vmatrix} 5 & 1 \\ 4 & -1 \end{vmatrix}}{\begin{vmatrix} 1 & 1 \\ 2 & -1 \end{vmatrix}} = \frac{-9}{-3} = 3$$

and

$$Y = \frac{[C]}{[A]} = \frac{\begin{vmatrix} 1 & 5 \\ 2 & 4 \end{vmatrix}}{\begin{vmatrix} 1 & 1 \\ 2 & -1 \end{vmatrix}} = \frac{-6}{-3} = 2.$$

As usual, the solution is $(X, Y) = (3, 2)$.

Matrix Inversion

Matrix inversion is the last method used to solve the simultaneous equations. The two equations written in matrix form are

$$\begin{bmatrix} 1 & 1 \\ 2 & -1 \end{bmatrix} \begin{bmatrix} x \\ y \end{bmatrix} = \begin{bmatrix} 5 \\ 4 \end{bmatrix}.$$

Premultiplying both sides of the equation by the inverse[2] of $\begin{bmatrix} 1 & 1 \\ 2 & -1 \end{bmatrix}$ yields

$$\begin{bmatrix} x \\ y \end{bmatrix} = \begin{bmatrix} \frac{1}{3} & \frac{1}{3} \\ \frac{2}{3} & -\frac{1}{3} \end{bmatrix} \begin{bmatrix} 5 \\ 4 \end{bmatrix} = [A^{-1}] \cdot \begin{bmatrix} c_1 \\ c_2 \end{bmatrix} = \begin{bmatrix} x \\ y \end{bmatrix} = \begin{bmatrix} 3 \\ 2 \end{bmatrix}$$

Since matrices that are equal must have equal elements, $x = 3$ and $y = 2$. Of course, all five solution techniques demonstrated here yield the same solution.

---

[2] The inverse of $[A] = \begin{vmatrix} 1 & 1 \\ 2 & -1 \end{vmatrix}$ is denoted $[A^{-1}]$; this inverse is

$$[A^{-1}] = \begin{vmatrix} \frac{1}{3} & \frac{1}{3} \\ \frac{2}{3} & -\frac{1}{3} \end{vmatrix}.$$

A method of finding the inverse matrix is explained in Frank Ayres, Jr., *Matrices* (New York: Schaum Publishing Co., 1962; Schaum Outline Series). Or, a method of finding the inverse matrix is explained in pp. 255 to 275 of Yamane's *Mathematics for Economists*, 1962. Dr. Francis has written matrix inversion programs in Fortran IV and Basic which will be supplied on request.

Appendix E

Quadratic Equations

Two major types of quadratic equations must be considered in portfolio analysis. The first type of quadratic equation is the equation in one unknown. Its general form is

$$ax^2 + bx + c = 0, \tag{E1}$$

where x is the unknown, a and b are coefficients, and c is a constant. Three quadratic equations in one unknown (x) are graphed in Fig. E.1. In the top equation in Fig. E.1, $a = 1$, $b = -6$, and $c = (13 - y)$. Only part of the three parabolas are graphed—actually the figures could be traced out infinitely far if desired. Not all quadratic equations in one unknown are parabolas that point up or down—some point to the left or right.

The second type of quadratic is the equation in two unknowns. Its general form is

$$Ax^2 + Bxy + Cy^2 + Dx + Ey + F = 0. \tag{E2}$$

Here, the two unknown variables are x and y, the coefficients are A, B, C, D, and E, and F is a constant. This equation is essentially the same as the formula for an isovariance ellipse. However, the variables x and y

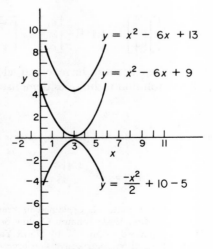

Fig. E.1   Parabolas

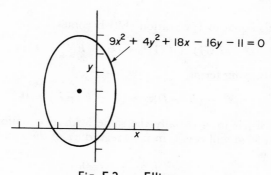

$$9x^2 + 4y^2 + 18x - 16y - 11 = 0$$

Fig. E.2   Ellipse

will be used here instead of w_1 and w_2. Figure E.2 is a graph of a quadratic equation in two unknowns. The particular equation graphed has $A = 9$, $B = 0$, $C = 4$, $D = 18$, $E = -16$, and $F = -11$.

Other types of quadratics exist, of course—those with three unknowns, four unknowns, and so on. However, all quadratics have one thing in common. The highest exponent of any variable in a quadratic equation is two.

Analysis of Quadratics in Two Unknowns

Depending on the signs and values of the different terms, the graph of a quadratic in two unknowns can take any one of several forms. The form depends mainly on the value of the coefficients A, B, and C and may be determined by the relationship $B^2 - 4AC$. The rules are:

(a) If $B^2 < 4AC$, the graph will usually be that of an ellipse. However, if $B = 0$ and $A = C$, the graph may be that of a circle, or a point, or may not exist.

(b) If $B^2 = 4AC$, the graph will be that of a parabola, or two parallel lines, or may not exist.

(c) If $B^2 > 4AC$, the graph is that of a hyperbola or of two intersecting lines.

In considering ellipses, we will be mainly concerned with the first, that is, (a).

The most common method of solving a quadratic equation in two unknowns is to set one of the unknowns to a constant and derive the value or values of the other. In other words, to solve a quadratic in two unknowns, we change the equation being solved to a quadratic in one unknown and solve enough points to enable graphing it.

Changing quadratics in two unknowns to quadratics in one unknown can be shown as follows for the general case. If we set one of the variables in equation (E2) to a constant (that is, if we set y equal to zero), equation (E2) becomes

$$Ax^2 + Dx + F = 0. \tag{E3a}$$

Or, if we set y equal to 1, equation (E2) becomes

$$Ax^2 + Bx(1) + C(1)^2 + Dx + E(1) + F = 0,$$

and, by rearranging terms,

$$Ax^2 + (B + D)x + (C + E + F) = 0 \tag{E3b}$$

Equation (E3b) is in essentially the same form as equation (E3a). The same general form will result, in fact, regardless of the value we assign to y. The form is

$$ax^2 + bx + c = 0, \tag{E1}$$

where $a = A$, $b = (By + D)$, and $c = (Cy^2 + Ey + F)$.

Quadratic equations in two unknowns that are converted to quadratic equations in one unknown (by setting one unknown equal to some real value as shown above) may be solved with the *quadratic formula* below.

$$x = \frac{-b \pm \sqrt{b^2 - 4ac}}{2a}. \tag{E4}$$

Analysis of Quadratics in One Unknown

Solving for x in terms of a, b, and c is done by "completing the square" as follows.

$ax^2 + bx + c = 0$	to be solved for x,
$4a^2x^2 + 4abx + 4ac = 4a(0) = 0$	multiply through by $4a$,
$4a^2x^2 + 4abx = -4ac$	rearrange terms,
$4a^2x^2 + 4abx + b^2 = b^2 - 4ac$	add b^2 to both sides of equation,
$2ax + b = \sqrt{b^2 - 4ac}$	take the square root of both sides,
$x = \dfrac{-b}{2a} \pm \dfrac{\sqrt{b^2 - 4ac}}{2a}$	rearrange terms. (E4′)

Equation (E4) is called the quadratic formula. It can be seen in equation (E4′) that the unknown, x, is equal to a constant $(-b/2a)$ plus or minus a constant $\dfrac{\sqrt{b^2 - 4ac}}{2a}$. Thus, there are usually two roots to consider. However, if the quantity under the radical is equal to zero (that is, if b^2 equals $4ac$), then there is only one value to the expression possible (that is, $-b/2a$). The quantity under the radical may also be less than zero. If this is the case, since we have no way to take the square root of a negative number, the roots will be imaginary numbers.

Because of the possibility of deriving imaginary points, the quantity under the radical ($b^2 - 4ac$) must be evaluated. This term is known as the *discriminant* of a quadratic equation. Regardless of the sign of b, it is obvious that b^2 must be positive. If a and c have opposite signs, the term ($-4ac$) must also be positive. If this is the case, the square roots of the quantity ($b^2 - 4ac$) will always be real, since the quantity will always be positive. Conversely, it is only when both a and c have the same sign that the term ($-4ac$) may be negative. If this term is negative and greater in value than b^2, no real roots are possible.

Solving an Ellipse

To illustrate the solution of a simple ellipse in two unknowns, consider

$$4x^2 + 9y^2 - 36 = 0. \tag{E5}$$

Here, the coefficients are as follows for the quadratic in two unknowns:

$A = 4,$

$B = 0,$ (that is, the Bxy term does not exist),

$C = 9,$

$D = 0,$ (that is, the Dx term does not exist),

$E = 0,$ (that is, the Ey term does not exist),

$F = -36.$

Since the coefficients of the quadratic in one unknown is a combination of the above coefficients,

$a = A = 4,$

$b = (By + D) = (0)y + (0) = 0,$

$c = (Cy^2 + Ey + F) = (9y^2 + (0)y + (-36)) = 9y^2 - 36.$

Plugging these values into equation (E4) gives

$$x = \frac{(0)}{(2)(4)} \pm \frac{\sqrt{(0)^2 - (4)(4)(9y^2 - 36)}}{(2)(4)} = \pm \frac{\sqrt{(16)(36 - 9y^2)}}{8}$$

and

$$x = \pm \frac{\sqrt{36 - 9y^2}}{2}.$$

To solve a few points now for this ellipse set y equal to zero.

$$x = \pm \frac{\sqrt{36}}{2} = +3 \text{ and } -3.$$

Setting y equal to one,

$$x = \pm \frac{\sqrt{36 - 9(1)^2}}{2} = +2.6 \text{ and } -2.6.$$

Setting y equal to three,

$$x = \pm \frac{\sqrt{36 - 9(3)^2}}{2} = \frac{\sqrt{-45}}{2}.$$

This last root is an imaginary, since the square root of a negative number is imaginary. (Figure E.3 shows the graphing of the ellipse $4x^2 + 9y^2 - 36 = 0$.) The point where the quantity under the radical becomes

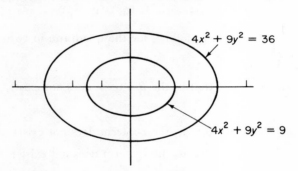

Fig. E.3   Ellipses

less than zero is, therefore, the effective limit of the ellipse. Determination of the values of y to set in order to find the limits of the ellipse with regard to x is possible, but rather clumsy. Therefore, it is sufficient to solve for x values at increasing intervals of y above and below the center until an infeasible solution is found.

The centroid of an ellipse is found from the general equation in two unknowns:

$$Ax^2 + Bxy + Cy^2 + Dx + Ey + F = 0 \qquad (E2)$$

by taking partial derivatives with respect to x and y as follows:

$$\frac{\partial}{\partial x} = 2Ax + By + D = 0,$$

$$\frac{\partial}{\partial y} = Bx + 2Cy + E = 0.$$

Solving these two resultant linear equations simultaneously proceeds below.

$2ABx_0 + B^2y_0 + BD = 0$ (multiply the first partial by $2B$),

$2ABx_0 + 4ACy_0 + 2AE = 0$ (multiply the lower partial by $2A$),

$B^2y_0 - 4ACy_0 + BD - 2AE = 0$ (by subtraction),

$(B^2 - 4AC)y_0 = 2AE - BD,$

$$y_0 = \frac{2AE - BD}{B^2 - 4AC}, \tag{E6}$$

$$x_0 = \left[\frac{-2C}{B}\right]\left[\frac{2AE - BD}{B^2 - 4AC}\right] - \frac{E}{B}. \tag{E7}$$

An Analytic Solution for Lines Tangent to a Set of Ellipses

The common method of finding the points where two equations meet is to rearrange one equation to solve for one unknown in terms of the other unknown, and then to substitute that equation into the other equation in place of the variable solved for. This may be illustrated for the ellipse and straight line as follows:

$$Ax^2 + Bxy + Cy^2 + Dx + Ey + F = 0 \quad \text{(ellipse)} \tag{E2}$$

$$y = Mx + K \quad \text{(straight line)} \tag{E8}$$

Substituting (E8) into (E2) yields

$$Ax^2 + B(Mx + K)x + C(Mx + K)^2 + Dx + E(Mx + K) + F = 0.$$

Simplifying,

$$Ax^2 + BMx^2 + BKx + CM^2x^2 + 2CMKx$$
$$+ CK^2 + Dx + EMx + EK + F = 0.$$

Rearranging terms,

$$(A + BM + CM^2)x^2 + (BK + 2CMK + EM + D)x$$
$$+ CK^2 + EK + F = 0.$$

In order to find the *one* point of coincidence of the two equations, take the derivative with respect to x, as follows:

$$\frac{d}{dx} = 2(A + BM + CM^2)x + (BK + 2CMK + EM + D) = 0,$$

and therefore

$$x = -\frac{BK + 2CMK + EM + D}{2A + 2BM + 2CM^2}. \tag{E9}$$

The value of y may then be found by substituting x into either equation (E8) or (E2) and solving. The benefits of this solution are two points that

lie on the critical line—that is, the centroid or minimum variance portfolio and a point of tangency of one isomean line with one isovariance
ellipse. Which tangency does not matter, since taking the derivative
ensures that *one* ellipse is coincident *at one point* with a specific straight line.
This is the result of dropping the constant term for the ellipse when its
equation is differentiated. The ellipse thus will assume the size necessary
to coincide with the straight line at one point.

It is now possible to derive an equation for the critical line connecting
the minimum variance centroid point and the tangency point. Where the
point of tangency is (x_1, y_1) and the centroid point is (x_0, y_0), solving
the following equation will result in the appropriate linear equation for the
critical line

$$(y - y_0) = \frac{y_1 - y_0}{x_1 - x_0}(x - x_0). \qquad \text{(E10)}$$

In this equation, the unsubscripted variables x and y are the general case.
To illustrate, suppose $(x_1, y_1) = (1, 3)$ and $(x_0, y_0) = (5, -2)$. Equation
(E10) becomes

$$y + 2 = \frac{3 + 2}{1 - 5}(x - 5),$$

$$y = \frac{-5}{4}x + \frac{25}{4} - 2,$$

$$y = \frac{17}{4} - \frac{5}{4}x,$$

$$4y + 5x = 17 \qquad \text{(equation for critical line)}.$$

This method of solution yields a specific equation for the critical line on
which all minimum variances for each return class must lie. Also, a
general equation for each return class follows:

Critical line equation:

$$I_2 x + J_2 y + K_2 = 0.$$

Isomean equation:

$$I_1 x + J_1 y + K_1 = r_p \quad \text{or} \quad I_1 x + J_1 y + (K_1 - r_p) = 0,$$

where I and J are coefficients of the x and y terms in equation (E10) and
the isomean, and where K is a constant. To find the points where these
two equations are common (that is, intersect), simply solve them simultaneously for each assigned value of portfolio return (r_p).

$$I_1 I_2 x + I_1 J_2 y + I_1 K_2 = 0,$$

$$-I_1 I_2 x - I_2 J_1 y - I_2 K_1 + I_2 r_p = 0,$$

and therefore

$$(I_1 J_2 - I_2 J_1)y + I_1 K_2 - K_2 K_1 + I_2 r_p = 0.$$

Rearranging terms,

$$y = \frac{I_2 K_1 - I_1 K_2 - I_2 r_p}{I_1 J_2 - I_2 J_1}.$$

Substituting the derived y into either the critical-line equation or the isomean equation will yield a value for x on the critical line where the particular isomean crosses it.

Once the points (x, y) are found for a given value of portfolio return (r_p), the portfolio variance of this point may then be found by substituting the x and y points derived into the general equation (E1):

$$Ax^2 + Bxy + Cy^2 + Dx + Ey + F = \text{Var}\ (r_p)$$

and solving for Var (r_p).

In Appendix F, which follows, is a program in Basic II language (University of Washington version) to perform this analysis.[1] The first part of the program generates the centroid point (that is, the minimum variance portfolio), the linear equation of the critical line, and a table of returns, variances, and weights. Note that it is not necessary to generate isovariance ellipses, although the second part of the program does derive plotting points for several isovariance ellipses, should they be desired.

Appendix F
Computer Programs for Graphical Analysis of a Three-Asset Portfolio

The programs that follow are written in Basic II language, the University of Washington version.[1] The programs perform the numerous, tedious, exacting arithmetic calculations associated with graphical portfolio analysis. The programs are written to handle three-security portfolios only.

First Program

The first program generates the centroid or minimum variance portfolio, the critical line, and a table of returns, variances, and weights for the efficient set. Although the algorithm used in the program does not require plotting the isovariance ellipses, the program generates points on the isovariances, which may be plotted if desired.

This appendix and the programs are based on the discussion and notation used in Chapter 4 and Appendix E. This appendix assumes a knowledge of the Basic language. Or, a knowledge of Fortran II will suffice—it is similar to Basic. The format for the input data is explained in the beginning of the first program and in Appendix E.

---

[1] W. F. Sharpe, *Basic* (New York: The Free Press, a division of Crowell-Collier and Macmillan, Inc., 1967). Basic is similar to Fortran II.

UNIVERSITY OF WASHINGTON
BASIC II COMPILER
9/69 VERSION

```
REM              PROGRAM TO SOLVE ISOVARIANCE ELLIPSES AND
REM              TANGENCY POINTS WITH ISOMEAN LINES
REM                      PROGRAMMED BY R. FLOCH
REM              READ IN THE QUADRATIC EQUATION COEFFICIENTS
REM              A IS THE COEF. OF THE X-SQUARED TERM
REM              B IS THE COEF. OF THE X-TIMES-Y TERM
REM              C IS THE COEF. OF THE Y-SQUARED TERM
REM              D IS THE COEF. OF THE X-TERM
REM              E IS THE COEF. OF THE Y-TERM
REM              F IS THE CONSTANT (WITHOUT VARIANCE RP) TERM
90   READ A,B,C,D,E,F
REM                      CHECK FOR AN ELLIPSE
     IF (B**2 − 4*A*C) LT 0 THEN 100
     PRINT ≠CHECK COEFFICIENTS A, B, AND C− NOT AN ELLIPSE≠
     GO TO 150
REM  READ IN LINEAR RETURN EQUATION COEFFICIENTS IX + JY + K = 0≠
REM     I1  IS THE X TERM COEFFICIENT
REM     J1  IS THE Y TERM COEFFICIENT
REM     K1 IS THE CONSTANT TERM (WITHOUT THE PORTFOLIO RETURN)
100  READ I1,J1,K1
REM                      FIND THE CENTROID
     LET Y0 = (2*A*E − B*D)/(B**2 − 4*A*C)
     LET X0 = ((−2)*C*Y0)/B − E/B
     PRINT ≠CENTROID IS AT          ≠
     PRINT ≠X EQUALS≠,X0
     PRINT ≠Y EQUALS≠,Y0
     LET V0 = A*(X0**2)+B*(X0*Y0)+C*(Y0**2)+D*X0+E*Y0+F
     LET R0 = I1*X0 + J1*Y0 + K1
     LET G = SQR(A**2 + B**2 + C**2 − 2*A*C)
     LET M0 = −B/(C−A+G)
     PRINT ≠VARIANCE AT THE CENTROID IS≠,V0
     PRINT ≠RETURN AT THE CENTROID IS≠,R0
     PRINT ≠SLOPE OF THE MAJOR AXIS OF THE ELLIPSE IS≠,M0
     PRINT
     PRINT
REM              FIND LINEAR EQUATION OF THE CRITICAL LINE
     LET M1 = −(I1/J1)
     LET K1 = −(K1/J1)
     LET X1 = −(B*K1+2*C*M1*K1+E*M1+D)/(2*(A+B*M1+C*(M1**2)))
     LET Y1 = M1*X1 + K1
     LET M2 = (Y1−Y0)/(X1−X0)
     LET K2 = Y0−(M2*X0)
     PRINT ≠CRITICAL LINE EQUATION Y = MX + K COEFFICIENTS ARE≠
     PRINT ≠M EQUALS≠,M2
     PRINT ≠K EQUALS≠,K2
     PRINT
     PRINT
```

```
REM                 COMPUTE RETURNS VARIANCES AND WEIGHTS
        PRINT ≠TABLE OF RETURNS, MINIMUM VARIANCES AND WEIGHTS≠
        PRINT
        PRINT ≠RETURN≠,  ≠VARIANCE≠,  ≠WEIGHT 1≠,  ≠WEIGHT 2≠,
          ≠WEIGHT 3≠
        PRINT
        LET I2 = −M2
        LET J2 = 1.0
        LET K2 = −K2
        LET K1 = −(K1*J1)
        DIM         Y(25),X(25),Z(25),V(25)
        FOR R = 0 TO 20
          LET Y(R) = (K1*I2 −K2*I1 − I2*R*.01)/(I1*J2 − I2*J1)
          LET X(R) = −(J2*Y(R) + K2)/I2
          LET Z(R) = 1.0 − Y(R) − X(R)
          LET V(R) = A*(X(R)**2)+B*(X(R)*Y(R))+C*(Y(R)**2)+D*X(R)+E*Y(R)
            +F
          PRINT R*.01,V(R),X(R),Y(R),Z(R)
        NEXT R
REM                 COMPUTE ISOVARIANCE ELLIPSE POINTS
        PAGE
        LET Y4 = (INT((Y0 + .05)*10))*0.1
        FOR R = 0 TO 20 STEP 5
        DIM         U(200), T(200), W(200)
          PRINT ≠ISOELLIPSE LINE FOR VARIANCE EQUALS≠,V(R)
          PRINT ≠POINT OF TANGENCY WITH RETURN EQUALS≠,R*.01,≠IS
            AT≠
          PRINT  ≠X EQUALS≠,X(R)
          PRINT  ≠Y EQUALS≠,Y(R)
          PRINT
          PRINT  ≠Y VALUE≠,≠+X VALUE≠,≠−X VALUE≠
          LET T = 0
110       LET Y3 = Y4 + T
          GO TO 130
120       LET Y3 = Y4 − T
130       LET B1 = B*Y3 + D
          LET C1 = C*(Y3**2) + E*Y3 + F − V(R)
          LET N = 100 + (Y3 − Y4)*10
          LET U(N) = Y3
          LET T(N) = 0
          LET W(N) = 0
          LET G =         (B1**2 − 4*A*C1)
        IF G LT 0 THEN 140
          LET G = SQR(G)
          LET T(N)=−(B1/(2*A)) + G/(2*A)
          LET W(N)=−(B1/(2*A)) − G/(2*A)
        IF Y3*10 + 100 = 0 THEN 140
        IF Y3 GT Y4 THEN 120
          LET T = T + .1
          GO TO 110
```

```
140      FOR N = (101 − T*10) TO (100 + T*10) STEP 1
           PRINT U(N),T(N),W(N)
         NEXT N
         PAGE
         NEXT R
150      GO TO 90
REM          DATA FROM EXAMPLE IN CHAPTER FOUR
REM          COEFFICIENTS OF EQUATION 4.5
DATA     .1838,.3422,.3190,−.2138,−.3690,.27
REM          COEFFICIENTS OF EQUATION 4.3
DATA     −.1147,−.0780,.1314
         END
```

The preceding program generates the following printed output.

```
CENTROID IS AT
X EQUALS          .0862878
Y EQUALS          .532088
VARIANCE AT THE CENTROID IS .162606
RETURN AT THE CENTROID IS .0799999
SLOPE OF THE MAJOR AXIS OF THE ELLIPSE IS −.680129
CRITICAL LINE EQUATION Y = MX + K COEFFICIENTS ARE
M EQUALS          −.227538
K EQUALS          .551722
```

TABLE OF RETURNS, MINIMUM VARIANCES AND WEIGHTS

RETURN	VARIANCE	WEIGHT 1	WEIGHT 2	WEIGHT 3
0	.24598	.911437	.344336	−.255773
.01	.226439	.808293	.367805	−.176098
.02	.209504	.705149	.391274	−.0964233
.03	.195174	.602006	.414743	−.0167487
.04	.183449	.498862	.438212	.062926
.05	.17433	.395718	.461681	.142601
.06	.167816	.292574	.48515	.222275
.07	.163908	.189431	.508619	.30195
.08	.162606	.0862868	.532088	.381625
.09	.163908	−.0168569	.555558	.461299
.1	.167817	−.120001	.579027	.540974
.11	.17433	−.223144	.602496	.620649
.12	.183449	−.326288	.625965	.700323
.13	.195174	−.429432	.649434	.779998
.14	.209504	−.532576	.672903	.859673
.15	.226439	−.635719	.696372	.939347
.16	.24598	−.738863	.719841	1.01902
.17	.268127	−.842007	.74331	1.0987
.18	.292878	−.945151	.766779	1.17837
.19	.320236	−1.04829	.790248	1.25805
.2	.350198	−1.15144	.813717	1.33772

ISOELLIPSE LINE FOR VARIANCE EQUALS   .226439
POINT OF TANGENCY WITH RETURN EQUALS   .15   IS AT

| X EQUALS | −.635719 |
| Y EQUALS | .696372 |

Y VALUE	+X VALUE	−X VALUE
−.1	.684845	.664556
0	.89984	.263381
.1	.918703	.0583375
.2	.896892	−.106032
.3	.85051	−.245831
.4	.785563	−.367065
.6	.60898	−.562843
.7	.498132	−.638176
.8	.370672	−.696897
.9	.223039	−.735444
1	.0469894	−.745575
1.1	−.183489	−.701277
1.2	0	0

ISOELLIPSE LINE FOR VARIANCE EQUALS .350198
POINT OF TANGENCY WITH RETURN EQUALS .2 IS AT

X EQUALS −1.15144
Y EQUALS .813717

Y VALUE	+X VALUE	−X VALUE
−.5	1.35523	.738891
−.4	1.46939	.438553
−.3	1.50816	.213607
−.2	1.5127	.0228809
−.1	1.49533	−.145932
0	1.46173	−.298506
.1	1.41501	−.437975
.2	1.35709	−.566235
.3	1.28917	−.684487
.4	1.21198	−.793484
.6	1.03135	−.985211
.7	.928044	−1.06809
.8	.815796	−1.14202
.9	.694065	−1.20647
1	.561956	−1.26054
1.1	.41806	−1.30283
1.2	.26012	−1.33107
1.3	.0843145	−1.34144
1.4	−.11664	−1.32667
1.5	−.360312	−1.26918
1.6	−.735802	−1.07987

ISOELLIPSE LINE FOR VARIANCE EQUALS   .24598
POINT OF TANGENCY WITH RETURN EQUALS   0   IS AT

| X EQUALS | .911437 |
| Y EQUALS | .344336 |

Y VALUE	+X VALUE	−X VALUE
−.1	1.00092	.348485
0	1.03722	.125997
.1	1.02831	−.0512679
.2	.993575	−.202716
.3	.940152	−.335473
.4	.871406	−.452908
.6	.693595	−.647458
.7	.585045	−.725089
.8	.46238	−.788604
.9	.323441	−.835846
1	.163887	−.862473
1.1	−.0260415	−.858725
1.2	−.278672	−.792275

ISOELLIPSE LINE FOR VARIANCE EQUALS   .17433
POINT OF TANGENCY WITH RETURN EQUALS   .05   IS AT

| X EQUALS | .395718 |
| Y EQUALS | .461681 |

Y VALUE	+X VALUE	−X VALUE
.3	.432649	.17203
.4	.429766	−.0112672
.6	.267571	−.221434
.7	.128191	−.268234
.8	−.125494	−.200731

ISOELLIPSE LINE FOR VARIANCE EQUALS   .167817
POINT OF TANGENCY WITH RETURN EQUALS   .1   IS AT

X EQUALS   −.120001
Y EQUALS   .579027

Y VALUE	+X VALUE	−X VALUE
.4	.324095	.0944038
.6	.179092	−.132955
.7	−.00797117	−.132072

Basic Language Program for Plotting Isovariance Ellipses

Given a function for the variance of a 3 security portfolio, it can be converted to an implicit function in 2 variables using the condition: $W_1 + W_2 + W_3 = 1$. Viz.,

$$\text{Var}\,(r_p) = W_1^2\sigma_1^2 + W_2^2\sigma_2^2 + W_3^2\sigma_3^2 + 2W_1W_2\sigma_{12} + 2W_1W_3\sigma_{13} + 2W_2W_3\sigma_{23}$$

$$= W_1^2\sigma_1^2 + W_2^2\sigma_2^2 + (1 - W_1 - W_2)^2\sigma_3^2 + 2W_1W_2\sigma_{12}$$

$$+ 2W_1(1 - W_1 - W_2)\sigma_{13} + 2W_2(1 - W_1 - W_2)\sigma_{23}$$

$$= W_1^2\sigma_1^2 + W_2^2\sigma_2^2 + \sigma_3^2 - 2W_1\sigma_3^2 - 2W_2\sigma_3^2 + 2W_1W_2\sigma_3^2$$

$$+ W_1^2\sigma_3^2 + W_2^2\sigma_3^2 + 2W_1W_2\sigma_{12} + 2W_1\sigma_{13} - 2W_1^2\sigma_{13} - 2W_1W_2\sigma_{13}$$

$$+ 2W_2\sigma_{23} - 2W_2W_1\sigma_{23} - 2W_2^2\sigma_{23}$$

A quadratic equation, i.e., $AW^2 + BW + C = 0$ is solved using the quadratic formula $W = \dfrac{B \pm \sqrt{B^2 - 4AC}}{2A}$. Treating W_2 as a constant, the above function may be solved with the quadratic formula by letting

A = all products of $W_1^2 = \sigma_1^2 + \sigma_3^2 - 2\sigma_{13}$,

B = all products of $W_1 = -2\sigma_3^2 + 2W_2\sigma_3^2 + 2W_2\sigma_{12} + 2\sigma_{13} - 2W_2\sigma_{13}$

$$- 2W_2\sigma_{23}, \text{ and}$$

C = all constants and terms treated as constants = $W_2^2\sigma_2^2$

$$+ \sigma_3^2 - 2W_2\sigma_3^2 + W_2^2\sigma_3^2 + 2W_2\sigma_{23} - 2W_2^2\sigma_{23} - \text{Var}\,(r_p).$$

The following program in Basic language will evaluate points on the isovariance ellipses using the above definitions. The user should fill in the numerical values for A, B, and C appropriate to his portfolio.

```
        $JOB
        $ID
        $EXECUTE
40        PRINT 'VARIANCE', 'FIRST W1', 'SECOND W1', 'W2'
50        FOR V = .1 TO .9 STEP .1
60        FOR W2 = −2.5 TO 2.5 STEP .3
61      LET A = some constant
62      LET B = some constant plus f(w₂)
63      LET C = some constant plus f(w₂) plus V
70        LET S = ((B**2) − ((4)*(A)*(C)))
80        IF S    LT    0      THEN 120
90        LET R1 = ((−B) + SQR(S))/(2*A)
100       LET R2 = ((−B) − SQR(S))/(2*A)
110       PRINT V, R1, R2, W2
120         NEXT W2
130         NEXT V
END
$EOF
```

Subject Index

Name Index